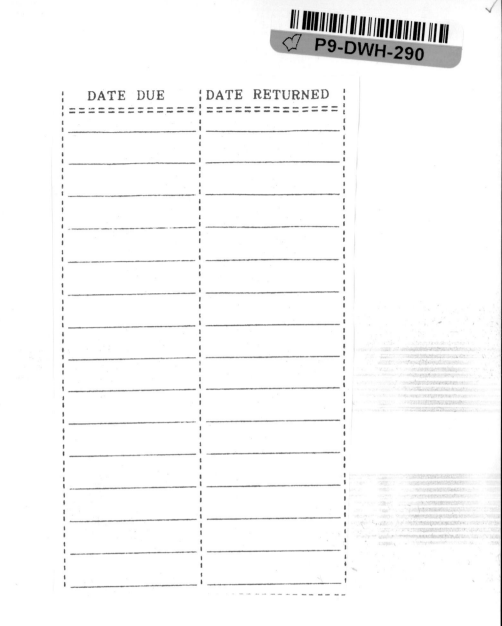

DATE DUE	DATE RETURNED

In memory of Ralph Leslie Collins

Peter Warlock

The composer

Brian Collins

Scolar Press

Published by
Scolar Press
Gower House
Croft Road
Aldershot
Hants GU11 3HR
England

Ashgate Publishing Company
Old Post Road
Brookfield
Vermont 05036–9704
USA

British Library Cataloguing in Publication Data

Collins, Brian
    Peter Warlock, the composer
    1. Warlock, Peter, 1894-1930 2. Composers – Great Britain
    Biography
    I. Title
    780.9'2

Library of Congress Cataloging in Publication Data

Collins, Brian
    Peter Warlock : the composer / Brian Collins
    Includes bibliographical references and index
    ISBN 1-85928-216-4 (cloth)
    1. Warlock, Peter, 1894-1930. 2. Composers – England – Biography
I. Title.
ML410.W2953C56   1996
782.2'092–dc20   CIP
[B]   96-20427   MN

ISBN 1 85928 216 4

Printed in Great Britain at the University Press, Cambridge

Contents

Acknowledgements		vii
Abbreviations		ix
Preface		xi
1	Contexts	1
2	The earliest compositions	13
3	New beginnings	22
4	*The curlew*: a portrait of the artist	54
5	Experiment and consolidation (1) The Winthrop Rogers songs	82
6	Experiment and consolidation (2) The early choral songs	120
7	Experiment and consolidation (3) Three more songs	139
8	Delius revisited and Warlock rediscovered	146
9	Rum, beer, good ale and other frolics	158
10	Refinements	176
11	The way forward (1) *Lillygay*	193
12	The way forward (2) *Candlelight* and *Jenny Gray*	206
13	Three pseudonyms (1) Amorous and pastoral	218
14	Three pseudonyms (2) Rumbustious and hedonistic	236
15	Three pseudonyms (3) Metaphysical and introspective	253
16	*Capriol* and some conclusions	327
Bibliography		344
Index		353

Acknowledgements

Any undertaking of this nature inevitably relies on the goodwill of many people. I now have the opportunity of publicly recording my appreciation and gratitude for the assistance and support freely given by individuals and organisations.

This project would not have materialised had it not been for an interest stimulated by the late Louis Pearson. Louis's own quiet passion for Warlock and, particularly, the festival he organised in 1970 at Bede College, Durham, gave me an extraordinary opportunity of confirming what I'd been able to work out for myself and encountering at first hand much music which had previously been only sounds in the head or, more importantly, totally unknown. In the ensuing years, until his death in 1986, in fact, he was both friend and correspondent; although our meetings were all too infrequent, his letters were always informative and thought-provoking. On the last occasion that I visited him, the research which would lead to this book was envisaged but not yet started. Among the things that he said to me then were words to the effect of "You will let me know what you find out?" This opportunity would, alas, never present itself.

No work on Peter Warlock can fail to recognise the contribution to the cause made by Fred Tomlinson. In addition to the material that has found its way into publications of one sort or another, Fred has an encyclopædic knowledge of Warlockian facts that he willingly makes available to those who share his enthusiasm. He also appears to have access to material that is obtainable from no other source and, in this and other respects, I have been grateful on more than one occasion to be able to prevail upon his generosity. We both recognise that our views on a number of issues do not coincide but this makes conversation and discussion the more stimulating and productive. I should also like to thank David Cox (my predecessor as editor of the Peter Warlock Society Newsletter) who put some of my ideas into print so regularly, also Michael Pilkington, Anthony Ingle and other members of the Peter Warlock Society for their encouragement and advice.

Other individuals and organisations I would like to thank by name are (in alphabetical order) Hywel Davies, Trevor Hold, Christian Kennett, Leicestershire County Council, Liz Mayne, Denis McCaldin/Music

Department of the University of Lancaster, Ronald Reah, Dennis Reynolds, Ian Roberts and Barry Smith.

In the light of recent changes in the law of copyright, there has been much discussion amongst Warlockians as to who – if anybody – holds the rights to Warlock's music. Warlock bequeathed them to Bernard van Dieren and they passed first to his widow, Frida, and then to their son, Bernard van Dieren Jr where the line is believed to end. In spite of enquiries by several people to ascertain the current holder, no name has become apparent. It is, therefore, impossible to acknowledge ownership in respect of the notated examples that are included in this book and I apologise to any person who may have a claim on these rights. Indeed, should such a person exist, I should be very interested to know of them.

In conclusion, and more positively, I gratefully acknowledge the assistance and advice given by my research supervisor, Anthony Pither, not to mention the sympathy and support, active and passive, afforded by my wife and children. Their tolerance has been stretched to the limit on several occasions.

BC

Abbreviations

Footnotes and the bibliography frequently refer to persons, organisations and sources listed below; they are abbreviated as follows:

A   Augener & Co.
B   Boosey and Co.
Ba   Banfield (1985)
BC   Brian Collins
BL   British Library
BvD   Bernard van Dieren
CG   Cecil Gray (1934)
Ch   J W Chester Ltd.
CP   Palmer (1976)
CT   Colin Taylor, one of PH's music masters at Eton and a corres-
         pondent for the rest of his life. Many of PH's letters to him
         survive.
D   Philip Heseltine (1923)
F   Fenby (1936)
FT   Fred Tomlinson; therefore:
FT1   Tomlinson (1974) and
FT2   Tomlinson (1977). These two volumes contain much valuable
         background information relating to PW's output as composer,
         arranger, editor and author, details regarding publication,
         poetic sources and general chronology; they can be referred to
         in parallel with this survey. To aid this process, FT's abbrevi-
         ations have been retained in the notes wherever practicable.
         (FT3 is, theoretically, in preparation but its completion is
         uncertain. An updated version of FT1/2 is possible, perhaps
         in a single volume.)
Gr   Cecil Gray.
IC   Copley (1979). Dr Copley amended and corrected earlier
         work on biography and chronology by Kenneth Avery (who
         wrote the Grove V entry) et al. Some of this is included or
         referred to in FT1/2; the publication date of 1973 for IC given
         in FT1 was speculatively optimistic because of production
         problems not relevant here.

MP	Pilkington (1989). This repertoire-guide to the solo songs is also a useful reference to editions, including any misprints.
NH	Nigel Heseltine (1992). This account of a father by a son who hardly knew him relies heavily on material that can no longer be substantiated. The principal source for the book is Nigel's grandmother, Edith ("Covie", PH's mother); her opinions and prejudices are often apparent. There are some obvious inaccuracies, some information is suppressed and some details are highly suspect; these facts may be grounds to doubt other material in the rest of the book.
O	Oxford University Press.
PH	Philip Heseltine and
PW	Peter Warlock. "Warlock" is always used in preference to "Heseltine" in the main text except where the latter is specifically referred to in, for example, letters or quotations. This survey does not seek to perpetuate the myth of the dual nature of one man's personality. Since the intention is to deal with the ouput of a composer, the composer's name is the one generally employed and it is left to others to speculate upon the use of pseudonyms.
PWS	The Peter Warlock Society; hence
PWSNL	The PWS newsletter.
T	Thames Publishing, London. T(i), T(ii) etc. refer to volumes of the PWS Collected Edition of the songs published by T (Vol 1, 1982; Vol 2, 1983; Vol 3, 1984; Vol 4, 1986; Vol 5, 1990; Vol 6, 1991; Vol 7, 1992; Vol 8, 1993). These contain all the songs with piano; other volumes now include works for other media.
W	Winthrop Rogers. Rogers was the first to put Warlock's music into print (in 1919) but PW's decision to submit work to him was partly made out of spite. (See IC pp. 15 & 66).

Preface

The title of this book is hardly original for, after all, how many others have been about "X – the composer"? But my choice of the wording is deliberate on two counts. To begin with I want to get away from the biographical emphasis that has become so much a part of the Warlock phenomenon. In pursuing or relating the details of his life with such concentrated vigour there is an unpleasant suggestion that his music was no good but it is always possible to fall back on sensational accounts of his drinking, womanising and occult delvings. However the music – or most of it – is worthwhile and does not need the unnecessary attentions that have become familiar. I shall say as much again in the first chapter.

But the title is also a quotation, of sorts, for Warlock wrote his own epitaph. In it he resorts to the denigratory manner that characterises much of his self-criticism and he equates his own calling to the job of his neighbour. Ironically, he also anticipates those who would become more fascinated by his personality than his achievements:

> Here lies Peter Warlock the composer
> Who lived next door to Munn the grocer.
> He died of drink and copulation,
> A sad discredit to the nation.

The family were far too respectable to have added it (even if they had known about it) to the marble stone that also marks the last resting place of Warlock's father, Arnold, and Arnold's first wife, Floie. Perhaps I should be thankful for that; it would have made writing this just that little bit harder.

BC
Melton Mowbray
January 1996

CHAPTER 1

Contexts

"Peter Warlock" is the most familiar of the pseudonyms used by Philip Heseltine (1894-1930) for, as this statement implies, there were others. At first, "Peter Warlock" was the author of an article[1] about the chamber music of Eugene Goossens where the name was used (for reasons which are not clear) to conceal Heseltine's real identity from the periodical's editor. Two more *noms-de-plume* adorn his least typical – and least significant – compositions while others were used to provide a degree of variety to the names of writers in *The Sackbut* of which for a while he was not only the editor but, also, a substantial contributor. Later, when "Warlock" became too well known, he had to invent further *personae* to sign the scathing letters he wrote occasionally to publications. The choice of the name "Warlock" has prompted speculation about its relationship to his interest in the occult; it is not the purpose of this survey to speculate on the use of or rationale behind this or his other authorial identities, but other biographical assumptions, however convenient or long held, will be shown to be erroneous.

While held in respect by many, Peter Warlock has rarely been the subject of extended investigation, even though books about song or English music in general may refer to him in positive, even superlative terms. Thus one encounters statements such as: ". . . this richly gifted personality . . ." (Eric Fenby);[2] "In the long history of English song his work holds an honourable place" (Ernest Walker);[3] ". . . the most remarkable talent in English song since the 17th century . . ." and "Warlock died . . . leaving behind him 100 songs not unworthy of the *oeuvre* of Hugo Wolf . . ." (Charles Osborne).[4] But the only extended literature devoted exclusively to this important figure of the inter-Wars years comprises Cecil Gray's biography[5] (a valuable account from one who knew the subject better than most but flawed by inaccuracy and opinion); Ian Copley's own survey (which posits no unified critique of the music);[6] and, more recently, Barry Smith's thorough and detailed biography (which deals with the music not at all).[7] Gray's biography contains two notated examples; neither is by Warlock!

Other books devoted to other composers contain interesting, often brief, observations or reminiscences about Warlock but these are usually of a biographical nature only; while they may offer some insight into the physical working practices of a creative individual, they rarely refer to the cerebral aspect. He is something of a biographer's dream in this respect: as is also the case with Sir Thomas Beecham of greater longevity and more recent memory, what he said (either in everyday speech or in letters and print) and how he behaved are more readily assimilable and more instantly appealing than his musical feats. In both cases craft has been overtaken by reputation, real or apocryphal. As a consequence – and the ubiquitous *Capriol* notwithstanding – casual conversation about the composer is more likely to be about his supposed involvement with the occult arts or some other, lascivious detail of his private life. This survey, therefore, will make no further mention of beer or black magick, motorcycles or Mog, sex or suicide. These aspects may be readily discovered elsewhere by any who feel deprived.

A few articles augment this otherwise limited treatment of a recognisedly important composer; however, the promotion of his music has been left largely to enthusiasts rather than academics. The labours of individuals such as Fred Tomlinson (whose own books, sleeve notes and arrangements have begun to remedy the situation) and other members of the Peter Warlock Society[8] are rarely accorded the credibility of scholarship, especially as their corporate activities can take place in surroundings as convivial as those frequented by the inspiration of their endeavours. Perhaps it is a combination of these factors, seasoned by snobbery (in which Gray himself, despite his fulminations against the guilty, also indulged), that has created an antipathetic environment in which, to the enthusiast, myopia appears deliberate. Nevertheless, close examination of the music readily reveals an inventive craftsman whose facility, a virtue mistaken for shallowness, enhances and is enhanced by the logical bases of his composition. Indeed, any apprehension that the music would not withstand the same analytical processes applied to the work of others has proved groundless and the emotional response which many – the writers above, perhaps – make upon encountering it has been constantly justified when the material has been closely scrutinised.

It is, of course, his own music that makes Warlock the subject of this investigation but it must be borne in mind that composition was only one of his musical occupations. Had he not been a critic, researcher, copyist, editor, arranger, author and aspirant impresario as well, the extent – even the diversity – of his compositional canon might have been greater. Tomlinson, in a corner of the first volume of his excellent and helpful *Peter Warlock Handbook*,[9] tabulates Warlock's contributions to most of these categories; when one understands that, but for a handful of items, his achievements cover a mere 15 years, the extent of his contribution to music in Britain this century can begin to be recognised. Because he died so young his full potential was never realised. He is the more to be mourned on this account.

The most positive lever on Warlock was, undoubtedly, his contact with Frederick Delius although, hitherto, the precise nature of the musical influence has not really been discussed. (There were other aspects of the relationship too: Delius and his strongly held beliefs were readily taken on board by the impressionable and fatherless Philip to the point where the opinion and invective of both become practically indistinguishable.) Very little of Warlock's music really sounds like that of Delius. The string *Serenade* is something of an exception, being an act of homage, while *An old song* imposes a formal discipline not found in the older man's work and the *Pieds-en-l'air* movement from *Capriol* contains some indulgently Delian harmonies. But, because these are instrumental pieces rather than the songs that constitute the majority of Warlock's output, they could be considered atypical anyway. Copley lists[10] a (small) number of other instances but they are largely passing references, eclecticisms even, rather than larger-scale statements over complete pieces. Yet it can be shown that one overt aspect of Delius's harmonic style, the characteristic, falling semitone, did affect the young composer but as a seminal feature, not as a model to be directly copied or a morsel to be unquestioningly regurgitated.

It is also necessary to address the real effect upon Warlock's output of the English High Renaissance and Bernard van Dieren, the other influences most frequently cited. While the infatuations with both Delius and van Dieren would fluctuate, these were all passions that would motivate him in one way or another for the remainder of his life. They have to be put into some kind of perspective: while no suggestion is intended that they were not genuine enthusiasms, it is both tempting and valid to evaluate the espousal of van Dieren and early music as snooks cocked at a conservative musical establishment. The same could be said of Bartók and Gesualdo; Warlock's propaganda on their behalf has been vindicated with the passage of time. Other objects of his commitment and energy, such as van Dieren himself or Leo Ornstein, have yet to be fully justified by posterity. His vociferous proselytising on behalf of what he saw as neglected causes is akin to his equally noisy denigration of respected figures such as Vaughan Williams and Holst. A revealing postscript of a letter to Colin Taylor[11] says that "when one is <u>actually</u>

[Warlock's underlining] making propaganda one has to be much more violently partisan than one really is. Out of the town atmosphere van Dieren's music is <u>unthinkable</u>."

Another letter[12] of 12.11.15 relates "the delights and surprises from the works of Byrd, Gibbons, Tomkins, Farnaby and many another astonishing composer who preceded J S Bach by more than a century" which he had experienced in the British Museum. His letter to Bernard van Dieren dated 8.6.16 refers to their first meeting. The Elizabethan encounter preceded that with van Dieren by six months or even more and is occasionally manifest in his music in the form of some rhythmic treatments such as metrical freedom (as in unbarred music, also a feature of the van Dieren stage) and some motivic usage (as mentioned by Copley.)[13] But the extensive use of modal material can be viewed as – and will be demonstrated to be – an extension of his chordal language, the driving force behind all his music. Under these circumstances, the Elizabethan references also become eclecticisms rather than the musical essence. It has been biographically convenient in the past to link Warlock's archaisms to his researches in Trinity College, Dublin, the British Museum and elsewhere. Their compositional origins will be shown to be otherwise. Bernard van Dieren's own musical pedigree attracted the young Warlock, anxious to extend his knowledge as much as he could, in a different way. Van Dieren had been in the Schoenbergian circle, if only on its outer reaches; he was familiar with Schoenberg's early work and his brother-in-law was the cellist in the first performance of *Pierrot lunaire*. Furthermore, his wife, the pianist Frida Kindler, had been a pupil of Busoni.

And why should Warlock choose to write lighter songs often (but not exclusively) about drinking beer? Gray, of course, leaps on this fact and incorporates it in his infamous theory about Heseltine/Warlock's dual personality. But the truth lies elsewhere. Once more, there has been an assumption that these songs are directly linked to his own lifestyle, a reflection of the reputation he has acquired – not without some justification it must be admitted – for womanising and wild carousing. Nevertheless, this aspect is not a major influence on Warlock's style and can be speedily dealt with.

This survey will often examine Warlock's output in the order it was written although, from time to time, such a path will not be taken for aesthetic or practical reasons. It makes sense to deal with revisions in the light of the original versions, or to examine some pieces in the context of others with which they are not contemporary. While the chronology breaks down sometimes for lack of evidence and supposition of one kind or another becomes necessary, there is neither the intention nor wish to question the work done on the date-ordering established by Copley (who corrected that of Kenneth Avery and others) and slightly revised by Tomlinson.

Virtually all of Warlock's output will be surveyed here. Only a few pieces are not considered: *The everlasting voices* (1915) presents material similar to that of its contemporaries in terms of chordal shapes and juxtapositions and, although a speculative completion has been published,[14] it includes Warlock's rejected vocal line. A *Chinese ballet* (1917), written under the pseudonym "Huanebango Z Palimpsest" exists in manuscript form only[15] and is written in an atypical idiom, as are the *Codpieces* (by "Prosdocimus de Beldamandis Jr"), parodies of popular dance-styles that, for all their humour and irreverence, lie outside the scope of these investigations. Otherwise, the limited attention paid elsewhere to the musical qualities of Warlock's output (rather than his life or lifestyle) makes coverage of as much as possible the more important.

Only Warlock's compositions will be dealt with; his many transcriptions and arrangements are ignored and, even then, not every aspect of his music is covered. As should become plain, his technique is based on chordal material and the emphasis is on those features of his style that relate to such practices. The relationship between words and music and the choice of texts, important considerations for one who was, primarily, a songwriter, will be considered relatively briefly; the principal structural interest in Warlock's songs lies in the instrumental rather than the vocal component. His sympathy for his texts is not in question but the evidence for chordal and chordally derived material being the basis for his music will dominate the argument. Neither is any sustained attempt made to place Warlock into a historical context. His relationship to his contemporaries, English or Continental, is not explored in any detail. The fact that all of these aspects are not dealt with means that there is still a substantial amount of work to be done before a full understanding of Warlock's place in British music between the Wars is possible.

For it is a fact that, to the casual observer, Warlock's music is the product of English late-Romanticism, so he gets lumped together with Elgar, Bax, Vaughan Williams, Butterworth, Finzi et al. The musical language of many of Warlock's pieces suggests otherwise: while they utilise features associated with tonality, structures are flexible enough to evade a sense of predominant key; others have only one fixed centre.

These two sorts of pieces, which could be termed respectively "para-tonal" (because they go beyond tonality) or "penetonal" (because they almost achieve tonal credibility), employ a selective diatonicism that incorporates modally or tonally derived material of one kind or another. In some, the relationship between centres can be idiosyncratic and achieved with a characteristic lack of subtlety that might be perfunctory if it were not itself eclectic, an individual response that avoids conventional procedures. Others, unambiguously diatonic, can eschew changes of key; the resultant melodic or harmonic material possesses a final but lacks the real test of tonal procedure, the establishment via modulation of a hierarchy of key relationships within and against which the principal key may be measured.

Warlock's manipulation, rejection even, of conventional tonal practice may go beyond these phenomena. A handful of early pieces can be described as atonal in that they evade references to specific key-centres. The atonality is, from their static qualities, more spiritually akin to Debussy than Schoenberg, although this is not to imply that there is a common vocabulary also. To regard a survey of Warlock's output, therefore, as a study in tonal usage (as might be the case for those whose knowledge of his music is limited to a few of the more familiar pieces) is to engender problems of nomenclature and derivation. Warlock is a genuine modernist in this respect: his chordal choice and adjacent ordering are governed by factors other than functional relationships. It becomes more pertinent, then, to think in terms of a chordal vocabulary rather than functional conventions and, for the most part, note-centres rather than tonalities.

Whatever its origins, Warlock's musical language depends funda-mentally upon a horizontally inspired but vertically dependent technique – the Delian "melody of chords". Both the identification and termi-nology are Warlock's own, a description of how he perceived Delius's style. Robert Nichols recalled an early meeting with him in the latter's rooms at Christ Church, Oxford. "The interest in Delius is vertical: one chord melts into another," Warlock told Nichols. "In fact you might call it a melody of chords. That's an exaggeration, of course, but perhaps it'll help you to see what I mean."[16] Warlock sought, ultimately, to rationalise it in his own music by means of melodic devices (as the vocal lines of his songs) and otherwise. A survey of his use of chords, therefore, must look beyond tonally familiar structures and juxta-positions. Nevertheless, Warlock is essentially a chordal composer; his choral music in particular is driven by its vertical qualities and, even when some works appear to have a more polyphonic basis, they too will be seen to have chordal origins. His music attests a constant search for a valid means of achieving chordal momentum and a striving for a balanced coexistence between horizontal and vertical components.

What was – or was not – Warlock's stylistic heritage? The matter of antecedents has inevitably arisen. Delius was the most powerful – if eventually the most maligned[17] – influence, a tonalist whose vocabulary employed a strong late-Romantic dialect. Warlock, who seems to have known the instrumental pieces better, imported a number of Delius's more colourful chords directly into his own panoply and they will be referred to continually throughout this survey. Nor can Warlock's early Wagnerian interest (a pre-Delian affection) be completely discounted. Overt manifestations of this enthusiasm are rare and of only minor significance in the context of this study;[18] yet, along with his contemporary European modernists, he is to be unequivocally marked as a post-Wagnerian if only in terms of the Delian lineage whence he springs. Warlock's life and brief compositional career spans a period of formative activity, not only the very different post-Wagnerian developments of Debussy, Richard Strauss and Schoenberg but the influx of material with other cultural derivations – Russia and Hungary, the gamelan, jazz and an increased awareness of the relevance of ethnic and popular styles in general. All of these aspects eventually made their presence felt in Britain either through the efforts of individuals (such as Henry Wood) or visiting groups (the Ballet Russe, the Original Dixieland Jazz Band).

In fact, Warlock had a wide knowledge of musical styles and genres including contemporary and popular movements. Some of it he acquired second-hand from friends although this could supplement what he had already found out for hmself: van Dieren would pass on both his enthusiasm for composers not currently fashionable as well as the knowledge of Schoenberg's music referred to above; but Warlock was already familiar with Schoenbergian theory as early as 1912 when his evaluation of the composer appeared in *The Musical Standard*. One of his masters at Eton, Colin Taylor, was unusual in that he possessed some knowledge of Debussy, Bartók and other contemporary composers and advised on the production of this, Warlock's first musical article.[19] Another friend would be Constant Lambert, the breadth and depth of whose knowledge of the contemporary European scene were probably unparalleled during Warlock's lifetime. We know that Warlock's knowledge of popular forms enabled him to compare Stravinsky with

Irving Berlin (not very favourably, as it happens) and he arranged his ragtime dance *The old codger*, one of the *Codpieces*, for the Savoy Orpheans (although there is no record of its ever having been performed by them and the arrangement is lost).

Despite a familiarity with continental trends, Warlock was sceptical of much of it; he had little time for Strauss, Skryabin or Stravinsky and his letters refer – in his uniquely scathing manner – to what he saw as their faults. In this sense he was something of a conservative, a stay-at-home, for his music is essentially British, English even. Like Gerald Finzi, he had a sympathy for the exotic but found his voice in native traditions and attitudes. He is one of a line of songwriters that stretches back to Sterndale Bennett and the Mendelssohnians and reached a late-Victorian flowering particularly in the work of Stanford (who was not reluctant to draw on his own ethnic origins). Butterworth, Gurney and Baines, together with Vaughan Williams also employed nationalistic elements, breaking with the formalism of the past and, like contemporary painters and poets, addressed proletarian subjects that would previously have been unacceptable. Roger Quilter, whom he admired, provides another link, parallel to the Delian one, with nineteenth-century Romanticism. (And Quilter was setting Shakespeare and other Elizabethan lyrics before Warlock.) For Holst Warlock had no time although he once considered approaching him for tuition. Both Vaughan Williams and Elgar found disfavour with him too but, in their case, he could also be a staunch and positive advocate.[20] In these respects, Warlock is the opposite of Delius the very diversity of whose background shaped his output. Warlock rejects many and retains only a few of his potential influences.

After Delius, who was his inspiration, Warlock discovered Bernard van Dieren who would become his mentor. But the true nature of the relationship must be examined with caution. There was something of the teacher-student about it but it was mainly catalytic in that tendencies already existed within Warlock's output which were confirmed and emboldened by the encounter; there was no wholesale stylistic importation. It is possible to observe similarities between a limited number of Warlock's pieces and those of van Dieren (the *Folk-song preludes* share some features of the latter's *Netherlands melodies* and the *Saudades* songs look similar on the page to works such as *Levana* or *Ich wanderte unter den Bäumen*). But it is difficult to say, most of the time, precisely where some aspects of Warlock's style originate. As a naïve composer – one whose formal musical education was negligible and whose musical interests and potential paradigms were esoteric – he is not easy to place into one category or another.

There are moments reminiscent of Bartók as well as van Dieren or Delius, composers whom he knew personally[21] and whose music he had discussed with them, but any overt influence they exerted is hard to prove. It is reasonable to suppose that harmonic material was acquired from Delius but Warlock's deployment is idiosyncratic; *Saudades* openly displays the influence of van Dieren in terms of its sonorities and textures but it is his line-led use of chords – used in a non-van Dieren-esque way – that is the real legacy. And it is tempting to ascribe to the influence (conscious or unconscious) of Bartók the justification for using modal material from outside the contemporary art-music aesthetic.

Some of Warlock's output makes undeniably tonal references and the innovative style of the songs mentioned above would appear, super-ficially, to be softened – some might say compromised – by such a situation. This should not necessarily be seen as symptomatic of retro-gression: the unashamed use of what appears to be conventional tonality by a composer, especially a British composer, working in the second and third decades of this century does not of itself imply a diminished vitality or credibility even though its use in some pieces seems incongruous alongside other examples from his output. The route by which Warlock attains what is, apparently (an important qualification), this more obviously tonal methodology demands contextualisation; at first sight, *My gostly fader*, *The bayley berith the bell away* and the other songs from 1918 seem to deny the more demanding language of *Saudades* (1916-17) or *The lover mourns for the loss of love* (?1915-16) in *The curlew*.

During Warlock's early years the semitone as a unit had been taking on a particular significance in contemporary European music. This was also the case in the establishment and execution of Warlock's compo-sitional technique in general, not just his chordal construction. The choice of the semitone as a constructional unit is significant. It is, in a Warlockian context, derived from Delius, as the opening of *A lake and a fairy boat* will demonstrate. But for Delius it served as a passing-note with harmonic associations; for Warlock (and his continental contem-poraries) it accommodates an emancipation from received tonal usage and becomes an initiating force in the exploration of new musical territory. Warlock depended upon the semitone as a means of modifying his basic material. At first, it was applied to chords; later it was to be the means of interchange between modes.

For the other principal element to be dealt with is modality and its derivation within Warlock's methodology. It is conveniently assumed that it emanates from his knowledge of and enthusiasm for the music of the Renaissance and early Baroque. But this assertion is questionable; it can be more relevantly considered as relating directly to his chordal choice. Modes and modality will be discussed in more detail as specific examples arise.

Notes

1   PW (1916); see BS p. 103.
2   F p. 106.
3   Walker (1952) p. 354.
4   Osborne (1974) pp. 235 & 236. Ironically Warlock "positively disliked Hugo Wolf" – Gerald Cockshott (March 1955) p. 128.
5   i.e. CG.
6   i.e. IC.
7   i.e. BS.
8   PWS was established in 1963 and is still active.
9   i.e. FT1/2; see p. 45 therein.
10   IC p. 36.
11   The letter is dated, in another hand (?CT's) "April 27(?) 1917".
12   FT (1978) quotes PH's entire letter of 8.6.16 to BvD and the reference it contains to their first meeting ". . . a few evenings ago . . .".
13   IC p. 42.
14   See note 2, Chapter 2.
15   by "Huanebango Z. Palimpsest", BL Add. Ms. 52904. There are many marginalia to this short-score, some of which have been obliterated (possibly because of their scatological content) by an unknown hand. IC pp. 222-3 relates its history and insignificance.
16   CG p. 63. Nichols's romantic account offers an early view of PW's musical outlook. The quotation follows an assertion that "The usual music – the music you hear most of, especially here, Bach and so forth – is mostly contrapuntal: that is to say the interest is horizontal. One tune moves in combination against another."
17   "Delius . . . wears very badly. His utter lack of any sense of construction . . . consistent thickness of texture and unrelieved sweetness of harmony . . . get on one's nerves" (letter to CT, 10th January 1929).
18   "Philip spoke rather of those he particularly admired, Grieg, Chopin, Wagner, Berlioz, than those he disliked . . ." (CG p.70). PW attended Richter's *Ring* cycle at Covent Garden in 1908 (FT1 p. 40). His *Valses: Rêves d'Isolde* (?1916-17) poke fun at the medium, "the characteristic *valse de salon* of the period at its most glutinous" (IC p. 221), rather than the material.
19   PH (1912) draws on material from Schoenberg's *Harmonielehre*.
20   In 1930 PW organised a letter, signed by many influential musicians of the day, supporting Elgar following criticism by Edward Dent.

21   PW's friendship with Delius and van Dieren is well known and documented; for information about (part of) his association with Bartók see Gillies (1989).

CHAPTER 2

The earliest compositions

The only complete, surviving pieces that predate the earliest attempts at what would become *The curlew* are the songs mentioned above, written during 1911-12. Other works were attempted but failed to reach fruition, were destroyed or have been lost.[1] (It must be made clear at this point that an unfinished song, *The everlasting voices*, also predates *The curlew* but is not included in this survey. It was written some five years after the three songs under discussion but the last bars of both the melody and the accompaniment are crossed out and the instruction "rewrite the end" – in a hand that is very similar to Warlock's own – added. It was not rewritten, at least not by the composer himself. A published version[2] retains the rejected vocal line although the crossing out on the manuscript applies to both parts. The language of *The everlasting voices* is very similar to that of its contemporary, *The water lily* which will be examined in Chapter 3.)

The three early songs display a self-conscious, effusive intensity through, first of all, an overzealous quantity of material and, secondly, the use of vocal-melodic devices that, by their subservience to the chord-oriented piano part, are inept. The employment of melisma in *A lake and a fairy boat* epitomises this phenomenon: melisma is a device that Warlock uses on only a handful of occasions within his entire *oeuvre* and he is not at all comfortable about its deployment in this particular song, as the treatment of the words "boat" and "sail" attests (Ex. 2.1). Such shortcomings mark these songs as juvenilia (they were written the year he left Eton) but, like the best of that commodity, they present embryonically features that will surface in a more developed or polished form in mature works.

Key- and chord-relationships in *A lake and a fairy boat* are regulated by the semitone, a unit that helps to shape the linear progress, although other, conflicting material (particularly whole-tones) has both a melodic and harmonic function. There is no key-signature and the first bar suggests no stable centre while it announces the semitone as a linear unit with harmonic implications. This, of course, is how Delius used it and the outcome is so obviously Delian that it verges on parody. Only then is F minor stated[3] (in bar 2); there are no dominant harmonies but a

Ex. 2.1: *A lake and a fairy boat* – bars 1-6

pseudo-dominant quality is suggested by the anacrusis, a rising 4th, in bars 2-3. The use of familiar features, but without their usual associations, is a feature that permeates later music but with the bonus of motivic justification. In this song there is no such substantiation either within the piano-part or elsewhere.

Otherwise, forward motion is generated by chords that could be either added 6ths on the flattened supertonic or minor chords on the flattened leading-note (bars 3 and 5). They resolve directly on to the tonic and, whatever their derivation, rely on the flattened supertonic – another semitonal relationship – to create harmonic drive and tension. It is an early and relatively crude example of the creation of shapes, chordal in this instance, that can be seen to have a number of origins. The element of dual or multiple derivations is an important feature of the Warlockian attitude that will reappear on several occasions in different forms.

Another feature that emphasises the semitone as a structural element appears in the opening bar. The G natural that begins the vocal line contradicts the tied, instrumental G sharp but, nevertheless, provides a continuation of the falling semitone motif initiated by the piano. In the context of later material, this is significant in a number of respects. It is a striking device when considered next to other weak or ugly melodic figures in the song; the consideration that Warlock must have given it in relation to these other shapes anticipates the importance he will place on vertical and horizontal integration as a feature of his constructional technique. There is a consequent reliance upon the vocal line that, despite its other shortcomings, anticipates the stronger shapes of the future. These, often in a strophic context, act as cantus firmi against which the piano can supply harmonic and motivic interest. It is noteworthy to see these criteria established in what may be Warlock's earliest extant work.[4]

More instability is introduced, first by a short circle-of-5ths (bars 7-8) and then by a progression that falls chromatically (bars 9-10); after this, F minor gives way to F major (the new mediant being a semitone-shaped shift) that is, in turn, allowed to become confused with its relative minor.[5] The D minor side of this ambiguity initially appears not so much in its own right but in the form of an added 6th to a tonic chord of F (Ex. 2.2) after which the new chord and a network of related ones is allowed to predominate. The added 6ths (indeed, added 9ths also) arise from

Ex. 2.2: *A lake and a fairy boat* – bars 15-16 (piano part only)

whole-tone displacements that start in bars 2 and 3 (see Ex. 2.1 again) and reappear in both the central, freely modulating section and the F major/Dminor-based one at the end. These added 6ths are of several kinds, minor on a major triad, major on a major triad and, most significantly of all, major on a minor triad. This produces the inverted *Tristan* chord, the shape that was to control large tracts of *The curlew* and which will be in evidence throughout Warlock's career. These added 6ths are related by inversion to chords of the 7th but, while Warlock will learn to control such ambiguous chord-shape derivations in later compositions, such is the profusion of shapes here that the song loses direction, over-relying upon the ephemeral sensuousness of individual chords (Hood's "Strings of orient pearls", perhaps) rather than a stronger formal logic. The same criticism can, of course, be levelled at examples from Delius's own music.

A similar plethora of features characterises *Music when soft voices die*, set in motion by three multiple-device bars from the piano. Whole-tones and falling semitones are again evident, as are perfect 4ths. All of these features have parts to play as the song unfolds but added 6ths and parallel chords (themselves based on 6ths – see bar 3 in Ex. 2.3) will be the principal units; they pervade the song both as a detail of the harmony and as an instigating force behind the chordal structure.

Ex. 2.3: *Music when soft voices die* **– bars 1-8 (originally a minor 3rd higher)**

The added 6th to the tonic chord recalls *A lake and a fairy boat* in that the F-centred introduction and the setting of Shelley's initial couplet are beset with Ds. In this song, though, there is a stronger gesture toward more usual tonal practices in the dominant-tonic quality of the first two bars and the circle-of-5ths figures (complete with Delian falling semitones) in bars 4-6. The pseudo-modulation (dominant of the dominant in bar 4) also suggests conventional procedures although it anticipates no similar move elsewhere in the song. The meandering figure in bar 5 creates, via its semitonal alternatives, a momentary, quasi-modal, musica ficta effect (E flat in the falling form, E natural in the rising), a foretaste of later works and interests.

The rest of the stanza is based on a quasi-modal D with flattened leading notes reminiscent of Mixolydian 7ths (another shape of things to come) in both melody and harmony. The added 6ths are still prevalent; they are developed to produce the pentatone-based chords and figures in bars 9-11. The A flat 9th that colours "quicken" (bar 13, Ex. 2.4) marks both the end of the first stanza and the D-based central section. It is,

Ex. 2.4: *Music when soft voices die* – bar 13

along with an F sharp 9th in the final, ultimately F-centred section, a further manifestation of the semitonal motion that had influenced *A lake and a fairy boat*. Appearances of this device are less evident here although, once more, it is first presented in the opening bars.

There are two surviving versions of this song; the foregoing analysis applies specifically to the later version[6] but is pertinent to both. Some of the differences are largely cosmetic – small rhythmic alterations and the notated arpeggio in bar 11, for example – although there are some larger changes to the second stanza. In the earlier version Warlock repeats accompanimental figures from the first stanza whereas, in the later one, he extends the falling semitone idea and amends the melody accordingly (Ex. 2.5). It is interesting to note that the A flat 9th in bar 13 (second

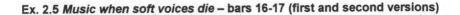

Ex. 2.5 *Music when soft voices die* – bars 16-17 (first and second versions)

version) was originally notated in terms of G sharp, the alteration confirming his conception of the chord as a semitonally shifted chord on the mediant, a process that recalls the F major/minor element in *A lake and a fairy boat*. There are other chordal alterations too, in bars 10, 12 and 14; in terms of what will emerge as Warlock's chordal vocabulary, they are significant, for there is usually a semitone difference between the two versions. The chordal choice of the last bars is quite different in the later version, though: Warlock rejects the sensuousness – the sensuality even – of his penultimate chord (first version) in favour of a more motivically and chordally structured conclusion (Ex. 2.6).

The wind from the west anticipates many songs with its dotted rhythms in compound time. *Robin Goodfellow* (1926), which uses similar figures, is more brilliantly frenetic but relates back to this one and the rising figures of bars 13 and 15-17 (Ex. 2.7). Although centred

Ex. 2.6: *Music when soft voices die* – closing bars
first version (bars 22-26)

second version (bars 22-24)

Ex. 2.7: *The wind from the west* – bars 13 & 16-17 (piano only)

and the rising figures of bars 13 and 15-17 (Ex. 2.7). Although centred on E flat there is no modulation. To begin with there is a brief conflict between tonic and dominant but the chordal usage, at times unnecessarily dense, is of limited interest in itself. There is nothing new here that has not already been observed (beyond the rhythmic interest already mentioned). Nevertheless there is a significant spin-off that points to future developments. It has been noted (regarding *A lake and a fairy boat*) that, in these early songs, Warlock favours the chordal progress; the vocal melody is thereby disadvantaged. In *The wind from the west* this is still largely the case although the deleterious effect on the melody is lessened in the outer sections by the easier (and, it must be said, more tonally conformist) nature of the harmonic motion. It is the central section (bars 9-18) that is striking, not for its beauty – the angular results are still gauche and clumsy because of their dependence on chordal adjacency – but as evidence of what Warlock regards, at this stage, as melodically acceptable. The same can be said, of course, with regard to the two contemporary songs but there is a greater fluidity in this one. The melodic chromaticism emanates from semitonal passing-notes in the piano part. Eighty-five years on these sound excessively cloying and self-indulgent but the kind of melodic outline they engender will be developed in future pieces, as *The water lily* will testify. Furthermore, the semitonal displacements in the final two bars of the piano accompaniment, which result in dissonance and proto-polyphony, anticipate by some five years the entry of Bernard van Dieren into his circle of friends and associates (Ex.2.8).

Ex. 2.8 *The wind from the west* **– bars 29-30 (piano only)**

Notes

1   See FT1 passim.

2   A completion by Anthony Ingle (T 1975 & T(i)).

3   All pitches, keys and centres refer to published editions where applicable. This song was originally a minor 3rd higher. For details of original pitches see FT1 and T editions. The situation is complicated, unfortunately. As is often the case with other composers, Warlock's songs appear in transposed editions for different voices. He disliked this practice and preferred to rewrite accompaniments to suit a new vocal range, but, of course, this was not always a practical consideration. With this in mind it might be thought preferable to cite all examples at the pitch initially decided by the composer. However, to aid investigation and comparison beyond this survey, the published pitch – or one of them – is employed in references and examples.

4   See IC p. 55. However, in the PWS edition (T(i)) FT places *The wind from the west* ahead of it.

5   Is this not a concentrated form (and only three years after the event) of the deliberately tortuous tonal scheme of Schoenberg's second string quartet? It commences in F sharp minor but the third movement suggests E flat minor, the relative of the tonic major.

6   See FT's preface to T(i).

CHAPTER 3

New beginnings

The water lily (1917) is roughly contemporary with *The lover mourns for the loss of love* (which constitutes the second movement of the *Curlew* cycle but was actually the first one to be written). Despite the Debussian instructions at the start, it represents an early manifestation of the effect on Warlock's music of his acquaintance with Bernard van Dieren and his music. It was to have been part of *Saudades* (see below), the work that displays the effect of the van Dieren encounter so strongly but was, in the end, left out. The style is more consciously dissonant than before and there is an increased rhythmic diversity. But, after examination, it can be seen to extend elements already experienced in earlier material.

The chordal vocabulary is familiar for the most part: only a handful of chords cannot be named. 79 chords constitute the piano accompaniment. Of course, the actual number of chords present depends on how they are counted! Cross-rhythms and appoggiaturas may, depending on interpretation, suggest more or less than the figure given but the total is offered as a fair one. The term "*Curlew*-chord" refers to the reshaped (inverted) *Tristan* chord that Warlock uses so frequently (and most overtly in *The curlew* itself); he acquired it not so much from Wagner but from Delius. In referring to it thus, any implications of spacing or resolution inherent in the *Tristan* chord are avoided.[1] There are:

    5 major chords;   7 minor chords;   8 minor 7ths;

    3 major 6ths (related to a minor 7th by inversion);

    2 major 7ths;   27 *Curlew*-chords;

    11 augmented 6ths (non-functional but in the German 6th/dominant 7th configuration).

There are also:

    1 minor 7th that has one note semitonally displaced;

    4 *Curlew*-chords that have one note semitonally displaced;

    4 diminished chords (a *Curlew*-chord with a particular kind of semitonal displacement);

    2 augmented chords.

Five others are more difficult to categorise. Three of them are chords built on 5ths (like that at the beginning) and the other two are shapes derived from pentatones. Substantially more will be said in due course about constituents of the latter grouping.

In this song, vocal and instrumental components are much less inter-dependent than had been the case; there are many instances where the former is semitonally displaced from the latter to create "wrong-note" harmonies reminiscent of the end of *The wind from the west*. Other semitonal aberrations are built into the vocal line: the E at the end of bar 3 is contradicted by the E flat in bar 5 and the F (also in bar 5) is cancelled by the F sharp in the following bar. These are just examples; like the "wrong" notes they are not isolated instances but permeate the entire song. Of 58 melody notes,[2] 15 (approximately a quarter) are at variance with the harmonic underlay (eight of them semitonally, making the consequent dissonances very astringent) and 13 are semitonal alternatives as described. The latter grouping constitutes one of those situations where the stimulus could be Bartók as much as van Dieren. It is wrong to assume that Warlock's modernism derives solely from van Dieren, a fact that must be made clear even at this early stage. Or, perhaps, it is more correct to say that Warlock's familiarity with Bartókian dissonance which, after all, began during his schooldays[3] provided something of a preparation for van Dieren's more robust style.

Some chords that have been placed in one or another category are fusions of two types. For example, in bar 7 the first chord presents elements of the minor 7th shape (in the total of which it is included) but it also has affinities with the 5ths-based chords (Ex. 3.1); the next chord too is classified as a minor 7th although it is shaped by the *Curlew*-chord as well. It is worth drawing attention to these chords that are formed by semitonally adjusting other shapes; they also are important in later works. It must be stressed that all of these chords are used in a non-functional manner. The opening approaches the pandiatonic and, from the above listing, it is apparent that (as if to emphasise the tonal instability of the piece) the accompaniment is peppered with *Curlew*-chords – they account for about one third of the total. The first chord of the piano introduction demands comment. It is built on 5ths and is so classified above; it could be described as a chord of the 11th but is also a spread form of the pentatone, a device to which Warlock returns, in one form or another, again and again. Although Warlock's pentatonic chords assume different characters as a result of spacing and inversion (just like triadic chords) they all possess essentially the same, familiar "black-keys" configuration. His relationship with the pentatone comes and goes over the next few years although it achieves total consolidation

Ex. 3.1: *The water lily* – bars 1-8

in the *Lillygay* cycle (1922). It can be viewed as another Delian legacy[4] but, as with the inherited semitone, Warlock imbues it with a strong, individual character.

Yet in many respects the harmonic armoury in *The water lily* – if not its actual deployment – is pure Delius. An examination of his *Twilight fancies (Abendstimmung)*[5] (1889) displays the utilisation of a similar chordal repertoire – *Curlew*-chords, diminished and minor 7ths and non-functional German 6ths (Ex. 3.2).

The cloths of heaven was a constituent of the original version of *The curlew*[6] and dates from 1916. It was to be recomposed in 1925 as *The sick heart* (to words by Arthur Symons)[7] but the original version will be discussed at this point. Its lack of barring identifies it visually with other van Dieren-influenced pieces although it is, for the most part, in conventional (Warlockian) compound time. This is how, suitably barred, it was later to reappear. Much of its harmonic material is familiar by now although it lacks the intense interrelationships which will be

Ex: 3.2 *Twilight fancies/Abendstimmung* (Delius) bars 3-6 & 14-17

evident in *The lover mourns for the loss of love*. Several chords have added notes, often 9ths but sometimes 11ths or 13ths and the resulting aggregations are used for their own sake, as with the interpolated 6ths in the 1911 songs, without recourse to textbook procedures; the song is loosely in C major/minor and the vocal entry is marked by a short pedal on C. For Warlock this is not so much a means of creating tensions within a clearly defined key-area as a way of restricting tonal growth, holding down any potential development. There is a brief utilisation of pentatone-based chords, but it is the end of the song, particularly the final chord and associated notes, where the principal interest lies as far as Warlock's harmonic procedures are concerned.

The arpeggiated chords of C, like those of a recitative, punctuate the vocal and verbal statement within which a B flat is given prominence both by duration and repetition. It forms an augmented (German) 6th shape with the piano but also presents a modal quality by announcing the flattened leading note. (It will be recalled that the terms "German

6th" or "dominant 7th" are used for convenience and merely describe the shape of the chord rather than any functional responsibilities it may possess.) It has been observed that, in the 1911 songs, Warlock failed to reconcile semitone and whole-tone elements. The latter feature is present in this song too: a B flat (rather than the A) would complete the whole-tone run of the final vocal phrase (Ex. 3.3) and it is tempting to look forward a little and interpret this in terms of Warlock's eventual espousal of modal elements where the whole tone and semitone both relate to the final as alternative 7ths. As a melodic manifestation of a

Ex. 3.3: *The cloths of Heaven* – conclusion (unbarred)

(no tempo given)

harmonic requirement (the German 6th is one of his "family" of frequently used chords) it is a solution to a problematical interval. Of course, there are also aesthetic implications but, at this stage, the situation is considered from the logical and practical viewpoint. The aesthetic argument will become more relevant in due course when the question of modality is addressed more fully, particularly in relation to the Winthrop Rogers songs.

A further multiplex device that confirms an interrelationship of chords within a Warlockian "family" can be identified in the piano's last chord and ensuing echo of the vocal phrase (Ex. 3.3 again). When the F sharp is sounded, the chord formed is a composite of another two of those that will often be experienced, the minor 7th and *Curlew*-chords – the resultant dissonance encapsulates both their linear similarity and difference. When the F sharp is replaced by G sharp the result is a fusion of minor 7th (held by the left hand) and augmented 6th – Italian rather than the fuller and, in the circumstances, more potentially confusing, German. Thus the "family" is consolidated – a relationship between chords that is shaped and controlled by the semitone, one that will later increase and be stabilised.[8]

For many years, the three songs that constitute the *Saudades* set were the only representatives of Warlock's early style readily available. Although written in 1916-17, they did not appear in print until Chester published them in 1923. By this time other, later, songs were already available (from Winthrop Rogers, mostly). The 1911 songs were not to be published until 1972 (by Thames). But before discussing the pieces further, it must be made clear that, like many groupings of Warlock's songs, they do not constitute a song-cycle. Perhaps *The curlew* is not really a cycle either but the original performance of 1920 may have been so considered. One can make out a strong case that *Lillygay* and *Candlelight* are true cycles but other collections (such as the two sets of *Peterisms* and the *Seven songs of summer*) are really just convenient aggregations rather than integrally conceived and interrelated groupings; the songs were often published individually. Unfortunately, songs from the cycles are sometimes performed separately.

The second song of *Saudades* and the first written, *Take O take those lips away*, is one of three settings[9] that Warlock made of Shakespeare's text. It has a remote sense of F minor although this is made the more difficult to appreciate by the frequent interpolation into chords of extraneous Cs (dominants or, given the intangibility of the tonic, theoretical dominants), the use of tonally non-specific chordal material (*Curlew*-chords and non-functional progressions in general), references to tonally distant areas (in terms of F) and, not least, anarchic vocal-melodic phrases that contradict piano harmonies. These combined factors could well be construed as "disillusioned hedonism"[10] but closer examination reveals a chordal vocabulary not so far removed from that which has become familiar. There is, once more, a reliance on particular kinds of chords such as minor 7ths and *Curlew*-chords, but there is a greater tendency, even more so than in *The water lily*, to distort shapes either by adding extra notes (such as suspensions, resolved or otherwise) or by the use of aggregate chords, fusions of two or more of the "family". Thus dissonance can be achieved by what are, largely, conventional processes; but there is also a degree of vocal-line independence, a continuation of *Water lily* techniques, created by harmonic discrepancy and semitonal aberration (Ex. 3.4).

Interestingly enough in the context of developments in contemporary songs, this one commences with a pentatone – or, rather, two of them. The relationship of the pentatone to the chordal family is demonstrable

Ex. 3.4: *Take o take those lips away (Saudades)* – bars 11-14

in a number of ways and will be considered from time to time in specific instances. In layout, it contains the notes of a minor 7th chord plus one that can be interpreted as a passing-note between 3rd and 5th or – and this phenomenon has already been noted[11] – an added 11th (Ex. 3.5a). Here the two pentatones employed are adjacent, that is, they are a 5th (or a 4th) apart. Consequently they not only have four notes in common but their respective remaining notes are only a semitone different (Ex. 3.5b). Warlock makes this relationship prominent by allowing the D flat

Ex. 3.5: pentatonic devices

(bar 2 – see Ex. 3.6) to fall on to the C, these being the pitches that complete, in terms of the two pentatone shapes, the rising figure of the opening bar. In the process, the F-centredness of the piece is stated but with a dominant bias (a van Dierenesque quality), anticipating the tonal instability that is to characterise the song. The C reappears in the next bar as an appoggiatura, then again in bar 4 within a horizontal motif in the bass against a chord to which it does not belong. In the latter case the resultant C-D flat interval is an inverted, octave-transposed echo of bar 2; it anticipates a number of similar occurrences where contradictory Cs are interpolated into harmonies in a linear manner, adjacent to D flats. The initial falling 2nd, D flat-C, is a gesture of mock resolution (or, more prosaically, an appoggiatura, as will be the case in similar

Ex. 3.6: *Take o take those lips away (Saudades)* – bars 1-4 (piano only)

instances later in the song) but it also relates back to the Delian falling semitone, *A lake and a fairy boat* and *Music when soft voices die*. By this stage, though, the semitone has been assimilated into Warlock's own vocabulary and imbued with a personalised usage. For this reason *Take O take . . .* stands at something of a watershed: in one sense it is the ultimate post-Delian piece, the luxuriance of its harmonies recalling Delius's own. building upon what he had acquired from Grieg; yet, in a different light, it possesses a new direction, a heightened sense of linear motif that both extends and links together banks of chords. In this circumstance it is not unreasonable to see it as the earliest manifestation of Peter Warlock the genuinely individual composer, finally discovering a personalised style that successfully transforms Delian infatuation into Warlockian self-assurance.

One small and, in some respects, unimportant detail of this song anticipates larger-scale manifestations in the future. Bar 21 repeats the vocal figure and associated words ("bring again") of the previous bar – the latter being dictated, as at the end of the verse, by Shakespeare's text (Ex. 3.7). The result is an example of word-painting, but differences in harmonic material prophesy the variations in harmonic emphasis that characterise Warlock's later, usually strophic uses of a similar but more extended technique.

The language of *Take O take those lips away* is Warlock's most consciously dissonant yet encountered and this despite the lack of tonal definition in *The water lily*. In *Heraclitus*[12] he refines the style, not without a backward glance or two. The clarity of line is more evident; it is manifest in the vocal part which has a powerfully lyrical fluidity for the angst of *Take O take . . .* has been sublimated and the dissonance softened as a result. The resultant tranquillity (without the desolation of *The lover mourns for the loss of love*) confirms the newness of purpose noted in *Take O take those lips away*. The reason for Warlock's

Ex. 3.7: *Take o take those lips away (Saudades)* – bars 19-21

rejection of *The water lily* from the set now begins to become clear. As Tomlinson suggests,[13] it is not excluded because it is a bad song, for this is obviously not so. In fact Warlock appears to recognise it as an anachronism belonging to an earlier stage in his development. If this is the reason, the situation regarding similar details in *The curlew* is made the more interesting; the appropriateness of the musical mood to the words aside, the mixture of chronological styles would suggest an autobiographical rationale to the whole work, an aspect which will be examined in the next chapter.

At this point, and before examining the rest of the *Saudades* set, it is worth examining the phenomenon of the *Curlew*-chord in a little more detail. The frequency with which it occurs in the songs so far discussed indicates its considerable importance in Warlock's constructional scheme. As a vertical element it contains the intervals of major 2nd, minor 3rd, perfect 4th, augmented 4th and minor 6th (Ex. 3.8). It also contains, by inversion, the intervals of major 3rd, perfect 5th, major 6th and minor 7th. It is this comprehensive quality that makes its Wagnerian

Ex. 3.8: Intervallic implications in the *Curlew*-chord

antecedent so strong and its consequent place in pre-modernist practice so significant. Interestingly enough, because it contains neither minor 2nd nor major 7th, it makes no reference to the semitone which also figures so strongly in Warlock's compositional armoury. The semitone and the *Curlew*-chord both complement and supplement one another, then. Indeed, they are combined at times when the former is brought to bear on the latter as a modifying force. The Delian heritage of the two devices, though, is transcended within Warlock's methodology; it is given a personalised logic and, hence, possesses a peculiar character. In a broader, more European, context there is a parallel with other devices that seek to encompass all intervals, if not actually all 12 semitones. A comparison with, for example, the note-row of Berg's *Lyrische suite* would not be out of place, not in the nature of the content or its deployment but of the rationale that underlies it.

Heraclitus[12] retains and extends the recitative-like quality of *The cloths of Heaven*, at least at the start. The voice here both disorients the chordal material and, paradoxically, completes it by extending horizontally the vertical shapes it utilises. To proclaim this point, the opening chord, a 9th, has its whole-tone and *Curlew*-chord associations exploited by the three notes of the vocal line, the prominence of the F sharp almost strong enough to convert the subsequent A minor chord into a *Curlew* shape (Ex. 3.9). Indeed, in this song there is a stronger

Ex.3.9: *Heraclitus* – opening (unbarred)

symbiosis between vocal line and accompaniment than had been the case before. The anarchic melodies of *The water lily* have been sublimated into a system that affords a degree of melodic and accompanimental independence, the aggregate effect being greater than merely the sum of its parts.

Ex. 3.10 demonstrates more instances of such a practice, announced initially by the opening declamation. The song drips with *Curlew*-chords. It is intriguing that they are frequently not in their pure state,

Ex.3.10: *Heraclitus* (unbarred – approximately a quarter of the way through)

"d7" indicates a dominant 7th/German 6th shape; "M7" is a major 7th; "–1" indicates one note in the shape has been semitonally adjusted. Some dynamics are omitted.

Warlock preferring to present semitonally adjusted versions or, often, *Curlew*-chords on to which additional notes have been grafted. Also, and most interestingly of all, he presents his semitonally displaced chords adjacent to the unmodified, "correct" versions, yet again confirming (just like the ending of *The cloths of Heaven*) the linearly inspired relationships within his chordal family. *Along the stream* maintains the cohesion between chordal and melodic elements. Here the effect is horizontal – more so than in any piece so far encountered – but the logic behind this motion remains vertical. In this respect it may be said that Warlock finally achieves what had evaded him for so long, the successful fusion of what, until this point, had been for him diverse, even incompatible, components. The piano introduction is constructed from elements of *Curlew* and other "family"-chords; semitones continue to amend chordal shapes but melodically they occur only as constituents of individual chords rather than independent features in their own right. At a first encounter – certainly graphically – it bears the van Dieren imprint. The lack of bar lines, as in *Heraclitus*, is genuine, there being a fluidity of movement that rejects regular metre, and this rhythmic flexibility, as in van Dieren's own music, complements the non-tonal progress. In the *Saudades* songs there is something of van Dieren's breathlessness (and, it must be said, congestion) as the second half of *Along the stream* illustrates. This is the same process that was recognised in *The water lily*, but now it has become more intense.

In the achievement of horizontal drive the *Saudades* songs are successful and they effectively employ Warlock's sophisticated and considered harmonic processes. But they are unique in Warlock's output for their employment of such a richness of elements – rhythmic profusion, polyphonic intensity, tonal rejection and consequent harmonic daring. They therefore pose an important question: why did he seem to turn his back on such a hard-won stylistic pinnacle, choosing to develop his attainments in a different direction? After these songs, Warlock's music appears to become even more eclectic. It is possible that, though he never totally abandoned it, this extreme form of the methodology offered by van Dieren provided too heady a mixture for general use. It does reappear, but only in a limited number of situations; in the last sections of *The curlew* to be written, for example, the special, autobiographical nature of the piece[14] creates an atypical situation. But, really, the pursuit of linear respectability (in an aesthetic sense) had gone too far and the harmonic requirement had become obscured. The rationale of the vertical component always predominates in Warlock's music and in these pieces the balance shifts too far to the horizontal. These interpretations may be over-speculative; whatever the reason, the next batch of songs demonstrates what is, on the surface, a stylistically dramatic change. The van Dieren experience made Warlock rethink his attitude towards horizontal shapes and the assumption of clearer melodic lines is the result. But the construction of these lines needed tight control. It is not possible to comprehend fully Warlock's changing attitude towards vocal melody without looking at two works contemporary with *Saudades*, a couple of rare, instrumental forays, and their implications. Not only do the constituent movements contain material that is of interest in its own right, but the nature of the melodic content is one that can be seen as influential in terms of the style of later work.

The five short pieces that constitute the *Folk-song preludes* are not his earliest surviving instrumental pieces. This distinction must go to the *Codpieces*, a witty and, at times, irreverent collection[15] that, for all its qualities, is not for discussion here. Reference to the *Preludes* at this point is not entirely accurate chronologically for they would only appear in their completed form in 1922. However, the first inspirational rush of activity dates from 1917, the time of Warlock's Celtic realisation, and the initial versions of movements II-V were produced then. A number of other tunes were similarly treated, although these have now been lost.[16] Warlock was not involved with the Folksong Movement to the extent that Ralph Vaughan Williams (whose music he appreciated in spite of his sarcastic remarks)[17] and Jack Moeran (whom he later befriended) both were. Nonetheless, he was an enthusiast and, among other issues, a supporter of Bartók's use of folk material; it is known that he sought to emulate him in the production of these preludes.[18] He was not a collector of material in the manner of Sharp or Karpeles (or those mentioned above) and so, in the strictest sense of the term, he can be described only as a peripheral figure who enjoyed listening to local singers[19] and this would appear to have been an early enthusiasm which predates the *Folk-song preludes* by several years.[20] He was, however, to set a number of texts (or variants) that are known to ethnomusicologists, so it is impossible to disassociate him entirely from the Movement.

What makes the *Folk-song preludes* (and, to a lesser extent, *An old song*) worthy of notice from a compositional point of view hinges on the order in which the elements of the piece were conceived and executed. It is evident that, up to this point, the melodic element (in the form of the vocal line) of the works discussed has been effected simultaneously with the chordal material or, as one must suspect is the case with the earliest songs, after it. Here the melodies – genuine folk tunes[21] – precede the chordal content and must, to some extent, affect chordal selection. But despite Warlock's affection for folk-music and his love of things Celtic, his choice of the tunes can be viewed as much from a compositional as a cultural standpoint, especially in view of his later revision and selection of the sketch material.[22] With the exception of the tune of *Prelude* IV, the themes employed are pentatonic, a shape which has already been identified as a component of some of the songs, and one which has also been shown to be part of the chordal family. It will be another folksong-related piece, the *Lillygay* cycle, that will confirm and strengthen the relationship.

The first of the *Preludes* has a sense of modes other than the pentatonic but, because the D-final melody lacks either a 3rd or a 6th it is not possible to define which particular one is in use (although the harmonies of the first bar suggest Dorian – see Ex. 3.11): Warlock can experiment harmonically with different 3rds (F or F sharp) and 6ths (B or B flat) as Ex. 3.12 summarises. The circumstances allow much

Ex. 3.11: *Folk-song preludes I – bar 1*

Ex. 3.12: D-centred modes

Dorian   Mixolydian   Aeolian

semitonal juxtaposition and juggling and not just with the notes stated. The result is, to some extent, familiar but with an increased use of conventional, triadic chords. These 3rds-based shapes are disguised in several ways – by inversion (particularly the second) or extension (to 7ths, 9ths and beyond); the harmonic vocabulary is centred on D. Yet the piece is not in D[23] partly because of the modal aspect and also as a result of the chord-choice. The Bs and Fs apart, chromaticism results, more often than not, from semitonal motion in the part-writing. But there is a dominant pedal – a quasi-drone – in the central section (Ex. 3.13); and, while there is no modulation to emphasise the D-centre, a chord of E, the dominant of the dominant, in bar 7 is echoed in bar 14 to form one of the alternative and adjacent cadences that close the movement (Ex. 3.14). These vestiges of tonal practice combine with the modes to produce a mixture of the familiar and the remote. There are references to E elsewhere but they are even more transitory and arise from chromatic insinuation affecting individual lines within the texture. Minor chords and their extensions predominate and the *Curlew*-chord, until now a measure of Warlock's non-tonal leanings, is reduced to a small number of appearances (one in the first section, two in the second and five in the third).

Warlock offers three treatments of the tune and these constitute the sections referred to. Copley's criticism of them is fair up to a point ("a rather laboured production . . . textures sometimes thick and clotted . . . harmonies often sound contrived rather than inevitable . . . very big

Ex. 3.13: *Folk-song preludes* I – bars 4-7

Ex. 3.14: *Folk-song preludes* I – bars 12-18. The small notation is Warlock's.

hands are required to cope with the widely spread chords").[24] They are logical rather than intuitive, but this objection can be applied to many a pivotal work. Some of the results, though, are striking in the most positive way – several harmonies in the last section are not unworthy of Bartók. Bar 13 possesses an element of conflicting ascending and descending modal forms that would not be out of place in a piece by him (Ex. 3.14 again).

Prelude II has two verses. (It is reasonable to regard these pieces as songs-without-words, given the simple, effectively strophic forms that they largely employ, the fact that the original themes were song-tunes, and the Warlockian context as a whole.) Copley points to the influence of van Dieren[25] to account for the rhythmic complexity of bar 8 but this is an unsatisfactory, if convenient, response. It is an extension of the multi-metre layout (Warlock uses 3/8, 5/8 and 7/8 as well as the 3/4 that predominates) which could equally be Bartókian or Schoenbergian in origin and it is likely that, since he did not record the tune himself in the field but took it from a reference work,[26] he has indulged in a little manipulation of the rhythms to create a quasi-spontaneous atmosphere. The *Allegretto rubato* instruction, the changes of tempo and the rhythmic differences between the melodic lines of the two verses substantiate this. Such a procedure is fully justifiable, and not necessarily inauthentic. Tunes notated in the field often appear on the printed page in a bare and multipurpose form, bereft of ornamentation or the variants that may be necessary to accommodate irregularities of verbal metre within a strophic structure. There is as much reconstruction and sympathetic conjecture necessary in the credible performance of ethnic material as in that pertaining to Baroque music. In these circumstances Warlock's version is likely to be as authentic as the next person's for, after all, he had firsthand experience of listening to folksingers and his melodic and rhythmic variants could have been suggested by them.

The harmonies he employs could not, although there are very few surprises in the first verse. The choice of chords is very restrained; Warlock succumbs readily to the arpeggios of the melody. Both the irregularity of the metre and the part-writing dilute this effect somewhat by distracting attention from the fact and, while there is a momentary modulation to the dominant – although not where one might expect it, in bar 6 of an eight-bar tune (Ex. 3.15) – it too is disguised, this time by a double appoggiatura and the unusual positioning of the fermata, another rhythmically disorienting detail.

Ex. 3.15: *Folk-song preludes* II – bars 1-7.

But all of these features cannot conceal the fact that, from a purely harmonic point of view, this is the most conservative passage of Warlock's music to survive since *The wind from the west*; it is made up principally of major chords with a few minor and dominant 7ths. There is only one *Curlew*-chord but two others are *Curlew*-chords with semitonal displacements. There is one chord based on 5ths and a dominant 11th. While these are not entirely the shapes of things to come (because they represent an extreme chordal reaction to a melodic situation), they demonstrate the continuing process of modification to a harmonic philosophy which had been evolving since *A lake and a fairy boat.* So Warlock has not abandoned his chordal family but it has become influenced by the nature of the melodic material, and none too successfully at that. Problems arise when he attempts to impose a more chromatic and less tonally secure vocabulary on a tune that has harmonic implications of its own and which is certainly strong enough to be sung unaccompanied or with only the minimum of support. Warlock had respected that situation in his initial harmonisation but, in seeking to personalise something that was not of his making, he falls, alas, into the trap of writing chords that are individually exciting but which have to vie for attention with the folk-tune.[27] There are the remnants of a tonal logic that might just succeed in holding the piece together were it not for the disfiguring effect of the polyphony (Ex. 3.16). Warlock was scathing about Cyril Scott[28] but he seems equally guilty of excess on this occasion!

Ex. 3.16: *Folk-song preludes* II – bars 11-18; melody with harmonic summary.

References have already been made (concerning *Music when soft voices die*) to Warlock's harmonic use of the pentatone shape and, in the third *Prelude*, he constructs a harmonic vocabulary around it. Some chords that have already been encountered are derived from the pentatone. The minor 7th shape uses four of the five notes – as do some of the 9ths that occurred in the early songs. This is the logic behind several chords in *Prelude* III but Warlock uses the first two bars as an exposition or statement-of-intent before embarking on a more abstract usage. The D flat in the first bar, emphasised rhythmically, creates a minor 7th chord when sounded against the E flat minor chord. The addition of a fifth note in the next, widely spaced chord is, both aurally and logically, the next step; as if to emphasise the point, Warlock completes the chord twice, once with the G flat and then with the F, thereby offering two different pentatone shapes bound linearly by his version of the Delian falling 2nd (Ex. 3.17). Once again, he is endeavouring to integrate vertical and horizontal elements: number II was doomed to failure in this respect because of the shapes created in an otherwise pentatonic melody. The fact that he realised this is suggested by his abandoning the pentatone in the short linking passages between the verses. The two bars can be interpreted as a purely chordal interlude but, in the context of the other material the highest notes assume the rôle of a melody. The A (bar 9) is only sounded once but extends the pentatone to six notes. Warlock was unhappy about these pieces[29] and, while he tended to be self-deprecatory about much of his output, the clash of interests between melody and harmony, something

Ex. 3.17: *Folk-song preludes* III – bars 1-2.

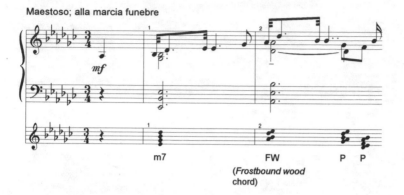

he perpetually attempted to reconcile (and had achieved in *Saudades*), makes him feel uncomfortable here. His use of pentatone-derived chords, seen in retrospect to have always been a part of his chordal vocabulary, is presented as a solution. At this stage it is a relatively crude method but later works, notably *Lillygay* again, will demonstrate a process of refinement.

The crucial chord in terms of this seminal pentatonic technique – in that it demonstrates further the relationship between the pentatone and other family chords – occurs towards the end of the piece (the penultimate chord of bar 18, Ex. 3.18). Although based on only three notes and not a complete chord that can be unequivocally defined as one thing or another, it could be derived either from a pentatone or a *Curlew*-chord. In this respect it recalls the conclusion of *The cloths of Heaven* where Warlock drew together a number of family chords, confirming their relationship by association. Here, ambiguity proves equally strong a process. But this knowledge may force a reappraisal of chordal patterns experienced earlier: the added 9ths of *A lake and a fairy boat*, although built into minor chords, can now be seen to assume a prophetic significance. They share a characteristic of chords in *Prelude* III and, while the chords in the earlier piece may have initially derived from more conventional horizontal/vertical interaction (appoggiaturas resolved or otherwise), it does not diminish their importance.

Prelude IV is exceptional in the set because the melody is not pentatonic. In spite (or because) of this, Warlock relates the first chord to a vertical pentatone. The E flat, conforming to the note-plan of the melody, is a semitonal displacement of the "correct" E natural which is

Ex. 3.18: *Folk-song preludes* III – bars 17-21.

Ex. 3.19: *Folk-song preludes* IV – bars 1-2.

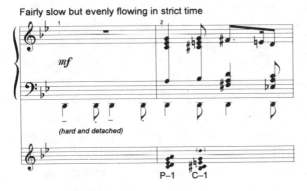

substituted for it in the following chord (Ex. 3.19). The first chord is also a *Curlew*-chord over a D pedal and further demonstrates the place of the pentatone, albeit in this modified shape, within the chordal family. However, the principal interest of the first half of the movement lies in the use of a bass pedal. In some senses this is unremarkable. The device has already been mentioned (in relation to *The cloths of heaven* and the first of these *Preludes*) and here Warlock uses it in much the same way that any pedal is employed – sometimes it blends with the chord above it, sometimes it is at variance with it. What is noteworthy is that he uses it at all for, while it is theoretically a dominant (in terms of the melody), there is no harmonically sustained sense of note-centre against which it can pull. In other words, the chords used reject any notion of a tonic and swamp the otherwise clear sense of G minor inherent in the melody (Ex. 3.20). The chordal juxtapositions – there is

Ex. 3.20: *Folk-song preludes* IV – bars 13-14.

no real sense of functional progression despite (or because of) the uncompromising semitone-dependent motion within parts – are too heavily reliant on the effects generated by individual note-aggregations to be corporately satisfying (This state of affairs deteriorates even further in the contrived part-writing of the second verse). The pedal here fails to be the supreme binding device that it will prove to be in, for example, *All the flowers of the spring* and, instead, creates an extra layer of information that only makes the texture more obscure. Warlock's intention may well have been to present a contrast to the accompanimental busyness of the second verse and, if this is the case, his conception of the device is less harmonic than linear.

Prelude V is a more successful – and less contentious – piece than the preceding one. The melodic pentatonicism is paralleled by a simpler harmonic outline, the more extrovertly dramatic elements being channelled into dynamic, rhythmic and textural statements. Chordally this *Prelude* has little that is new beyond a restraint not noticeable in some of its companion pieces. Its rhythmic bravado is not particularly satisfying as a compensation for this.

A more extended work, contemporary with and related to the *Folk-song preludes*, is *An old song* (1917). It is a treatment of a Celtic melody too, pentatonic to boot, but within a more rhapsodic structure than is normally associated with Warlock and one that is overtly Delian. However, to what extent its derivative nature is essential or merely superficial must be discovered by examination of the material.

The first chord is a fusion of several, not necessarily compatible, elements. Horn and low strings hold a three-note chord that anticipates the opening notes of the "old song" while the violins – in four parts as in Delius's *On hearing the first cuckoo in spring* – play a minor 6th that falls a semitone (Ex. 3.21). The vertical build-up that results is complex and dissonant (but not harshly so because of the spacing and scoring). It breaks with Delius not only in terms of the material per se but because of its linear integration. It is, in fact, a single pattern superimposed on itself a tone higher, but the upper figure has been semitonally distorted. Because of the spacing, the violin figures appear to be at variance with what is happening lower down; it is really the other way about as the resolution of bars 7 and 8 indicates.

Ex. 3.21: *An old song* – bars 1-8 (actual sounds)

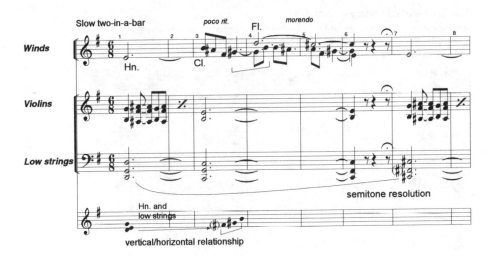

The Delian shift in bar 3 – lower parts move semitonally, bass falls – announces pentatone or 4ths-based harmonies; the clarinet figure (blatantly reminiscent of the oboe at the outset of *First cuckoo . .*) cuts across the underlying chords. Bars 7-11 answer bars 1-6, reducing their tensions in Warlockian terms by resorting to chords that conform to the family. The complex build up of bar 1 is modified into a semitonally adjusted *Curlew*-chord in bar 7 and the pentatones with conflicting unessentials are transformed into a chord that can be interpreted as two semitonally adjusted *Curlew*-chords, each an inversion of the other.

To herald the theme, though, there is a device hitherto unexploited – at least not in such an extended fashion as here. It has already been established that Warlock can associate family chords by juxtaposition. The eight chords of bars 12(i)-14(i) present the chordal panoply in a particularly ordered fashion with the *Curlew*-chord itself established as the link, the parental chord of the family, perhaps, that literally maintains the order (Ex. 3.22). Within the progression successive chord-types differ from one another by a semitone: thus chords 1, 2 and 3 conform to the scheme, as do chords 4, 5 and 6, then chords 7 and 8. Chord 7 is chord 6 with an added note; chords 3 and 6 are *Curlew*-chords. But rather than employ the semitone-dominated logic which will be experienced in *The lover mourns for the loss of love*, Warlock uses a technique here that is more like the pandiatonic introduction of *The water lily*, transfiguration rather than stasis – a philosophy appropriate to a landscape composition.

Ex. 3.22: *An old song* – bars 1-8

4/5 indicates a pentatonic chord from which only four notes have been used.
FW indicates the *Frostbound wood*-chord, a particular 4/5 shape.

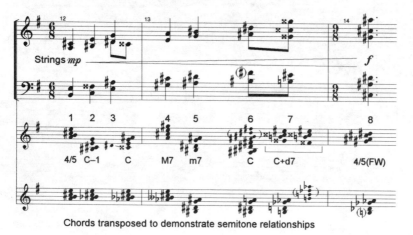

Chords transposed to demonstrate semitone relationships

Warlock found the melody structurally attractive, although he expressed his liking for it in emotional rather than formal terminology.[30] His treatment of it is similarly inspired but demonstrates the innate, constructional integration which has become increasingly typical. As to whether it is Delian or post-Delian is not in question. Some wag has apparently christened it *On hearing the second cuckoo in spring*[31] but that misses one point in the desire to make another. In broad, formal terms it is more subtle than those of Delius's orchestral works that Warlock would have known well (such as *Brigg fair* or the *Two pieces for small orchestra*) as the melody, although fixed and predetermined, appears to grow from other, essentially chordal material that simultaneously generates more – but consequently related – ideas. The chordal palette is strictly controlled and, while it does not possess the restricted choice of *The lover mourns for the loss of love*, there is a similarity in the way that the harmonic range is regulated.

It is evident by this stage that, while Delius was a stimulus (as van Dieren was a catalyst) it is Warlock's use – always more intellectual – of Delian borrowings that is the interesting feature. *An old song* is the last time that the Delius factor is so pronounced (except for the *Serenade*, a tribute and, therefore, something of a special case) and, because Warlock was never an innovative orchestral composer, there is rather too much of the older man's scoring in it for comfort. Warlock's passion for Delius was beginning to pale. He would never completely abandon his enthusiasm but it would be subject to moderation and, if *Saudades* had not adequately shuffled off the Delian mantle as a result of its extremism, by appearing to be so dependent on the stylistic paradigm, this particular piece achieves that effect. Nonetheless – and paradoxically – one is left to wonder whether or not, given the largely unsatisfactory nature of the *Preludes* and the successful, if spectacular, situation regarding *Saudades*, Warlock uses *An old song* as a way of getting back to his musical roots, an opportunity to reassess and retrench, at a time when he was undergoing a degree of emotional and aesthetic disturbance. His treatment of the received melody is more cautious then in the piano pieces and his harmonic panoply less blatant. The scoring is largely incidental, although it clouds other, more important compositional issues by enhancing the Delian superficiality. Warlock's orchestral output is tiny and, although his orchestration is competent, it is hardly remarkable and certainly not a crucial feature of his style.

Furthermore, while they are undoubtedly a turning point, the *Folk-song preludes* must be seen in the context of the *Saudades* set. It has been illustrated above that, in the songs, Warlock had achieved a genuine fusion of horizontal and vertical elements, establishing (the van Dieren influence notwithstanding) a highly individualistic yet musically valid vocabulary in the process. It is inappropriate to imply that in the *Preludes* he merely reverted to a more conventional methodology that had always been at the back of his mind. Such an implication would be unfair to the integrity revealed hitherto. What is recognised in the production of the piano pieces is that melody has a function within the otherwise chordal process. The new way of working is not a change of direction but an extension of previous practices. Just as a heavy reliance on chords now accommodates the rôle of melody, so is the way open for through-composition to be modified to a form of strophism that incorporates continual change. Characteristically, Warlock will employ his tunes in his own way; they will be lines made familiar by repetition against which the piano can exercise a degree of harmonic invention. The *Preludes* are the earliest example of the technique.

The songs that ensued and which were published by Winthrop Rogers would bring a degree of public recognition; they present a view of the composer that, without the benefit of the context of works discussed hitherto, could appear more conventional than is really the case. Closer examination will suggest that this conventionality is only superficial. It was claimed at the outset that very little of Warlock's output sounds like Delius. The same is true of van Dieren, *Saudades* and the *Folk-song preludes* aside. But Warlock's presentation of more overtly melodic procedures is a distillation of the van Dieren experience, the adoption of a linear process that, nevertheless, binds together and is, in fact, derived from the chordal rationale. The success of the songs sent to Rogers (in putting forward Peter Warlock) does not necessarily result from the way that they corporately endeavour to develop a compositional identity. The same could be said of Gray's opinion of them.[32]

A small diversion is necessary at this stage, partly for the sake of completeness, more to provide information that will only be fully relevant at a later point. *A Christmas hommage* [sic] *to Bernard van Dieren* is a brief piece in short score for unspecified resources. It precedes *I askèd a thief to steal me a peach* by a week[33] and, like the latter piece, it was intended as a seasonal greeting to a friend.[34] But, unlike it, the language is startling, more akin to the compositional style of its dedicatee. It utilises the same, abstracted, post-Delian mannerisms of the *Folk-song preludes* and, just as they did, seeks to provide a pre-composed melody with a chromatic, chordal underlay and ends up by overwhelming it. On this occasion, the melody is that of the well known Christmas hymn *The first Nowell* chosen, perhaps, because its scalic shapes are ripe for improvisation at the piano. While it has a certain interest as a novelty, it would have little or less importance in Warlock's output as a whole had not a short section of it been lifted out and inserted into a more significant piece, the second of the two Cornish carols. It has a seven-bar introduction motivically related to the main theme, a harmonisation of the melody of one verse, the refrain (the section transported into the later work) and a four-bar coda. As in the *Preludes*, the harmonic implications of the imported tune are at variance with those imposed by the composer and the result, though culturally amusing, presents an aesthetic conflict. Perhaps the *molto lento* instruction at the outset recognises this for it allows more time to savour each chordal statement (although it is moderated to *andante* at the start of the verse-melody).

Most of the harmony is based on family chords although there are several aberrations where the tune is not really compatible with the preferred chord. This is particularly noticeable where the melody, moving at but a steady speed, is considered to include passing-notes (see Ex. 3.23). One of the excesses modified in the later manifestation is a forced tonic pedal that accompanies the penultimate bar of the melody although, apart from cadence points, it has little regard for the A flat-centre that regulates the melody and upon which the entire piece eventually settles.

Ex. 3.23: *A Christmas hommage to Bernard van Dieren* **– bars 23-5**
(Warlock's notation)

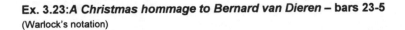

There have been so many references to a family of chords that the moment has arrived where some additional comment is necessary. The term implies not just a frequency of, but a relationship between, a small group of chords. These chords, used in their several inversions – a relevant consideration as will shortly be seen – do not necessarily have any functional character either with one another or with other chords from outside the family; progress between them depends on stepwise motion within individual lines, real or implied. The relationship has become increasingly evident in those pieces that have been discussed and it will continue to develop in works yet to be examined. In addition to unmodified major and minor chords (which play a subordinate rôle at this stage), the family consists of the chords of the minor and major 7ths, the (non-functional) German 6th (or dominant 7th) shape and the *Curlew*-chord. The Delian origin of these chords has already been noted but, by an extension of the relationships to be described in relation to *The lover mourns for the loss of love*, this group of four shapes can be viewed as related to one another linearly, the regulating factor that binds them together being the semitone. So (as Ex. 3.24 indicates) the *Curlew*-chord, when one note is semitonally modified, becomes a minor 7th. Subsequent semitonal alterations produce the dominant 7th/German

Ex. 3.24: Warlock's chordal "family"

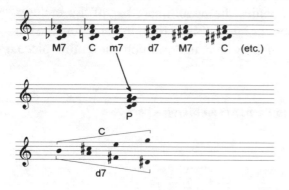

Ex. 3.25: Dr Day's chords, family chords and pentatonic derivatives

6th and then the major 7th configurations. The *Saudades* songs have been seen to employ these shapes continually, sometimes with further modification, particularly by semitonally altering one of the constituents. Later works will also be seen to use them extensively too. The fifth chord of the family is the pentatone and its relationship – to the minor 7th shape in particular – has already been commented upon in the discussion of *Take O take those lips away*. But the pentatone is not simply an addition to the others, an unrelated afterthought. The link to the minor 7th apart, the true relationship between the four modes is not yet fully established; but the last songs that Warlock was to write will show how the pentatone can encapsulate figures derived from or otherwise related to the other three.

There is some additional evidence of the way that Warlock thought: he reveals little about his compositional methods in either his formal or informal writings but a letter to Colin Taylor covers a number of issues.[35] On the nature of harmony Warlock assures his former teacher that it is the:

> . . . easiest department of all music to master. The great thing to remember is that our system is not based merely upon 1-3-5 but upon 1-3-5-7-9-11-13. (There was, I believe, a certain Dr Day[36] who vainly tried to establish this elementary fact in the musical world.) In any key these two chords – major and minor [Ex. 3.25a] explain everything – with their inversions.

Both of these composite chords can be seen as an aggregation of four of the family chords (Ex. 3.25b). As a consequence, the linear link between chords that is established by the modifying semitones is complemented by the common vertical component that exists between them. Warlock's reference to inversions is also important, for, as has been noticed, the family shapes appear in different guises that may suggest other kinds of chord. The most common of these is the minor 7th which, depending upon spacing and inversion, can sound like a major 6th. For convenience, it will be referred to as a 7th although, from time to time, comparisons may be drawn with chords of the 6th in the songs of 1911.

The same letter refers to the organisation of chordal material. Warlock favours four-note chords; this should not be interpreted as a preference for four-part harmony although it is often the result. Apart from the pentatone, the family is made up of four-note chords; but the pentatone itself is often reduced to a four-note chord by a process of omission.[37] If one note is left out, then, and excluding the minor 7th, three other types of chord emerge (Ex. 3.25c). One is a major triad with an added 9th, one is a minor triad with an added 11th and the third, produced in two different ways, comprises two major 2nds separated by a minor 3rd. This last named aggregation (which might be named the *Frostbound wood*-chord because of affinities with that song which will become evident in due course) can be written in terms of two separate pentatones a 4th (or a 5th) apart. It can also be described as a 4ths- (or 5ths-)

based chord, as can the complete pentatone shape when deployed vertically. These configurations will be encountered many times in the course of further investigations.

Notes

1   This is a much simpler use of the term than that employed in Ba (p. 265 and passim) and stems from the fact that it occurs so many times as a separately definable entity in Warlock's output. As described above it has been an accepted term within Warlockian circles for many years and will be used thus in this survey.

2   The groups of repeated notes in bars 13 and 22 are each counted as just one note because the harmony remains constant during each respective group; the repeated notes in bar 20 are counted individually because of harmonic changes at these points.

3   See CT (Autumn 1964).

4   CP pp. 19-22.

5   PW's knowledge of this piece is not known beyond his catalogue in D. PW refers to the song as *Evening voices*, a better translation than the usual one.

6   A fifth song, *Wine comes in at the mouth*, is now lost and, along with *The cloths of heaven* was given at the first performance in 1920 (IC p.182).

7   FT1 pp. 11, 12 and 20.

8   The chordal family is discussed more fully on pp. 47-50.

9   Two further settings, one of which is now lost, were made in 1918. See FT1 p. 21.

10   IC p. 62.

11   See p. 25.

12   The spelling on the original Ch edition (1923) was "Heracleitus" but this has been amended in T(i). FT's note to this edition gives the background to the alteration. In PH's letters to CT he invariably uses the "ei" spelling. There are extensive notes in IC (pp. 154-6) regarding the differences between printed and manuscript versions and, also, PW's corrections to the published version (although these do not affect the pitches).

13   FT: preface to T(i).

14   See Chapter 4.

15   *Suite for pianoforte* (*Liber I*) BL Add. Ms. 48303. The full titles of the four pieces that comprise this offering (written under the pseudonym "Prosdocimus de Beldamandis Junior") are listed in FT1 p. 11 and IC pp. 217-221. The latter also includes a short descriptive analysis. The *Valses: Rêves d'Isolde* (see note 18, Chapter 1) are also included in the collection of manuscripts.

16   See FT1 p. 13.

17 PW appears to have respected Vaughan Williams as a composer except, ironically, in his treatment of folksong! He refers to him as ". . . that big man . . . who looks as though he ought to have straw in his boots . . ." but considered the *Pastoral symphony* to be ". . . a truly splendid work". Yet ". . . this composer's music . . . is all just a little too much like a cow looking over a gate. Nonetheless he is a truly great composer and the more I hear the more I admire him" (CG pp.78-79). Yet ". . . a composer named Williams . . . is one of those for whom mysticism means mistiness and vacuity . . ." (CG p. 193) and PW writes of ". . . the usual idiotic harmonic restrictions that faddists like . . . V. Williams and Co. like to impose on themselves." (a letter to CT quoted in IC p. 227).

18 In a letter to CT of 17th July 1917 (BL Add. Ms. 54197). Also in a letter to Gr, again quoted in IC p. 227, PW relates his folksong arrangements to those of Grieg and BvD.

19 See Augustus John's "Introductory" to CG pp. 13 and 14.

20 See Robert Nichols's contribution ("At Oxford") to CG pp. 78-9.

21 PW did not name the tunes he employed but Copley succeeded in identifying all but the first of them and he gives this information in IC pp. 229-231. The titles are summarised together with their Gaelic names in FT1 p. 13. The tune of the first one is *Cholla mo rùin* (Colla – or Colin – my love); see Margaret Fay Shaw: *Folksongs and folklore of South Uist*, Routledge and Kegan Paul, 1955, pp. 130-1and BC: "The theme of the first of Warlock's *Folk-song preludes*", PWSNL no. 46 (March 1991), p. 10.

22 See FT1 p. 11.

23 The ascribing of key-centres to many of Warlock's pieces is a dangerous and tedious business! As is explained within the text, after taking into account modal and other considerations, the use of labels such as "D major" is inaccurate and unnecessary.

24 IC p. 228 *et seq*.

25 IC p. 230.

26 IC p. 249 suggests Alfred Moffat (arr.): *The minstrelsy of the Scottish Highlands*, Bailey & Ferguson, Glasgow (no date). PW refers to this volume himself (". . . an admirable collection of songs, as such . . .") in a letter to Gr – see IC p. 227.

27 Christopher Palmer cannot possibly have had this particular movement in mind when he said that the *Folk-song preludes* (CP p.154) "seem hardly to have dated at all; . . . they are the first echt-English [sic] music (excluding that of Delius himself and

Percy Grainger) to show that Delian harmony can adapt itself to a folksong context."

28   PH (14 June 1917): ". . . Cyril Scott . . . continues to develop the harmonic style of Joseph Barnby in the spirit of Oscar Wilde." See also PH (1 February 1922): ". . . a great deal of music . . . is built up of fragments discovered more or less fortuitously at the pianoforte and afterwards unskilfully glued together . . ." [footnote] ". . . examples may be found in the work of Cyril Scott."

29   IC p. 232.

30   In a letter to CT dated 15th August 1917.

31   Cited in CG p. 158.

32   "The above-mentioned songs [*The bayly berith the bell away, My gostly fader, Whenas the rye, Lullaby, As ever I saw* and *Take O take those lips away* (1918)] . . . are not merely among the best he ever wrote, but works of genuine originality, quite unlike anything else." CG p. 159.

33   The second version of the song is dated December 31st 1917 (FT: preface to T(ii)) – PW's Christmas greeting to BvD is dated December 24th 1917. See p. 85 and note 1 in Chapter 5.

34   The recipient of *I asked a thief . . .* was CT.

35   Letter dated 24th September 1917 (BL Add. Ms. 54197). In addition to the information given in the main body of the text PW also writes about what he calls "pot-boilers" and refers to the "most exciting" act of selecting four notes from a potentially five-note chord.

36   This is Dr Alfred Day (1810-49 – the title is a medical one) whose *Treatise on harmony* (1845) expounds a hypothesis referred to variously as "Day theory" or the "Day system". To confirm Warlock's opinion, it "no longer holds serious attention" (*Oxford Companion to Music*, Tenth Edition, London, 1970). In fact, Day's views did colour later nineteenth-century harmonic teaching and analysis but had fallen out of favour by PW's time. This fact alone was sufficient for PW to give them credence.

37   See note 35 again.

CHAPTER 4

The curlew: a portrait of the artist

The curlew is a nature-poem and, as such, displays Warlock's spiritual indebtedness to Frederick Delius. Here, the bird-imagery of *Sea drift* is translated from the ocean to the moors, but not to those of Yeats's Ireland; rather, they are of the Wales[1] that was, from the age of thirteen, Warlock's sporadic home. Edith Heseltine, Warlock's mother, widowed in 1897 when her son was only a couple of years old, later married Walter Buckley Jones of Cefn-Bryntalch, Montgomeryshire. There were no other children.[2]

In the metamorphosis from Delian panorama to Warlockian waste-land, the music is made more emotionally intimate, more stylised, more pastoral even. Full orchestra is reduced to chamber ensemble and all the vocal resources, baritone and chorus, are condensed into a lone tenor voice. The shift of emphasis is symbolised by the instruments that supplement the string quartet – flute and cor anglais; this latter, in preference to oboe, evokes the darker side of Arcady. While both can produce onomatopoeic birdsong, they also suggest, in their disparate timbres but similar – though not identical – tessituras, the relationship between the protagonists, defined or allusive, of the verbal texts.

The curlew has often been described as Warlock's "masterpiece"[3] but this statement needs a certain amount of interpretation. In a cultural context where large works are considered important, his small songs – the duration of some of which can be counted in seconds rather than minutes – are deemed to represent a paucity of invention and he is condemned (rather than celebrated) as a miniaturist. Now, *The curlew* is a fine, even a remarkable, piece and one that plants the banner of Expressionism firmly into British soil. It tackles, in its own way, the tritone, that most contentious of tonal intervals and thereby anticipates Frank Bridge's third string quartet by some seven years. But its structural unease is more than a parallel statement of the emotional instability inherent in Yeats's words. Despite the force projected by its very size, it lacks the confidence both of mood and technique that marks *Lillygay*, its chronological successor and a work which is much more representative of Warlock's maturity. *The curlew*, though, lies at the core of his compositional career. In this one piece he develops from confused neophyte to competent executant, from an explorer of "clotted and sepulchral"[4] chords to lyrical melodist. Not only from this standpoint but from others too the work becomes autobiography, a composer's chronicle of his own progress that records both his personal experience and the techniques he accumulated.

It is not known precisely when Warlock started work on *The curlew*. On 22nd January 1916 Delius wrote to him after receiving some songs. "Your song the 'Curlew' [Delius's punctuation] gave me the greatest pleasure . . . There is real emotion in your song". It is not at all clear whether Delius had been sent *The lover mourns for the loss of love*, destined to become the second movement of the cycle, or another setting, now lost. Whichever it was, it demonstrates that, although the piece we know today would not be completed until 1922, it was an ongoing project since early 1916 or even late 1915. This was a crucial time in Warlock's personal life that witnessed not only several impassioned sexual relationships and, eventually, the birth of his son[5] but the intensification of the Great War (for which he had no sympathy) and the prospect, however remote, of conscription.[6] His marriage to "Bobbie" Channing (known as "Puma") was always doomed and was entered into at her insistence;[7] his subsequent sojourn in Ireland was partly Celtic exploration, partly escape from marital,[8] family and military life (although, like Arnold Bax but not to the same extent, he was drawn by the people, language and cultural heritage of that country).

In addition to these private upheavals, his attempts at composition were also insecure. Delius was still too powerful a rôle-model and the younger man's attempts at emulating the established style of a very different personality had been inconclusive and in vain. Meanwhile, the poetry of W. B. Yeats had held a fascination for Warlock for some years and it is no exaggeration to say that he was one of the first Englishmen to appreciate its qualities. But the moods expressed in the poems that he chose to set in *The curlew* – isolation, frustration and rejection – evoke sentiments akin to those he felt about his personal and artistic predicament. Yeats wrote in terms of relationships. Warlock's position was more complex; his emotional involvements were compounded by financial constraints, his search for valid, artistic expression and his social perception.

The gestation of the work also covered stylistic influences and progress beyond the seminal, Delian aspect. Its early development coincides with the first contacts between Warlock and Bernard van Dieren.[9] It spans the more experimental early works (*Saudades* and the

Folk-song preludes) as well as the Winthrop Rogers songs which strongly manifest and establish what would, eventually, become the true, mature, Warlockian style.

But there are other reasons to justify the claim for *The curlew* to stand as autobiography. In certain respects it is atypical of the Warlockian canon. It was written over an extraordinarily long period of time – approximately seven years – and was subject to considerable alteration including the rejection of two settings after an unsatisfactory performance in 1920.[10] But Warlock was a composer who worked in frenetic bursts and, when the mood was right, could produce a song a day. It survived the destruction that befell other settings of Yeats's verse following disagreements between poet and composer that arose, largely, over attempts to get the work in question published and Yeats's general reservations about musical treatments of his verse.[11] *The curlew* was one of only a handful of Warlock's compositions to generate critical acclaim during his lifetime – it was given a Carnegie award in 1925 – and one of an even smaller number with which he expressed any satisfaction.[12] Given the context, such rare self-approval can be considered as much an emotional reaction as an aesthetic one.

A chordal examination of the second movement, *The lover mourns for the loss of love*, puts into perspective the neurotic stasis of Yeats's text as well as managing to articulate the creative standstill that Warlock had been experiencing for several years. This is achieved not only by means of a concentrated brevity (that also marks *The water lily*) but a reliance on a very limited chordal palette. Basically, Warlock employs only two chords, the *Curlew*-chord itself and the minor 7th. These chords are linearly (rather than functionally) related in that one is a semitonally adjusted version of the other although, at this stage, it is difficult to establish which derives from which.

Of the 46 chords that constitute this movement, 16 are pure *Curlew* types and a further 16 are minor 7ths. Additionally, six *Curlew*-chords are subject to further semitonal adjustment of one of the notes, as are two minor 7ths; four chords are made up of superimposed elements of both sorts of chord. One chord, at J5(ii), is an unmodified minor that announces the second vocal phrase. It may be possible to ascribe a sense of D minor to the movement, a fact briefly substantiated by this chord and some prominent C sharps but, given the ambiguity of the majority of the chordal material, the ascription is theoretical only and moments in the section approach, in effect, atonality. There are very few contemporary British composers whose music could warrant this term.

One further chord cannot satisfactorily be defined in conventional terms. It is basically a chord of E minor with an added F sharp (a 9th?). The interpolated note is placed in the bass to disorient the rest of the chord by pulling against both the E and, particularly, the G (Ex. 4.1). While it has an intrinsically dramatic quality, like the individual chords in the early songs, it upsets the movement's integrity.

Ex. 4.1: *The curlew* **– bar J10 (part)**

At this point, it is worth reflecting upon Warlock's harmonic method. He chooses chords that appeal to him for their individual qualities; their juxtaposition often depends on the motion of the instrumental lines but the technique is, as yet, imperfect. The concentrated chromatic motion promised at the start (in bar J1) is not maintained at the same density. While it is certainly a continual element, it does not predominate. Similarly, the chordal choice, although substantially based on the semitonally related *Curlew* and minor 7th chords, is subject to sporadic modification; a suspension here or a chromatic passing note there can dilute the potential intensity. However, it is also worth pointing out that other manifestations of a dependency on the semitone (such as false-relation and semitonal alternatives within the same line) maintain the mood of personal desolation.

It is equally important to remember Warlock's attitude towards chordal inversion. Because he works outside the context of functional harmony, he regards different inversions of a chord to be equal manifestations. This process continues even in later works where, although his language appears more conventionally diatonic (and very much more so than is the case here), he uses 6/4 chords in locations that are far from conventional. He suggests as much in the letter to Colin Taylor that has already been referred to.[13]

The semitonal displacement of any one note in either the minor 7th or *Curlew*-chords results, as Ex. 4.2 demonstrates, in both familiar and unfamiliar shapes. The chordal vocabulary of this piece, then, is more

Ex. 4.2: *The curlew* – bars J1-12 with summary.
(Dynamics, phrasing etc. omitted)

tightly integrated, the semitone having increased its hold on the harmonic choice while maintaining its importance as a linear unit; part-motion often (but by no means exclusively) employs the interval and melodic aberrations – already encountered in *The water lily* – are in evidence. It is also worth pointing out here that *The lover mourns for the loss of love* demonstrates a significant development in Warlock's compositional philosophy: until this piece, which was conjectured before his meeting with van Dieren,[14] his musical language had been principally Delian; here he utilises the stylistic qualities of a more sophisticated, abstracted and, above all, significantly personalised vocabulary to complement the poem's theme of sexual frustration. It is

ironic that this should be so; it was his own frustration at being unable
to control the linear deployment of vertical entities that stimulated his
development of the material utilised in *The lover mourns . .*; he had
initially sought to create a means whereby chordal progress would be
facilitated: in this case he achieves his most static piece of writing – the
tempo direction is "Slow and very still". The "clotted and sepulchral"
quality may yet have been inescapable although, in this concise and
chordally incestuous structure, it provides the ideal match for Yeats's
poetry.

A precise chronology for the composition of the four Yeats songs that
comprise *The curlew* is difficult to determine. Little survives in the way
of sketch or other autograph material that could solve the problem and it
is, therefore, impossible to discuss it in a chronological context that is
wholly accurate. Indeed, the situation is further complicated by the
passage of time because what must be dealt with here is the published
version, the only one that has survived, and there is verbal evidence that
this is not as originally formulated by Warlock.[15] It is not unlikely that
earlier, seminal attempts differed from what is now available. So, while
it may appear that the composition of *The curlew* dates from the same
time as the Winthrop Rogers songs, the first choral pieces and other
items, it must be understood that refinements of the original material
may not be immediately contemporary with them.

The songs of 1917-19 published by Rogers demonstrate a shift in
Warlock's compositional emphasis but in detail rather than essence.
They reaffirm and expand the relationship between vertical and
horizontal components stated here; they have a more overtly diatonic
bias, created largely by the development of modal elements. As a result,
a comparison between them and these settings of Yeats (an enthusiasm
of his teens and early twenties) may give one the sense of a backward
look. By 1920 all of the Rogers songs had been published but *The
curlew* must still be considered as a work in progress, even though a
version of it was performed in that particular year.[16] *The withering of
the boughs*, the long, multi-stylistic song that constitutes the third
section of the piece, and which would exhibit something of the
composer's increasing modal fascination, was yet to be written. *The
lover mourns for the loss of love* is in place along with the two outer
movements. *He reproves the curlew*, with its introductory fantasia,
commences the whole piece; in the remarkable finale, the
unaccompanied voice, reminiscent of the opening of Holst's *Sávitri*[17]
and its idiosyncratic use of the semitone, declaims *He hears the cry of*

the sedge. It must be made clear now that, while it is convenient to deal with *The curlew* as a cycle of four songs with instrumental interludes, the way it is usually considered, it should really be thought of as an extended work of a single movement with a number of sections in which the instrumental writing is as important as the vocal. Only 25 of 106 bars employ the voice in the settings of the first two texts (*He reproves the curlew* and *The lover mourns . . .*), a comment on the rôle of the instrumental component in the output of Warlock the songwriter.

In *He reproves the curlew* and *He hears the cry of the sedge*, the vocal style is largely declamatory. There is none of the accessible, if chord-led, lyricism of some other songs nor, indeed, of their developing strophism. In *The curlew*, Warlock employs the through-composition associated with many early songs but the timespan over which it must now be sustained is much greater. It is not just in this respect that the opening suggests the effects of his association with Bernard van Dieren; horizontal, intervallic constructions suggest note-centres only in the most indirect and tenuous fashion and rhythmically fluid, linear statements, although precisely notated, demand a degree of metrical freedom in performance. These practices will be as much a feature of the unaccompanied vocal melody at the end of the work as they are of the two monophonic, instrumental phrases that both anticipate it and set the whole piece in motion.

The first of these, from the cor anglais, contains a linear form of the *Curlew*-chord itself. This motif, or sub-cells of it, will figure strongly throughout in both vertical and horizontal formats; it is completed in this instance by a descending, chromatic line that asserts and enlarges upon Warlock's Delian past. The sub-cells themselves will be the basis of extension and development (see Ex. 4.3); the first three notes, an interval-ratio of a rising whole-tone and a minor 3rd common to both the horizontalised *Curlew* and minor 7th chords, will appear extensively in a number of guises. The viola uses them in its own answering phrase (bars 2-5) as a springboard (with a semitonal adjustment) but the cor anglais has already sounded the same pattern, inverted, with an interpolated chromatic note. This inversion, which also closes the viola answer, derives from the family chords of the minor 7th and German 6th; the linear *Curlew*-chord, inverted, makes a German 6th formation, a detail also included in Ex. 3.24. In addition to the inverted form, the three-note figure also appears as a retrograde (in bar 3). This motif, which is also a constituent of pentatonic material, will assume a greater importance not only as this work proceeds but in later pieces, especially

Ex. 4.3: *The curlew* – bars 1-A4 (actual sounds)
(Slurring, phrasing and dynamics omitted)

And wilt thou leave me thus (1928 – indeed, it will be a convenient shorthand to refer to it as the *And wilt thou*-motif). While its presence in pentatonic (or pentatone-derived) constructions is inevitable, it has a limited currency elsewhere as examination of some melodic passages in *My lady is a pretty one* (1919) will demonstrate. Another sub-cell of the *Curlew*-chord, the diminished triad (and consequent tritone), can also be seen as devices that shape the growth of the viola phrase. In addition, the span of a perfect 4th inherent in the three-note motif will be a constituent of developmental techniques after rehearsal-letter B.

The linear exposition of this material is followed by a chordal presentation in which the *Curlew*-chord, either in its basic or a modified form, is again crucial. When the flute and violins enter they make a statement that becomes rhythmically distinctive, an onomatopoeic curlew-cry. The whole of this vertically deployed figure employs four chords, two of them played several times, in collaboration with the held viola C sharp. One is an F sharp minor chord – of which more later; the others consist of one unaltered and two semitonally adjusted

Curlew-chords. One of these forms a minor 7th and therefore – given Warlock's attitude to inversion – briefly implies a linear relationship between chords that is the driving force behind *The lover mourns for the loss of love*. The viola, having achieved a high D in bar 3, continues the descent it began before the chordal interruption, ending on C sharp, the most prominent note of this opening section. In the course of the descent it develops intervallic relationships already encountered; the motif of a rising whole-tone and minor 3rd becomes a rising whole tone and falling minor 3rd shape which is extended to create a semitonally modified retrograde of the opening idea (bars 7-8).

Such relationships that regulate the material in this sort of way are the stuff of late-Romanticism and early Modernism. In his use of linear, intervallic relationships within a tonally fluid environment, Warlock seems to be demonstrating a methodology similar to that of his continental contemporaries, techniques that are unusual in a British composer but particularly so in one whose formal musical education was extremely limited. Those pieces that survive from his early attempts at composing (the songs of 1911) exhibit a preoccupation with favourite chordshapes. But the use of these is rudimentary, the material is poorly organised in mundane or uncontrolled structures and forms – there is too much emphasis on momentary delight rather than longer-term development and implication.

What is being encountered in *The curlew* is very different; there is an increased sensitivity to the texts, material is deployed in an altogether more sophisticated way and there is, consequently, a sustained intensity that earlier work did not and could not possess. The precise process whereby the composer of *A lake and a fairy boat* reached this level of refinement is not easy to discern. No compositions or sketch-material from the intervening years survive although there are references in a few letters of the time to prospective pieces; whether these were abortive, destroyed or lost is impossible to tell. One must conjecture that, in this interim, there was much deliberation, experiment and soul-searching but, in the absence of other evidence, the position of Bernard van Dieren in Warlock's life becomes provocatively more important. Van Dieren (1887-1936) had a wider musical awareness and experience than Warlock and, while in particular respects he was an amateur musician, had sophisticated tastes, had the publication of his music supported by Busoni and was familiar with the music of Schoenberg. His musical tastes were wide and included composers such as Liszt and Alkan who were not as widely appreciated then as they are today.[18] Warlock certainly looked on van Dieren as an enlightened mentor and a significant composer; his (and Cecil Gray's) promotions of van Dieren's music are well documented[19] but it is worth speculating that some of this enthusiasm arose from the sense of gratitude that Warlock felt as a result of their association. After all, Warlock not only rejected his family in name, he further dissociated himself from them by willing that van Dieren be his sole heir.

Obvious examples of the influence of van Dieren have been noticed in the *Folk-song preludes* and the *Saudades* song-set. In the two outer settings of *The curlew*, the melody of chords[20] (the chief characteristic of *The lover mourns for the loss of love* – it dictates the vocal melody) has a linear manifestation. The vertical configurations are still present but in a horizontal form; given the contrapuntal nature of van Dieren's own music, it is hard to resist attributing the development to his influence.

The start of *He reproves the curlew*, then, is tonally unclear. By the time the viola has completed its falling passage all 12 pitches have been heard, indeed most of them had been sounded before the flute and violin chords. But the initial, cor anglais figure comes to rest on C sharp, as do both halves of the viola formation, and the same note is used as a drone during the chordal statement. It can be regarded, if retrospectively, as a dominant pedal subject to interruption and decoration that eventually resolves, however incompletely, at bar 9 (letter A). The incompleteness results, primarily, from false relations inherent in the chordal material at that point and, secondarily, from the reinstituted C sharp drone that creates second inversion chords of F sharp. One of the false relations (in A3) is a dispute between mediants promoting F sharp minor in addition to the major. But the dichotomy has been prepared for in the preceding material; although A natural is ignored in the opening cor anglais and viola phrases in preference to A sharp, the flute and violin chords have it the other way about, hence the F sharp minor chords mentioned above. The continuation of the viola line had reinstated the sharpened version. The use of such alternative notes will prove an important feature of Warlock's style and a particularly vital component of *Lillygay*.

The device at letter A – a statement of what Copley aptly terms[21] the "gloom" motif – is an amalgam of patterns, chords and other procedures; it creates the heavy atmosphere that is the emotional tenor of the piece. Sustained C sharps – two of them now – restrict tonal progress in what is developing into a stylistic fingerprint. Part-writing depends on the intervals presented by the cor anglais, minor and major

2nds and minor 3rd, the limited palette already referred to in the second half of the viola passage. The false relations can, in the light of an accumulating knowledge of Warlock's *modus operandi*, be viewed as semitonal adjustments but with a strong Bartókian quality (as in *Mikrokosmos*[22] numbers 103 and 106) but without any bitonal implications.[23] Parallel major 3rds also have a connection with whole-tone scale techniques; this may have prompted Copley's comment about a Debussian similarity.[24]

Two birdsong-phrases (in first violin bars B1-3 and flute bars B3-8) extend these linear techniques but within a chordal environment in which the drone has become a *Curlew*-chord; there is, significantly, an F sharp/C sharp, double-stopped cello 5th in the bass. The initial added dissonances swiftly resolve. Semitone displacements, in the form of wrong-note melodic shapes, are sounded against the held chord, especially by the flute. The use of this kind of linear aberration was also a feature of *The water lily*; as well as clouding any note-centre implications, it relates to other semitone-interplay techniques such as the discrepant 3rds witnessed a few bars earlier. More examples can be encountered in this particular work.

At letter B, the violin line begins by relating the three-note motif (whole-tone and minor 3rd) to the pentatone, in this case the reduced, *Frostbound wood* version (Ex. 4.4). The presentation is disturbed by the A natural at the end of its first bar (B1 – A sharp would have been pentatonically correct); the note conforms to the underlying chord and alludes to the A natural/sharp discrepancies of preceding sections. The flute line that follows, static at first as repeated notes generate surface activity within the held chord, becomes more intervallically active (the semitone is the first step away from the monotone) and utilises many more dissonant notes than its string precursor. The intervals in both lines have become bigger, spanning 4ths, 5ths and wider; they can be seen in terms (sometimes as inversions) of those already contained in or implied by the cor anglais shape. They confirm relationships referred to during earlier discussion of the *Curlew*-chord and its rationale as part of Warlock's chordal panoply; but, it will be recalled, the *Curlew*-chord contains, either directly or by inversion, all intervals except the semitone, presented separately in the opening statement. This relationship – or lack of one – explains why, firstly, Warlock keeps the two components apart at the beginning, employing the one as a continuation of the other and, secondly, why the intervals not immediately associated with the opening are retained until this later stage in the proceedings.

Ex. 4.4: *The curlew* – bars B1-8
(Slurring, phrasing and dynamics omitted)

Although the different statements which constitute this instrumental opening are associated by common intervallic and chordal material (which are themselves related), textural rather than timbral differences distinguish them. At letter C, therefore, the drone is replaced by a viola tremolando against which the cor anglais can continue its intervallic widening and use of dissonant melody notes, techniques from the previous section, and which largely continue, with timbral variety, until the entry of the voice 18 bars later. There are some amendments to this usage – chordal thickening at C5 and a reappearance of the "gloom" motif at D – but the emphasis is still on the single melodic line, one that continues to be principally shaped by material from the opening two bars at that, even if monody sometimes substitutes for monophony.

Such practices are a part of the van Dierenesque phase of Warlock's career. While at no stage in this song does he abandon the chordal basis of his compositional outlook, the contact with another composer who had developed procedures that enabled his music to progress linearly, if idiosyncratically, encouraged him to explore similar methods. Warlock's own music had become bogged down by his search for a purely chordal methodology. However it must be understood that the deployment of vertically conceived material in a horizontal texture is not so much an emulation of van Dieren's techniques as Warlock's response to them, one that absorbs the essence of the former while remaining true to the latter's first principles. It is a matter here of a horizontal gesture being given credibility as a result of its vertical origins. Warlock's personalised usage can be re-examined in *Saudades* and the *Folk-song preludes*; in the latter the pentatonic tunes are, at least to start with, not so much a melodic entity as ready-made, horizontal forms of a vertical component which was already becoming established in his output. But, if the technical origin lies with van Dieren, its genius is Delius, *On Craig Ddu*[25] revisited. The bleak landscape of Yeats's verse is encapsulated in the call of the curlew, a symbol of human relationships. Warlock mirrors this in his own distillation, the *Curlew*-chord, an ambiguous, indecisive aggregation that aspires to other shapes but is semitonally prevented from achieving them.

The cello solo that immediately prefaces the vocal entry encapsulates both the philosophical and technical basis of Warlock's development of expositional material (Ex. 4.5). The whole- and half-tones and the minor 3rd are represented as before; the diminished triad components of the *Curlew*-chord are now inverted to produce wider intervals (major 6ths). The diminished triad is, of course, unaltered by inversion and its use in

Ex. 4.5: *The curlew* – bars D6-8

this context both validates and exploits the technique. The perfect 4th, though, appears not just in its own right but as the encompassing interval that marks the extent of the whole-tone and minor 3rd cell. Now, however, the motif is semitonally modified to form an amended retrograde which ends the short passage. It has been preceded by another amended figure, this time of a whole-tone and a major 3rd; this could be considered as a semitonal alteration of either the inverted opening shape or a descending diminished triad. The model is not so much English techniques of motivic development but continental ones; there is a parallel with pieces such as the scherzo of Schoenberg's second quartet where initially distinct motifs are modified so that their precise and separate origins become unclear.[26] The use of the major (as opposed to the minor) 3rd is important. It is not only a semitonal alteration but relates back to the major/minor debate of the opening. There are comparable uses in other songs already examined but, more pertinent to the work under discussion, it introduces elements of the major 7th, the only family chord not yet alluded to in the motivic manipulations.

The eventual entry of the tenor voice at letter E is startling, and not just for its verbal or timbral properties. The unison string G sharps that announce its own, identical starting-note suggest a previously unheard centre a 5th above the recurrent C sharp of the opening rather than a 5th below it, and the metrical arioso that supersedes the instrumental recitative demands the strict crotchet pulse that has frequently been flexible hitherto. The voice reasserts the rising, linear *Curlew*-chord that launched the whole piece, but semitonally alters its continuation so that it returns to G sharp rather than the A sharp that would have been transpositionally correct (Ex. 4.6 – cf. Ex. 4.3 bars 1-2).

Ex. 4.6: *The curlew* – bars E1-3

Processes already described account for the remainder of the material associated with the first text (until immediately before the second song at letter J) and are employed both in vocal and instrumental lines. Dissonance continues to be an important feature of the style even when the texture is dependent on reduced or otherwise thinned resources such as the viola and cello at bars E5-7 or voice and strings at G6-8. A nice fusion of these two phenomena occurs at F3 where the voice has a semitonally modified version of the *Curlew*-chord figure, the F double-sharp being the altered pitch. The cello simultaneously supplies the "correct" F sharp (Ex. 4.7). The six lines of the poem (except for the third and fourth which constitute a continuous verbal statement) are separated from one another by instrumental passages; they further insist that the work as a whole is really a piece of chamber music that employs a text rather than a regular song cycle.[27] The voice is but another timbral

Ex. 4.7: *The curlew* – bars F2-3 (expression markings omitted)

element with, at this stage, no sustained, distinctive and autonomous melodic line. Thus is the true relationship between melody and accompaniment in a Warlockian context further examined and a redefinition of those two terms therein is demanded.

Instrumental material that completes the song repeats previously heard ideas. The fact that these devices belong to the text – rather than being merely an interlude before the next song – is suggested by the reappearance of the "curlew-cry" figure, already heard in bars 6 and E4, before the text-setting is completed. The other birdsong lines are also heard again, as is the "gloom" motif, twice. Its first restatement is very similar to that initially encountered (although the focus has moved from C sharp to E flat) then it occurs very briefly, a distorted echo, in a modified form without the false relations. In this respect it offers a little moment of note-centre stability (E after the E flat of the preceding bars) between the restless material that went before and the nervous stasis of *The lover mourns for the loss of love.*

In some respects the fourth song, *He hears the cry of the sedge*, displays marked similarities with the first. It begins with an instrumental prelude which exhibits constructional procedures already met in *He reproves the curlew*. Not only are these procedures common to both but so is the basic material as the first violin quickly attests at bar X2 (Ex. 4.8) via major and minor 2nds and minor 3rds. As before, this line is sounded with a metrical flexibility (the variability is suggested) over sustained devices, the first of which is a chord built on 4ths. Reference

Ex. 4.8: *The curlew* – bars X1-3

has been made briefly in the past to the relationship of this sort of chord to the pentatone; the fundamentality of the pentatone to the compositional thought at this point is stated in the course of the succeeding bars. In bar X4 the cello and (double-stopped) viola combine with the tremolandi of the second violin to form alternately, a four note, pentatone-based chord (with the E) and a *Curlew*-chord (with the D). (The rising 4th pattern is to be modified in X7 so that the aggregate effect becomes a pentatone with one note semitonally adjusted (the viola F). The "correct" note, F sharp, is sounded by the first violin at the end of X8, one of several discrepant melody notes it presents at this stage.)

But the use of the pentatone, even in these abstracted guises, is short-lived, just as it was in the first song, and it is necessary to investigate its relationship with other parts of the work. It will make a stronger appearance in *The withering of the boughs*, though, and so raises questions about the stage at which Warlock composed these bars. If they were written before the song that eventually would immediately precede them they must relate back, however remotely, to the 4ths of the limited pentatonic sections (B1 and H8) in *He reproves the curlew*. This is difficult to justify and it is more satisfying instead to think of them as emerging from the peculiar pentatonic usage at the words "I know of the sleepy country" in *The withering of the boughs*. And if this is the case, it complicates even further the issue of chronology raised earlier.

The main exception concerning the general relationship of this song to shapes announced earlier is the passage between letters Y and Z. The emphasis is on the semitone which, of course, has been employed throughout although not in the manner displayed here. Earlier manifestations have the interval as a linear unit, a device for modifying chords and – a combination of these two – a means of manipulating horizontal shapes so that there is dissent between coincident melodic and harmonic material. Bars Y1-3 utilise all 12 pitches, a practice briefly and horizontally proposed in bars 2-8; the notes are now dispersed throughout all parts rather than within a single line and, while their deployment is variable (some notes occurring more frequently than others), they are presented with a degree of linear freedom that suggests their being used for their own sake (like the chordal deployment in the 1911 songs) rather than as representatives of another order. The dependence upon predetermined motif that has been such a feature of the writing is abandoned here as Warlock prefers other shapes or processes: semitone runs are extensions of the chromatic passing-note (as with the continuation of the *Curlew*-chord motif in the cor anglais's opening); melodic amendment is of the kind witnessed in *A lake and a fairy boat*; there is an increased use of dissonance. There is no single, paramount technique. The preference, as is the case throughout these two songs, is for a multiplicity of ideas that derive from a limited number of stimuli. the same tendency is also apparent in the alternating whole- and half-tones of the second-violin line (Y7-9) and the semitonal juggling of arpeggios at Y13-14 (see Ex. 4.9).

All of this material, regardless of its diversity, must be seen as anticipating the entry of the voice at Z15. The most adjacent preparation is the flute line of Z6-13, delivered over a drone that is the modified pentatone-chord from bars X7-8. Like some of the material that immediately precedes it, it employs all 12 pitches. Again, the distribution within the 31 constituent notes is not consistent – some, A and G sharp in particular, receive more attention than others. The technique is wayward for it merely self-borrows and extends one of the birdsong phrases from *He reproves the curlew*, a device that was itself

Ex. 4.9: *The curlew* – bars Y13-14

something of a novelty when it was first sounded. It has not been heard since B8 and will not be heard again, hardly a case of significant development. Nevertheless, the intent of a chromatic and centreless melody fused with a motionless, diatonically associated yet tonally uncommitted chord is more straightforward. It represents, like *Saudades*, a sustained and overtly modernist attitude to composition and so prefaces a style that, while it was to develop, deserted the more obvious elements of that modernism, particularly dissonance and pitch-order. This action could imply that the adoption of a more diatonic technique can be interpreted as a regressive move. Whether this is the case in actuality, though, depends on the use of other devices, especially modality. Meanwhile, an examination of the constructional basis of the vocal line that is about to emerge shows it to be both uncompromising in its assertion of note-centre independence and competent in its handling of motif.

Yet this very virtue produces a Warlockian curiosity. There is no chordal content in this word-setting either as an underlay towards and against which a melodic component can relate and react, or as an inherently vertical device which can, nevertheless, be given a horizontal format. This had seemed to be the intention at the outset.

So, the unaccompanied melody that constitutes the setting of *He hears the cry of the sedge* takes a stage further the intentions of the flute line that precedes it. The utilisation of all 12 pitches is retained as is, in the context of the work, its relatively long duration – the flute's eight bar statement is unbroken by rests of any significant length or interruptions from other instruments or ideas; eleven continuous bars for the voice may seem unremarkable but, given Warlock's tendency elsewhere to separate lines of text, the contrast is climactically outstanding. Coincident harmony is relinquished so that the vocal line must stand alone, relating only to itself. It therefore needs the internal logic that is provided by references to motivic material by now so well established. And if the modal material that will be so apparent in contemporary songs is absent, there is a similarity of derivation in that both procedures are derived from chords of the family.

Although there is no pedal, there could be one implied. Is it not the E that begins the line (supported by the viola), which is referred to frequently throughout and is picked up again by the cello in Z25? The note is heavily used when the voice resumes in Z27. It is reasonable to think in these terms for an extended E-based section can be seen as a pseudo-dominant, a leading-note to the open 5th chord (F and C) that ends the work, a tonal procedure concealed almost to the point of atonality.

The first performance of *The curlew* in the form known today was given in December 1922 although *The withering of the boughs* had been completed in June.[28] In some respects this is three songs rolled into one for the stanzas of Yeats's poem, some common motifs apart, are set in different ways. Thus, the music matches the separate moods evoked by the poet, but what is interesting from a Warlockian standpoint is that the settings represent different aspects of his compositional development and, consequently, support the suggestion of autobiography.

The first stanza/song is written in the motif-oriented style that is a characteristic of *The curlew* as a whole. (Because Warlock can not be seen to work so intensively in this particular way elsewhere, it is, presumably, the scale of the piece under discussion that demands such an approach.) It starts at letter K, immediately after the end of *The lover mourns for the loss of love*; an instrumental prelude is regulated by the semitone, just like the preceding song, but with an emphasis on parallelism (Ex. 4.10), a feature that the earlier movement anticipates in its last two chords. The cor anglais figure, shaped by the major 2nd and minor 3rd found in other sections, forms a decorated falling semitone

Ex.4.10: *The curlew* – bars K1-3 (actual sounds)

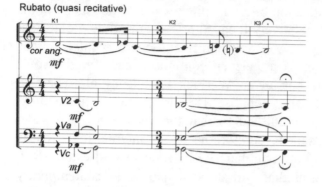

Ex. 4.11: *The curlew* – bars K1-O8

that, though rhythmically offset, matches the parallel chords – indeed is part of them, creating major 7ths. The chromatic roulades that ensue emphasise the semitone as a unit although in a more exposed, less subtle, manner than previously. Ex. 4.11 summarises material between rehearsal letters K and P.

A modification of the "gloom" figure (M6-9) prepares for a vocal entry based on similar material. The music is driven by a genuine polyphony; the voice is offset by the flute and viola that work in parallel 3rds over an A pedal, always with another held note, first C (which indirectly confirms an A centre) and then D (which makes it more ambiguous). The voice, though, uses a strict Aeolian mode centred on E, at least until letter P, although it could, perhaps, be construed as a Dorian on A. It demonstrates further the relationship between the pentatone and the other modes with the three-note, *And wilt thou*-motif once again stating its universality (bars N9-11). After P there is further motivic interplay; the harmonic implications, though, become more dissonant and more difficult to categorise. Parallel motion is still important and a figure of a falling minor 3rd and a rising whole tone, a derivative of that other three-note motif, is more prevalent and culminates in the string tremoli of bar Q6. This figure, then, combines the techniques of parallelism and false relation, a link with the "gloom" figure which it anticipates by a few seconds.

But, before this latter device can be sounded, the voice has a declamatory and isolated figure ("The boughs have withered because I have told them my dreams") based on the *Curlew*-chord and with a distinctive rhythm. This phrase will reappear. The shapes used in the section between letters P-R are summarised in Ex. 4.12.

Ex. 4.12: *The curlew* – bars P1-Q15

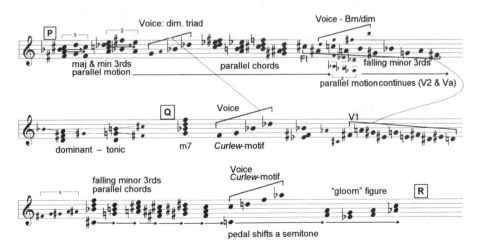

The next stanza/song, frenetic and even neurotic, is separated from the preceding material by the fermatas of bar Q15. It starts as a serpentine, semiquaver viola line that is extremely chromatic – it has no single note-focus. There is no tonal implication of the short C pedal; it is there to provide a foil to the coincident rapid pitch-motion – a rôle also taken by the vocal E flats as the flute plays a reminder of the cor anglais's opening line. But the busy viola shapes predominate and form the basis, via a number of developments and distillations, for this particular section (R-U, Ex. 4.13).

Ex. 4.13: *The curlew* – bars R1-T17

The first amendment is a reduction to semitone or whole tone, trill-like alternations, often with parallel motion (R5 et seq.). These are extended into sextuplets that then reassume the flexibility and freedom of the earlier manifestations. This technique frequently creates situations in which all twelve notes are in close proximity to each other and searching for a note-centre within the instrumental parts is pointless. The voice too is subject to this lack of a stable centre although it does gravitate towards an E Dorian (from bar R10) that is then influenced by the linear form of the *Curlew*-chord. Probably because of the intensity of the chromaticism and the conscious avoidance of a note-centre, the headlong plunge in S8 once again has a Schoenbergian quality about it.[29] This provides additional, though circumstantial, evidence of the influence of van Dieren. Warlock knew about aspects of Schoenberg's methodology from his own investigations[30] but he may have acquired a greater, if vicarious, familiarity through his friend.[31]

The last two lines in each of Yeats's stanzas are the same; Warlock employs the same vocal figures this second time as he did before but, as in his strophic songs, the instrumental component is changed, particularly that associated with the second line of the pair. Here, the cor anglais drone is replaced by a *Curlew*-chord – but a different one from that upon which the vocal figure is based.

The third stanza/song maintains the polyphony that has been a continual feature of the setting of this poem. But now the frenetic, van Dierenesque atonality gives way as the more serene qualities evoked by the verse utilise modal material; the voice employs a hexatone formed by two overlapping pentatones although it is, actually, purely pentatonic much of the time. This factor, in combination with instrumental false-relations, produces ambiguities of centre which the A pedal, frequently doubled at the octave, does not resolve. The first violin appears to use an A-based Dorian mode but semitonal (rather than chromatic) adjustments, as well as the aberrations created by the false relations, distort this; the voice could be centred on A or D. There is no resolution to the situation when, at bar V6, the harmony settles on to a pentatone shape – not so much a lute- as a guitar-tuning chord[32] – that is different from either of those employed by the voice (though it has notes in common – see Ex. 4.14).

The cor anglais reintroduces the *Curlew* motif at V10 and effectively announces the beginning of what turns out to be the coda to this song. Harmonically, it contains much *Curlew*-chord material – melodically too, even though the three-note motif derived from the chord is subject

Ex. 4.14: *The curlew* – melodic and harmonic pentatones in bars U8-V8

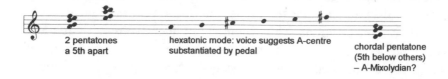

2 pentatones
a 5th apart

hexatonic mode: voice suggests A-centre
substantiated by pedal

chordal pentatone
(5th below others)
– A-Mixolydian?

to much semitonal change. The climax is a statement of the line that closes each stanza; the rhythm is exactly as in the previous two hearings and a *Curlew*-chord drone (though a different one from the previous occasion) accompanies it. This time, however, the pitches are not notated and the result – largely as a result of the prescribed rhythms – is a kind of sprechgesang though not of the sort used in *Pierrot lunaire*.[33]

The curlew remains a perplexing piece despite its obvious qualities, especially the marriage of musical material to the sentiments expressed in Yeats's texts – a less easily quantifiable commodity than the identification of chord-choices, the linear material derived from them and the subsequent modification of both by the semitone. Although it contains material that could only have been written in 1922 (the use of the pentatone in the last section to be described), it is a piece that largely looks back on past achievements. This is, perhaps, inevitable because of the time that it took to write. It is a complex work; so much is obvious from the foregoing. Its emotional power may never be in doubt but much of that comes from the intensity of the processes at work, a manifestation of the personal and artistic turmoil that he was experiencing. Again, if it exudes van Dieren's polyphony, it possesses his congestion too. Like *Saudades* and the *Folk-song preludes*, it demonstrates a musical vocabulary which Warlock would never again assume. This is not to say that he throws out the baby with the bathwater; the Winthrop Rogers songs exhibit a distillation of the techniques used embryonically in *The curlew* and also the development of a language that integrates his chordal origins and his contrapuntal conversion in a manner with which he seems altogether more comfortable. So, what it is important to realise about the whole piece is that it demonstrates an increasing awareness on his part of the significance of motif as a structural component. By doing so he is not only remaining true to his chordal basis (in the nature of the figure he employs) but sowing the seed for the next phase of his career.

The curlew expresses, despite the motivic material that binds it together, disparate qualities and contains other, largely chordal, details that do not fit the general trend. Its use of dissonance can be akin to the way harmonic aggregations are employed in the early songs, as moments of excitement rather than integrated occurrences. But this comment is not intended to denigrate one of the most significant pieces of British chamber music of the inter-war years. It displays a genuine quest to extend musical vocabulary, especially in the British-music context that Warlock considered stuffy, conservative and complacent.

Notes

1   Parrott (October 1964).
2   See NH passim.
3   Received wisdom has it thus, an opinion frequently trotted out by, for example, the BBC when the work is broadcast.
4   PW described some choral pieces written c. 1916 in these terms (see FT1 pp. 32 & 38).
5   According to NH, PW fathered two children at about the same time; Nigel was not the son of PW and his wife, "Puma"; her son was adopted but is thought to have died. These details have resulted in much discussion in Warlockian circles.
6   See NH p. 119.
7   A letter to Phyl Crocker, wife of PW's friend Boris de Croustchoff, makes this fact clear (BL Add.Ms. 57794).
8   Puma visited PW during his time in Ireland and, indeed, was his companion on a number of occasions despite the fact that they hardly lived together after their marriage. See NH passim and Smith (1991).
9   PW and BvD first met in early June, 1916. See FT (1978) p.8.
10   See IC p. 182.
11   Yeats's antipathy to settings of his poems (and his reasoning) is well known but a BBC radio programme (The music of W. B. Yeats, BBC Radio 3, 12/06/87) traced the poet's attitude to music in general.
12   ". . . for the first time in my life I really feel pleased with something I have written." Letter to CT dated December 7th 1922.
13   See note 35, Chapter 3.
14   See note 12, Chapter 1.
15   IC (p. 181, note 7) relates Hubert Foss's recollection of an early performance.
16   Idem. Settings of The cloths of Heaven and Wine comes in at the mouth were removed afterwards.
17   Sávitri was first performed in 1916 but it is very unlikely that Warlock was familiar with it.
18   BvD's collection of essays, (1935) although a personal view of several musical issues, nevertheless, displays an unusually wide knowledge.
19   In, for example, CG and IC passim.
20   See p. 6 and note 16, Chapter 1.
21   IC p. 261 and passim.

22   *Mikrokosmos* was written in 1935 (after PW's death) but the comparison is still pertinent.

23   IC suggests there are bitonal elements in PW's music (p. 39, using Cockshott as a starting point).

24   "One wonders whether he had Debussy's *Syrènes* [sic] at the back of his mind?" IC p. 174. But is this not an example of coincident technique rather than a matter of direct influence?

25   See pp. 146 et seq.

26   By making this comparison there is no intention of drawing close parallels between PW's and Schoenberg's emerging styles or suggesting that the former was influenced by the latter; the issue is one of stylistic coincidence within an Expressionist context.

27   Is it possible to resist a further comparison with Schoenberg's op. 10 at this point? PW certainly knew the quartet; BC possesses PW's own copy which is, unfortunately, not annotated.

28   FT1 p. 43.

29   As in the descending, chromatic, parallel 3rds in Schoenberg's op. 10 (again) bars 160-3.

30   Such as his *Musical Standard* article (PH (1912)).

31   See p. 4.

32   See note 5 in Chapter 11.

33   PH (4th August 1923) suggests that he was already familiar with the work before its London première, although what he wrote could be gleaned from an examination of the score.

CHAPTER 5

Experiment and consolidation (1)
The Winthrop Rogers songs and their contemporaries

Before looking at the two groups of songs that Winthrop Rogers published in 1919 and 1920, two other pieces need examining. *I askèd a thief to steal me a peach* dates from the end of 1917 although it looks towards the later songs. It contains more material that conforms to the popular image of a Warlock song – diatonic context, skipping rhythms, chordal sensuousness, amorous words – than has been the case to this point. It is a successful venture with a musical directness to match the verbal material, texturally leaner than works that immediately precede it and more overtly tonal too. It sets in motion the period of stylistic modification that characterises the Rogers songs and professes a shift towards diatonicism (and its inherent tonal demands) that the Rogers songs will regulate. In this song through-composition is still preferred to strophism – a necessity given the brevity of the text – and thereby demonstrates a structural link to earlier material. But although it was not to appear in print until 1972,[1] it is close in spirit to the batch of songs written or completed in 1918-19 and published shortly afterwards by Rogers.

Tonal appearances notwithstanding, there is a chordal ambiguity in the opening bar as intriguing as any so far encountered; it confirms the relationship of this song as much to those that precede it (in its content and the resulting sound) as to those that follow. The E flat tonic is briefly concealed and, instead, an aggregation is presented of three family chords, namely *Curlew*, minor 7th and pentatone (Ex. 5.1). The upper, horizontal, element is pentatonically derived (a rogue A flat notwithstanding) and will be balanced by the last bar in due course. Dissonances within the opening bar anticipate and are subsequently stabilised by the tonal implications of the following one. The dominant-of-the-dominant here can be related to a modulatory procedure although Warlock uses it more like a punctuation mark, a kind of semicolon to imply that more is to come.

References to – though not necessarily a confirmation of – a defined tonal centre occur chiefly at the start. Parallel 6ths in the accompaniment reinforce the vocal melody (Ex. 5.2) and present a cosy,

Ex. 5.1: *I askèd a thief to steal me a peach* – **bars 1-2**

Ex. 5.2: *I askèd a thief to steal me a peach* – **bars 2-8**

if contrived, reassurance that is set up only to be knocked down later, a complement to the post-lapsarian imagery of Blake's poem, perhaps. Once the E flat-centre is established it persists largely in the listener's imagination; there is no support from the piano although the voice is more conformist. The situation is like that recognised in the *Folk-song preludes*, in fact, although now the relationship between melody and harmony is less strained. While the instrumental material may be familiar, the real point of interest about this song is Warlock's ability to combine these apparently disparate elements so successfully without compromising the achievements of *Saudades* or *The water lily*. It is too easy to latch on to Delian features such as the falling semitone appoggiaturas (bar 9 – Ex. 5.3a) or the (falling semitone) bass passing-note (bar 17 – Ex. 5.3b) without recognising the progress of the chordal selection. By this stage such details are more decorative than essential.

Ex. 5.3: *I askèd a thief to steal me a peach* **– bars 9 & 17 (piano only)**

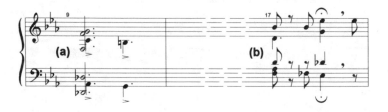

To the memory of a great singer was subject to modification before its eventual publication in 1923[2] and the original version is now referred to as *Bright is the ring of words*, the first line of Stevenson's poem. While it employs a chordal vocabulary similar to that of *I askèd a thief to steal me a peach*, it presents elements of melodic construction that are in themselves noteworthy and will be considered shortly. Chordal choice relies heavily upon the family and *Curlew*-chords in particular (which dominate bars 11-13 – Ex. 5.4) and is reminiscent of concentrations in earlier pieces, such as the opening of *Heraclitus* (although there is no associated linear component here). Nevertheless, apart from a climactically rhythmic and harmonic abstraction at bar 15, the piano writing is much simpler than in the previous song. This is achieved partly by restricting the deployed pitch-range but mostly by making transition between chords dependent on stepwise often semitonal, motion. As if to emphasise this the metrical interpretation is also greatly simplified; the predominating 3/4 is usually divided as

Ex. 5.4: *Bright is the ring of words* – bars 10-14
(originally a minor 3rd higher)

minim-plus-crotchet, an unobtrusive shape that enhances the newly found lyricism. The four couplets of text occupy insufficient space to warrant a strophic treatment, especially given Warlock's preference for setting a note to a syllable. The result, as in many of these less mature pieces, is a lack of sustained focus, although this is less important in a piece that lasts only a minute and a half. (Warlock seeks to remedy this somewhat in his revision, *To the memory of a great singer*, by writing a short epilogue to emphasise the true centre.) The Winthrop Rogers songs can, however, be seen as attempts to achieve a degree of credibility, not by the application of mere ingenuity but by the development of a technique based on integration of material and mutually appropriate structural procedures. The next songs to be examined are those that eventually appeared in 1919.[3]

In one respect, the early part of 1918 was a lean period for Warlock as far as composition was concerned for nothing was committed to paper. Nevertheless, it was just the opposite in terms of inspiration; the Irish Year is chronicled by others[4] but principally included an enhanced appreciation of things Celtic and the continued discovery of the English Renaissance.[5] The latter aspect resulted from an encounter with William Ballet's Lute Book in the library of Trinity College, Dublin. This produced no immediate transcriptions or hard copy of any kind; along with similar experiences, it would develop into a passion that permeated his musical career as editor, arranger, musicologist and, in particular ways, as composer. However, considerable care needs to be exercised about conveniently attributing specific aspects of Warlock's style to his interest in early music; this phenomenon will be addressed more fully in due course in relation to actual moments in individual songs.

Seven songs were published by Rogers in 1919; they had been written the previous year, possibly based on ideas conceived in Ireland[6] and were submitted speculatively under the pseudonym "Peter Warlock". Heseltine had alienated himself from Rogers by criticising the latter's refusal to publish van Dieren and the pseudonym, although providing only temporary cover, remained.[7] The songs demonstrate a change of direction in Warlock's output but not a completely new one. The relationship between vertical and horizontal components is strengthened but material is more diatonic than has hitherto been the case. There is a shift, though, towards modality rather than unequivocal tonality; textures are simpler and more utilitarian than anything already seen. Most of the harmonic vocabulary is established and family chords are much in evidence, but the proportion of major and minor chords is now greater than before. Another feature of these songs is the emergence of a developing sense of vocal melody, the derivations of which will be described in due course.

Take O take those lips away is another setting of Shakespeare's text from *Measure for measure* already used in *Saudades*. It recalls the earlier version in the nature of some chords, concealment of note-centre, the rhythmic fluidity of the vocal line (characterised here by changes of metre) and the falling semitone that opens the vocal line, although it lacks the chromaticism in either vocal or piano part of its predecessor. It is as though Warlock had come through the more intense aspects of the van Dieren experience without effect; this is, with an important exception, *The cloths of Heaven* revisited.

The element that is new – not just in this but all of the Rogers songs – and which will be a feature of virtually the rest of his output, is the constructional content and, thereby (as suggested above), the rôle of the vocal melody. As has also been noted, the number of accidentals is reduced and there is a consequent effect upon chordal choice within the accompaniment; the introduction belies the F sharp minor qualities of the vocal part but, thereafter, it is less readily denied, despite the ambiguities of *Curlew-* and pentatone-derived chords or harmonic diversions at the cadences. It is as though Warlock, after the manner of the *Folk-song preludes*, seeks to disguise the orientation of his tune by employing an array of Delian and post-Delian resources. But he does not resort to the same textural density as before – that is a feature which will never reappear.

In addition to family-related chords, only 12 are unequivocally major or minor. The eight minor chords are, but for two, those on the tonic (the repeated tonic at the conclusion is counted as a single chord) and two of the four major chords are dominants. Several of the 7th shapes, used in earlier songs for their own sake, begin to assume a functional importance so a picture emerges of a revised attitude towards the relationships that exist between adjacent chords. This is not to say that earlier practices have been abandoned for, in some ways, they have become more obvious or blatant, especially in their new context. The penultimate chord is a 7th on D; given the functional relationships that have been allowed to develop during the second half of the song this would suggest a chord of G as a resolution. In actuality, the result is a semitone away, F sharp (minor), an outcome confirmed by repetition (Ex. 5.5).

Ex. 5.5: *Take o take those lips away* **(1918) – bars 15-18**

By contrast, the most striking feature of *As ever I saw* is the proliferation of major chords. Of the 188 chords in the piece just 100 are major, and this number excludes those with a major component such as the 7ths of different kinds. Between these can be found familiar shapes in various guises: even apparently incidental notes create family-related aggregations, especially those derived from a pentatone. Because Warlock mainly uses 4-note chords (except where the piano is exposed between the verses and for emphasis in the last verse), pentatone-based chords omit one note out of the five. These are designated 4/5 in Ex. 5.6 and elsewhere (but also look again at the introduction to *Music when soft voices die* for earlier examples); the C flats that pervade the piano part derive from the Mixolydian 7th presented in the first bar (Ex. 5.7).

Ex. 5.6: *As ever I saw* – bars 26 & 30-31

Ex. 5.7: *As ever I saw* – bars 1-8

C flat affects both melody and harmony throughout. The chord at 1ii is effectively a dominant 7th which, supported by the tonic minor at 2iii and the A flat minor 7th at 3ii creates the impression of a G flat centre when the voice enters. This stimulates a modulation to the real tonic in bar 5, a process which occurs again during the remainder of the stanza. The strongly tonal references and relationships that arise as a result necessitate some crude remedies such as interrupted cadences, a tonic pedal and a sharp-side modulation (in bar 21) and, eventually, several modifications to the vocal line (variably successful – the fluid simplicity of the original is relinquished) to emphasise D flat at the beginnings of the remaining stanzas. Nevertheless, the incidence of C flat remains high within the piano-part, especially in the fourth verse, necessitating the balance (a tonal relic) of another dominant modulation. The final verse, however, in which the original melody is virtually restored, reduces their appearance to a minimum. But, in the brief piano coda, they predominate and suggest that the piece depends on the Mixolydian mode rather than any strict sense of key.

Such comments about chordal vocabulary also apply to *My gostly fader*, a texturally more restrained piece in which the relationship between voice and chordal underlay recalls that of a recitative. The piano punctuates the vocal line rather than – the Warlockian norm – stating it as part of the harmonic flow. The proportion of major chords is less, and minors slightly more than in the previous song but this is explained by the nature of the modal deployments. Harmonically, this is a turbulent song with conflicts of material. The nature and meaning of the eclectic text and the declamatory style aside, it demands a sparser texture and restrained articulation in the piano part.

In a gesture similar to that of *As ever I saw*, the opening evokes a dominant/tonic scenario except that, here, the C in the voice is the 7th on the dominant and the note-centre is confirmed by the resolution rather than its creating ambiguities. The first three bars constitute a dominant 7th but, given their position and their extent, suggest a brief, D-based Mixolydian mode that leads not into the G major implied by the key-signature but to G minor (Ex. 5.8a). The statement is unexpected: B natural has been prominent in bar 3, emphasised by the instrumental duplication of the vocal note in exposed octaves. The B flat component of the G minor chord in bar 4 is open to interpretation as a Warlockian (or Delian) shift of a semitone; but it can also be considered as a resolution, not just of the dominant 7th but of the B natural that succeeded it and whose aural incongruity is enhanced by emphasis.

Ex. 5.8: *My gostly fader* **– bars 1-6, 15-20 & 30-35**

The song becomes a chronicle of the discrepancy between Bs flat and natural. The flattened version (and resultant minor chord) of bar 4 is confirmed in bar 6, although the next section (bars 7-14) supports B natural (apart, briefly, from 12i-13ii) and closes with it (G major at bar 14). Meanwhile the E flat at the beginning of bar 13 (part of a C minor 7th chord) is an early warning of things to come. The E natural that replaces it, a constituent of a decorated suspension, helps shape a vertical pentatone.

Bars 15-17 duplicate 1-3 but, instead of the G minor chord that would follow, there is a chord of E minor that evokes B natural. However, it is immediately succeeded by a (real) German 6th, albeit one unconventionally quitted, that includes both B flat and a further E flat to anticipate the now imminent move. Bars 19-20 correspond to 5-6.

The new note-centre of E flat is announced by a change of key-signature, a unique, mid-song occurrence in Warlock's output. This could be construed as a late-Romantic gesture but, given the rarity of such a situation, it should be seen more as an indication of the state of flux in which Warlock's attitude towards keys, modes and note-centres finds itself. The choice of the new key is less in need of conjecture: apart from uncompromisingly including B flat (the previous key-signature implied a natural) it is also a semitone away from the D chord that opened the song and that had become, by association, a signal for the natural/flat duel to begin or resume. Additionally, by being one flat further away from G minor, it heralds the further flat-side moves that are about to take place: a D flat is introduced in bar 23 (another distortion that can be interpreted either as an extension of the Delian falling semitone or a Mixolydian inflexion). G flat and C flat appear in bar 24; these are counterbalanced by two circle-of-5ths progressions that appear to be heading for G minor at bar 29 but are interrupted the first inversion C minor chord is almost a chord of E flat (the C is heard as a suspension that resolves on to neither B flat nor B natural) before a pivotal *Curlew*-chord allows the return of the D chord. Once again this announces the dichotomy: now the melody is modified (at 32) to favour B flat; then B natural is preferred (in bar 33 – the German 6th of bar 18 is rendered Italian and more non-committal), followed by B flat (in 34) but – finally (in all senses) – natural in the last chord. Exx.5.8a-c show bars 1-6, 15-20 & 30-35 above one another to aid comparison.

The B natural of the final chord proclaims not so much a *tierce de Picardie* as another manifestation, even the resolution, of the discrepancy. B flat and B natural have come to signify different modes or keys during the song. Although Warlock's handling here is complicated by other material, their adjacent relationship, both linear and harmonic, is increasingly important in Warlock's developing methodology.

The harmonic underlay of *My gostly fader* is a means to an end, a chordal progression that occasionally includes the shape of the vocal outline. The piano part of *The bayly berith the bell away*[8] has a greater sense of autonomy with its own, exclusive motif. Doubling of the vocal line here is virtually non-existent, although the piano does employ motion in parallel with it from time to time and maintains a homorhythmic contact with the voice throughout, also the case in the majority of the songs. A feature of this accompaniment is the manner in which material conforms to the chordal family, thus (as in bar 13 of *My gostly fader*) devices such as appoggiaturas, suspensions and even passing-notes, far from being incidentally decorative, are essential to the logic.

The use of unmodified major and minor chords is again reduced; together they account for about 40 per cent of the harmonic choice and, once more, alternative 3rds are presented in the form of G or G flat with an E flat centre. The opening favours G natural while G flat is approached via the flat-side move at 3iii-4i (Ex. 5.9). G natural can now

Ex. 5.9: *The bayly berith the bell away* – bars 1-10

be reintroduced (bar 8) as a pseudo-leading-note to the A flat chord in 9; it then monopolises the next bars as a signifier, not for an E flat mode but for one centred on C. (This allows some E/E flat interplay in the manner of the opening.) G flat is not reinstated until bar 41, largely the result of a vocal initiative based on the original figure. In fact the melody is given a degree of independence also; this is not to suggest the discrepancies between the two parts that are found in earlier songs but, in addition to the lack of voice-doubling, there are several occasions on which the voice completes the chordal logic inherent in the piano writing. This is a rare element in Warlock's style despite being a feature of the lute-song that is supposed to have influenced him so much.

Thus is revealed another indication of the changing rôle of melody in his music, although the rule is to substantiate the voice-note harmonically by duplicating it somewhere within the piano-chord, not necessarily at the top. The chordal component is still supreme even when it has become less clear whether composition of the vocal line preceded that of the piano part, the other way about, or whether the events were simultaneous.

For the first time, it is necessary in this song to assess any possible influence of Elizabethan or Jacobean music on Warlock's output. Much of the song's content can be described in terms of the composer's past practice, both chordally and melodically. But the specific chord-choice, particularly in the relationships that exist between adjacent shapes, displays a closer similarity to the style of the 16th century than anything so far witnessed (Bars 6iii-10i, for instance). Of course, such progressions are principally a means of avoiding functional relationships but the question relates particularly to Warlock given the received wisdom about his supposed influences. When these songs were written he had only just begun his exploration of early English music[9] and none of the fruits of his labours had been published. Indeed, and from a biographical standpoint, at this stage there is no indication that early music would assume the importance in his musical affairs that was to prove to be the case. The question to be addressed is whether Warlock uses what can be termed "Elizabethanisms" as a starting point for his songs or whether they are incidental moments of delicious but transitory eclecticism that enhance the individualised harmonic logic without taking it over. On the evidence of this one song the latter would appear to be the case but it is obviously necessary to examine a larger sample to reach a satisfactory conclusion. The extensive use of homorhythms between voice and piano is not so much a manifestation of an infatuation with the Renaissance as a result of Warlock's chordal approach, a tendency since the earliest songs.

There is a lady sweet and kind belongs to the second group of Winthrop Rogers songs although its composition is contemporary with the first. The three-verse, strophic structure is further broken down in that each line of the poem is set as a complete entity, separated from the others either by a longer note or a rest. On several occasions the voice is exposed over a held piano-chord thereby placing a greater emphasis on the melody; earlier manifestations of a similar phenomenon (as in *The cloths of Heaven*, *Heraclitus* or even *My gostly fader*) have been of a declamatory nature. Here the result is more lyrical.

The song employs very simple resources in terms of overall shape and individual components. Chordal choice is generally familiar, even unremarkable at times and its success is limited, especially in comparison with the later, more resolute and less inhibited setting.[10] It demonstrates, though not as completely as *The bayly berith the bell away*, a reluctance to emphasise vocal line with piano; the unsophisticated quality of *There is a lady sweet and kind* has not the character of its immediate predecessor. There are, nevertheless, a number of notes within the vocal part that are melodically autonomous in that they do not contribute to or coincide with the prevailing chord. They are passing-notes, accented or not and, as such, cannot be deemed extraordinary. But they suggest the increasing importance of the vocal line. Other songs will demonstrate that the bases for Warlock's melodies (if such they be) may be different from those of his accompaniments (and that may not prove to be an accurate term either).

The expectation of D minor inherent in the key-signature and proclaimed by the first chord of *Lullaby* is modified by the subsequent B natural. This accidental is emphasised by its inclusion in the inverted mordent that gives character to the brief introduction. The resulting chord of G major suggests, collaboratively, a D-centred Dorian mode, a tonal discrepancy that is extended by other disputes between F sharp/natural and B flat/natural. This suggests a network of linear elements, all springing from D but implying, variously, Dorian, Mixolydian and Aeolian tendencies. Add the occasional use of a raised 7th (C sharp) and the implications of major and minor keys also impinge. Ex. 5.10 illustrates these modes. Other songs have exhibited similar states of affairs but their discrepancies were incidental rather than essential. (*My*

Ex. 5.10: D-centred modes in *Lullaby*

Aeolian   Dorian   Mixolydian

gostly fader was beginning to express such a relationship but less forcefully and, in the shift of centre, with an eye on compromise.)

The entire song derives its energy and impetus from the way these discrepant notes vie with one another. It makes no real sense to describe it in tonal terminology for it lacks the modulatory procedures that are essential to that process (in other words, it is penetonal). Apart from the signifier-accidentals mentioned there are no chromatic notes except for two occurrences of an E flat (falling semitone) passing-note and a G sharp in a *Curlew*-chord that may suggest a vestigial modulation.

Whenas the rye reach to the chin has an audacious self-confidence that epitomises the growing assurance of the Winthrop Rogers pieces. This quality emanates from the manner in which diatonic material is handled but, in contrast to the last song, diatonic restraint (as a result of modal statement) gives way to abandon as all points of the tonal compass are visited, the result of circle-of-5ths progressions of varying length. The vocal line is ebulliently chromatic; this element is more obviously chord-dependent and, hence, more predictable than was the case with earlier songs. The profusion of major chords from the piano recalls other recent pieces; their functional quality derives not only from the circles-of-5ths for they possess a naïve strength (many chords have six or more notes). The deliberate, overstated, dominant-tonic relationship of the opening is the precedent for the progressions that follow, a set of pseudo-sequences[11] that start well sharp of the nominated G-centre then push it away in a rush to the flat side, a caricature of a process that will attain a degree of refinement in *Rest sweet nymphs* and elsewhere. The ultimate return to G may never be in doubt, especially as it is periodically revealed, but the blatant peregrination that precedes it and which lasts half a minute has a tongue-in-cheek quality that parallels the words.

With its arpeggio-based piano part and heroic dotted rhythms in the vocal line, *Dedication* is something of a sore thumb in Warlock's oeuvre. The only other piece of his with which it has any affinity is the flamboyant and Quilteresque[12] *Consider* (1923). The arpeggios here are less relentless than in the later work as a result of their being replaced by block chords at strategic points, and almost completely in the last verse. The drive is still chordal and emphasises Warlock's continuing search for a logic to the deployment of vertically inspired material. But the deluge of semiquavers creates an air of grandiose overstatement, a didacticism bordering on the mock-heroic that is an uncharacteristic feature of the rest of his output. (However ironic or sarcastic Warlock's verbal comments and criticisms were, these qualities do not spill into his compositions, an additional consideration that affects the evaluation of this particular song.) Once more, family chords predominate alongside the major and, to a lesser extent, minor chords that have already been commented upon. It must be noted that the shape previously referred to as a minor 7th takes more the quality of added 6th chords, a feature of the 1911 songs.

The song begins with three functionally incompatible chords; they can be thought of as preparations for note-centres referred to in the course of the whole piece (Ex. 5.11). Their roots lie a major 3rd apart and they

Ex. 5.11: *Dedication* – **bars 1-4**
(originally a minor 3rd higher)

Allegro molto, con fuoco

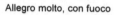

establish, albeit clumsily, some of the harmonic basis for the rest of the song. The B flat of the opening bar announces the most frequently used centre and is, effectively, the tonic although it lacks the inevitability inherent in *Whenas the rye reach to the chin* ; it is also something of a red herring as an expositional harmonic statement. The ensuing D and F sharp arpeggios flagrantly contradict the first bar (and each other);[13] they anticipate, and are validated by, bar 15 where an arpeggiated chord of D6 (in the lower half of the keyboard) is interrupted by B minor chords (in the upper). A sense of B had already been briefly stated in bar 4, a pivot between the F sharp major of the preceding bar and the F sharp minor that occupies the remainder of bar 4. Significantly, B lies a semitone away from the initial B flat centre; here, then, is more evidence that Warlock has not abandoned his original, Delian inspiration, even if it has undergone some changes. The D chord in bar 2 is included for completeness, confirming the relationship before it is established – a Warlockian paradox.

To return to bar 15, an added 6th chord on D redistributes the notes of a minor 7th on B so any implied bitonal relationship is hardly startling. Other manifestations are more adventurous, as in bars 13 and 16 (Ex. 5.12). The circle-of-5ths at the end of the stanza is not surprising in the

Ex. 5.12: *Dedication* – bars 10 & 16

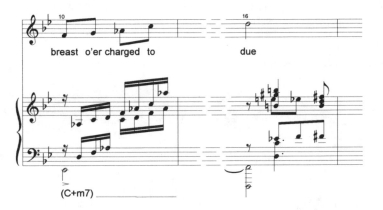

light of his contemporary songs and can be seen here as a fluid but recognisably tangible progression in the song. It is, therefore, worth commenting that the same device can mean different things to Warlock in different contexts: it can be used in an overtly tonal situation to symbolise abandon or lassitude; in a more tonally dubious environment it offers momentary stability.

The form is essentially strophic although there is a four-bar block in the third verse where the melody is subject to considerable alteration and must be justified only in terms of the changes that take place in the piano part. This presents the first real opportunity to examine Warlock's treatment of strophism. *There is a lady sweet and kind* had employed the form but not with any real degree of imagination; the harmonic treatment there varied little from stanza to stanza, depending as it did upon decorations of the original chords (such as passing-notes and thickening of the texture) rather than chordal change. This minimal variation of harmonic treatment and the truncation of the verbal text[14] are interrelated phenomena as the technique could stand but little repetition of material. In *Dedication*, though, the principle of harmonic decoration is maintained but here there is also – as implied above – an element of chordal alteration that necessitates changes to the vocal line. In later songs Warlock will construct melodies that tolerate chordal variation without needing modification; in the light of this and the composer's technique observed so far, it makes sense to see the chord-choice affecting the voice-part rather than the other way about.

Some of the chordal constructions, especially in the second half of the song, derive from the triadic aggregations implied by the introductory bars. While there are no actual superimpositions of two chords a 5th apart, a manifestation of the overt tonal, dominant-tonic procedures of *Whenas the rye reach to the chin*, they are implied in some figures and persist in added 9th chords (Ex. 5.13).

Ex. 5.13: *Dedication* – bars 67 & 70-71

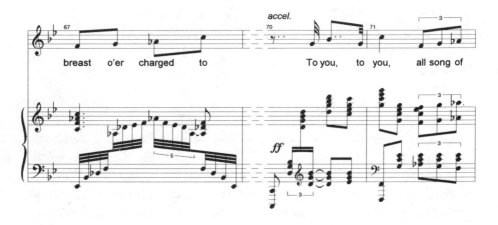

Dedication is a song weighed down with notes and ideas. Despite its shortcomings, it offers an insight into Warlock's methods and his view of the problems with which he had to contend. It is also the last of the songs that Winthrop Rogers published in 1919. Four others were composed in this same year and (with *There is a lady* . . . discussed above) appeared the following one under the same imprint. But *Love for love*, despite its rhythmic and harmonic simplicity after *Dedication*, displays a similar situation to its predecessor in the matter of relating chordal choice to overall structure. It sets five stanzas of anonymous verse,[15] the first, second and fifth of which employ the same vocal outline; to correspond with this, the piano-part employs material in the first verse which becomes the basis for the other two. The deployment of material in these two verses is subject to small alterations: the bass is dropped an octave to begin with and some chords are thickened out by, for example, the addition of an upper line (bars 15-17). But apart from the substitution of a C sharp minor chord for one of E major (bar 12 –

an interruption at the head of the verse) and a pseudo-modulation (caused by a momentary A sharp in the bass), there is no substantial alteration to the harmony. The fifth verse reverts to the chordal choice of the first except for a brief climactic progression (bars 41-42) and a modification at the end of the verse in both vocal and piano parts. Chordal thickening is another feature of the pre-cadential writing.

The second verse, meanwhile, employs a different combination of vocal and instrumental material that is reused, little changed, in the fourth. There are several moments of identical harmony: the last chords of the first and second bars and most of the fourth and fifth bars correspond to the equivalent locations in the outside verses. Likewise, the rhythmic and textural deployment is the same. Given the brevity of the verses (8 bars each of Allegretto con moto) one might have expected the same melodic line to have served five times but Warlock appears to have been unable or unwilling to vary his choice of chord sufficiently with this tune. Certainly he offers little in the way of harmonic modification in the three verses in question. And having elected to change that material for the two remaining verses he seems to have gauged that extensive development of it would be inappropriate.

Warlock came upon the text of *My little sweet darling* during his delvings into early music. The words are taken from a song by William Byrd of 1581. One of the striking features of Warlock's piece is the occasional substitution of an expected minor chord by an unexpected major one (and vice versa, a technique already apparent in *My gostly fader*). Material, especially the melody, is uncluttered; combined with some of the chordal substitutions, this creates an ayre-like atmosphere. But there are many accidentals that suggest flat-side shifts. These semitonally inspired modifications can again be related to the influence of Delius so it does become tempting to describe the song as "a fusion of the Elizabethan and the modern."[16] The accuracy of this evaluation must be seen in relation to the facts.

Although semitonal interplay once more creates a sense of residual modulation to the dominant in bar 2, chordal motion depends on surprise as much as, if not more than, functional smoothness, a technique akin to interruptions or shifts. Apart from a very few, genuinely chromatic, passing-notes, nearly all the accidentals derive from relationships between linear elements that are modal, not tonal, in origin. The exception is the brief denial of a conventional move to the relative minor at bar 7. The preferred use of the major at this moment (which recalls *Music when soft voices die*) confirms the major/minor supplanting referred to above and draws attention to the semitone as a (continuing) instrument of modification; most importantly, it denies tonal expectations within a relatively simple context that retains diatonicism as a working practice. In this last respect it anticipates some of Warlock's later songs (*Cradle song* is one example among many) in which he experiments with different environments to control his chordal progress.

The modal bases of the material are suggested by the minor chord (instead of the expected major) at the end of bar 8. This clue suggests a chordal choice based on a number of modes with the same final (Ex. 5.14); the A flat and D flat based chords of bars 4, 11-12 and elsewhere can be viewed in terms of Aeolian modifications. Even so, other details could suggest both tonal practice and current technique: the penultimate chord of D flat (written in terms of C sharp) contains E natural rather than the E sharp (enharmonic F) of previous D flat chords. This is a substitution of minor for major but one that retains the leading note to herald the final F chord (Ex. 5.15).

Ex. 5.14: F-centred modes in *My little sweet darling*

Ionian   Mixolydian   Aeolian

Ex. 5.15: *My little sweet darling* – bar 22

Andantino – poco lento e rubato

When Warlock made a string quartet arrangement of this song in 1927 he added a short, two-bar introduction to replace the single note of the earlier version with which it is otherwise materially identical. He used this as an expositional statement;[17] the minor chord at the end of the first of these bars is not only an anticipation of similar substitutions but a means of introducing the Mixolydian 7th (Ex. 5.16). It is important,

Ex. 5.16: *My little sweet darling* – introduction from version for string quartet
(originally a tone higher)

then, to consider *My little sweet darling* not so much as a fusion, or even a reconciliation, of two apparently separate aspects of Warlock's style; rather it is a demonstration of something more crucial to understanding him as a composer and, even, as a person. In this song it is possible to encounter two manifestations of a single stylistic output that should not *per se* be so much considered as being in conflict with one another as being variants on a single purpose, akin to the multi-modality gradually becoming an important feature of his composition.

The introduction to *Mourn no moe* is more intensely chromatic than anything encountered elsewhere in the Rogers songs. It employs eleven of the possible twelve pitches in the space of its two bars and is heavily dependent upon the *Curlew*-chord. In some respects it is incongruous in the context of the song as a whole but it can be justified in terms not of what it is endeavouring to emphasise but what it wishes to avoid, and it does suggest something of the chord-choice that ensues. Its function, therefore, is not to announce the C that is the basis of the chord underlying the first vocal note and which closes the song; rather, it is to avoid a major/minor preference since, as in the previous song, there is a continual discrepancy here too. The original introduction to *My little sweet darling* cleared the way for both alternatives; the beginning here consciously denies them.

The C chord, when it is sounded, has no inherent stability. Note-choice suggests that the real centre is the F (minor) achieved at the end of bar 6 because the Mixolydian 7ths are strong and frequent and the evasive introduction has provided no reference points. It is possible again to consider the material in terms of C-centred modes, Mixolydian and – initially – Aeolian; the A natural that might declare a Dorian influence is largely avoided at first. This was the only pitch not referred to in the chromatic piano introduction and it remains unheard until bar 8 where it is suddenly, and prominently, revealed. Its appearance at a point where A flat would have been equally acceptable is significant for it breaks with the principally Aeolian material that has preceded it and heralds the brief Mixolydian emphasis that starts at bar 11 (Ex. 5.17).

Ionian and Mixolydian 7ths vie with one another in bar 14 before Aeolian references reappear but, despite the modally derived material that has become so much a characteristic of the Winthrop Rogers songs, other aspects of Warlock's harmonic logic here display an essentially late-Romantic attitude towards note-centres. The D flat that strengthened the tendency towards an F-centred language in bar 6 reappears enharmonically as the leading note of D major (bars 12-13), creating a relationship similar to that experienced in *My little sweet darling*. Additionally, the final chord of C is reached via the family chord of a major 7th. This is essentially an F minor chord that relates to the earlier bars of the song but D flat, the F minor signifier of bar 6, (a note which could also be a semitonally adjusted C) has been added.

Copley says[18] that *Sweet content* is "the apotheosis of the false relation" although its semitonal discrepancies can also be credited to musica ficta, modal or post-Delian (the Warlockian semitone) derivations. The E natural and E flat that are the initial and continual contestants can be considered Ionian and Mixolydian signifiers respectively but E flat is usual in falling, and E natural in rising, figures. The piano part has an F-centre while the voice, at least to start with, favours C; in this latter context, the two notes declare a major/minor discrepancy.

The alternative Es prompt similar occurrences: B flat and B natural highlight the F (instrumental) and C (vocal) centres respectively of the first seven bars. This technique is neither modulation – there is no resolved outcome – nor bitonality (which demands dissent through simultaneity) although it could be related to both. What Warlock actually offers is the scenario of interchangeability that has become more and more apparent in recent songs. The process develops throughout this one. The F natural/sharp interchange of bar 13 recalls *My little sweet darling* (and even *Music when soft voices die*);

Ex. 5.17: *Mourn no moe* – bars 1-12

contemporary practice suggests its technical origin but it could, at the same time, be thought of as deriving from the *tierce de Picardie* (and there is a further example at 20-21, this time depending on sharp and natural Cs). Herein lies another of Warlock's strengths: this will not be the last time that his style will be seen to develop simultaneously from different origins, the familiar and the invented.

These pairs of discrepant notes shape the remainder of the song. The only other accidental is a G sharp that effects transitory modulations, to A minor at 43 and A major at 50. Thus the minor/major interchange is maintained, although the time span is elongated. The earlier Rogers songs had witnessed an increase in the use of major and minor chords in comparison with other, family chords. At that stage they came as something of a surprise because, while the songs in which they appeared were often successful, the material seemed out of character. But it must also be recalled that *The cloths of Heaven* had also relied on a major/minor relationship albeit in a looser context. By this stage – *Sweet content* is the last of these early songs to be published by Rogers[19] – Warlock has been able to effect a relationship between them that is in keeping with his developing style. This style, while it lacks the radicalism of the continental composers that he admired, nevertheless addresses a similar question, namely how to incorporate and contend with the semitone as the interval of change. His solution involved the retention, to a greater or lesser extent, of diatonicism as a working practice. But it is important to view his attitude to tonal practices as a progressive one in which he establishes and exploits working procedures that add a new dimension to received usage. It is interesting to conjecture that, in this respect, he can be seen as a precursor (philosophically if not in terms of specific material or results) of other, better known (and more respectable) British composers such as Tippett or Britten.

Warlock's technique is still in a state of flux in 1919; he is not to abandon the more extreme, overtly modernist, processes of 1916-17 but extensive reappearances will be restricted to just a few pieces. The Rogers songs, composed over a comparatively short time,[20] do suggest an evolving attitude to handling material and strategies that, for all the imperfections and inconsistencies, is positive and credible. Warlock is not unique in his employment of modal material, of course, although this is a feature that is more likely to be associated with Vaughan Williams, George Butterworth or the composers of the folksong revival in general. Nor has his handling of the semitone as a structural force yet achieved the degree of refinement that will be encountered in *Lillygay* or *The withering of the boughs*. But, taking these groups of songs as a whole, they can be shown as representing a cumulative shift of emphasis in Warlock's developing style that answers more questions than it asks.

And, because he is concerned about the relationship between linear and chordal elements, there are additional features, principally the melodic aspirations of the vocal lines, that must be dealt with.

In 1916 Warlock had been living in Chelsea, an area of London to which he would return several times during his life. Like many young artists in the capital he frequented the Café Royal where he met Cecil Gray, Jacob Epstein and, through the latter, the Dutch composer Bernard van Dieren, a remarkable personality whose knowledge of European music Warlock found fascinating. The two were to remain friends thereafter and what Warlock learned from van Dieren was the closest he came to an advanced musical education. Quite what was the precise nature of the instruction is difficult to discern. It probably did not take the form of strict exercises; the two men would have discussed their own and other people's compositions. What is clear is that the sort of pieces Warlock wrote after meeting van Dieren were different from those he produced before. Van Dieren the contrapuntist made him aware of the importance of linear motion and, while the transformation was not immediate (as the *Folk-song preludes* show) Warlock appears to have acquired a different attitude towards the relationship between melody and harmony, between the horizontal and the vertical. From this point Warlock felt more able to establish his own working practices: an examination of the vocal material in the Rogers songs reveals an important link between the bases of the harmonic and melodic material.

In considering these songs so far, references to modal devices have become inescapable, although these have concerned not so much the choice of individual chord-shapes as their deployment. Examination of the vocal lines reveals similar starting points, though; they represent the earliest attempts at what will eventually be recognised as the mature Warlockian style. Not all of these songs do display modal features; however, by observing occurrences it is possible to explain origins in the context of Warlock's own developing style. But it must be made clear now that any assumption that modality derives solely from his knowledge of early music is erroneous. His musicological interests may have been catalytic but they are not basic to the sort of material that he employs. (And it would also be possible to argue – but not here – that his pursuit of early music arose as much because it chimed with his own methods and outlook as vice versa.)

I askèd a thief to steal me a peach immediately demonstrates a feature of Warlock's writing for the voice that persistently recurs, even in the most mature songs: while there is a sense of melody and accompaniment it is achieved texturally rather than formally. The vocal part depends on the piano harmonies for the line only makes sense as an extension of the coincident choice of chord. In these conditions, melody as a term requires clarification. If the word implies both the element of continuous generation that goes beyond simple manipulation of motif and also a degree of autonomy that stems from the same, self-contained, structural logic, then Warlock's vocal lines rarely achieve this, either because the particular kind of strophism he will favour does not allow it or his through-composed pieces are too short to permit melodic growth. Warlock's melodies are generally tied to his harmonies; in this respect, the rationale of the 1911 songs is not abandoned although, as time progresses and his style develops, the tunes become more sophisticated and can convey the impression of autonomy. In this survey, therefore, "melody" is really a convenient shorthand for "vocal line" or "voice-part", a term that describes a textural delineation (voice-surface as opposed to piano-substance) without any other constructional implications. Similarly, in choral contexts, melody as a term is used to define the highest sounding part, another device that is texture-dependent. So, to summarise and emphasise, the piano has the most important material in Warlock's songs, although they exhibit his endeavours to produce vocal lines that are credible and have an inbuilt rationale.[21] In this respect, the anarchic melody lines of *The water lily*, etc., rather than displaying independence, merely draw attention to the piano's hegemony.

Melodic material, then, in *I askèd a thief . . .* is consistent with an E flat centre; accidentals suggest a move to the relative minor (bar 14) but only after references to that key's dominant (in bar 7). These references are not necessarily substantiated by the associated chordal material, a far from isolated phenomenon in these and later pieces. Warlock's attitude to his melodies as adjuncts, afterthoughts even, to the keyboard harmonies sometimes produces such a disparity of material between the two parts rather than any process of integration. The melody of *I askèd a thief . . .* is angular. In this respect, it looks back to the crude lines in the songs of 1911 while representing the next stage of Warlock's progress, seeking to recognise the melodic demands experienced in the still-evolving *Folk-song preludes* yet adhering to the chord-choices he was making six years previously.

Bright is the ring of words commences with a short pentatonic phrase that recalls the *Preludes* by association though not by actual motif. While there are additional, brief and sporadic references to it during the remainder of the song, the device is unsustained and, like those Elizabethanisms referred to in earlier discussion, gives the impression of being more in the nature of a passing eclecticism than an essential. But, in its later manifestation, *To the memory of a great singer*, Warlock totally changes the second vocal phrase so that the pentatone is retained a little further. Bars 7-8 employ four notes from a pentatone different from that which opened the song, 16-19 use the initial shape without modification while 25 introduces a single, foreign note into the rising figure. The melody does not dispute the chordal underlay although, in the light of the longer notes from the piano, the voice is more exposed than has usually been the case as if to emphasise the constructional point. Interestingly, Vaughan Williams's setting also presents a flexible attitude towards pentatonicism and commences with a big chord and a similar falling figure. See Ex. 5.18.[22]

Ex. 5.18: *Bright is the ring of words*
settings by Warlock and Ralph Vaughan Williams

After the G flat-centred statement of the first line, suggestions of E flat minor are flawed by an A natural (bar 6), a C flat final (bar 12) and then a B double-flat (bar 14). The E flat element is strong in a song that purports to be in G flat – the melody comes to rest on it at the end producing an added 6th to the final chord, thereby recalling the earliest songs. Indeed there is a good case to be made for stating that the melody is centred on E flat (with the C natural in bar 20 as a Dorian signifier, perhaps) rather than on G flat, although it would again be misleading to suggest, especially at this early stage, that there is any element of bitonality (or bimodality).

The melody of *Take O take those lips away* conforms perfectly to F sharp minor. The only accidental with which the singer must contend is an E sharp leading-note in bar 5. Elsewhere, the 7th is either avoided (as in bars 6-10) or E natural is preferred, invariably in descending shapes. These procedures create a sense of the Aeolian mode that is, apart from a few strategically placed F sharp minor chords, unsupported by the piano. The melody ends on C sharp, achieved via a scalic descent of an octave, producing a Phrygian quality (although the piano firmly states F sharp minor at its end – see Ex. 5.5 again). A Phrygian element may seem far-fetched as the underlay claims a firm close in the tonic; but other practice suggests that discrepancies between melodic and harmonic material are not so infrequent that this instance, despite stronger relationships with the piano part, cannot be seen as a gentle precedent.

The conflict of 7ths in *As ever I saw* is taken to greater lengths than was the case in *Take O take . . ;* the melody essentially conforms to a D flat-centred Mixolydian mode with a C flat 7th that is raised to C natural after the manner of musica ficta in ascending passages (see Ex. 5.7). With one exception, there are no other accidentals in the vocal line. The only occurrence of the raised 7th in a descending figure (bar 26 in Ex. 5.6) effects a modulation to A flat. Significantly, the melody avoids using the new leading-note itself at first and it is presented by the piano; it occurs in the voice at the departure point of the next section which, as might be expected, reverts to D flat, a move effected sequentially and homophonically. Cs flat and natural continue to present their respective cases but, at the very end of the tune, the issue is avoided; the D flat final is approached via a B flat and a plagal, rather than a perfect, cadence from the piano.

Modal references, then, were alluded to but left in an ambiguous state in *As ever I saw*. The situation is more intense and equally as unresolved in *My gostly fader*. Some of the confusion is created by the harmonic implications imposed by the piano so that, to start with at least, a Mixo-lydian mode on D is suggested. However, this is quickly amended so that the true centre of the song is heard as G. But since both B natural and B flat are heard in the first six bars, it is not clear whether the piece is written in terms of G major or minor, or whether there is a modal allusion here too. When the centre shifts to E flat in bar 21 Fs are natural, of course, and the change can be considered, if only in retro-spect, to have been briefly anticipated in bar 12 by the piano (Ex. 5.19).

Ex. 5.19: *My gostly fader* – bars 10-13

Ensuing melodic accidentals are consistent with F sharp minor. In a tonal scenario this is the dominant of the relative minor of D, the centre suggested at the start of the song though rapidly negated. B major is briefly achieved at 10ii but is only transitory and there is no real sense of modulation. In the light of experience, it makes more sense to consider the F sharp passage as manifesting a semitonally regulated shift away from the established G-centre that, complete with discrepant 3rds, is to be reinstated in bars 13-14. There is no musica ficta context here to explain their divergent presence although they can be interpreted as statements – signifiers indeed – of different G modes. When a similar situation arises in the central, E flat-based, section, the G/G flat interchange is either an extension of the technique of alternative 3rds witnessed earlier in the song or – again the overall situation has to be considered – a semitonal amendment of the previously established centre. The B/B flat argument continues to the end; it is difficult to avoid calling the eventual G major chord a tierce de Picardie, especially in the context of the melodic B flats (doubled by the keyboard) that precede it. But the song has relied so much on the interchangeability of these two notes that, especially as they involve the 3rd (rather than the 7th as in the last piece) and there is no consideration of the melodic minor to cloud the issue, they must be thought of as elements of G-centred modes (or keys) stated consecutively.

For, while it is possible to consider the G-based areas of *My gostly fader* as products of a major/minor scenario as much as a modal one, it is difficult to state categorically which because of the limited amount of material that they generate; each covers only a 5th (G-D) so there are no 7ths to suggest the one or the other. The others, focused on F sharp and E flat, offer no solution because they present both alternatives, the raised and then the lowered 7th respectively. At this stage in his development Warlock appears, by design or accident, to be keeping his options open, unprepared to commit himself fully to a clear cut area of usage. Tonal procedures are still in evidence, though only simply, and there are suggestions of modal derivations but, as yet, he appears unwilling to exploit them to any extent.

Nor does *The bayly berith the bell* away offer much in the way of further clarification or commitment one way or the other. At the heart of the piece is the E flat major/C minor link already noted, another appearance of the relationship between centres that has been and will be witnessed in other songs too: E flat/C minor in *I askèd a thief to steal me a peach* and G flat/E flat minor in *Bright is the ring of words* are recent examples. The start of *The bayly berith the bell away* suggests, with its C and D flats, an E flat Aeolian mode (Ex. 5.9). But this is immediately superseded by a C-based section that could also be Aeolian, although the lack of a 7th once again prevents precise identification. It would be wrong to ascribe these relationships exclusively to a tonal scenario; they represent and evolve from relocations of centre within a modal note-distribution and, despite his current uncertainty, this is how Warlock is beginning to use them. They also have affinities with the simultaneous use of D6th and B minor 7th chords in *Dedication*.

From bar 38 the relatively straightforward material already encountered undergoes a process of modification similar to that experienced in preceding songs. Significantly, it starts with repeated B flats to recall the opening but which, of greater importance, are the Aeolian mode signifiers missing from the last section (Ex. 5.20). It announces a reversion to the E flat (Aeolian) of the start which rapidly gives way to four bars of G minor material, a temporary disturbance before the E flat Aeolian returns to complete the song. Once again melodic material is at odds with the piano in which E flat major is the finishing point. The voice assists the dichotomy to some extent by withholding the 3rd

Ex. 5.20: *The bayly berith the bell away* – bars 35-40

immediately prior to the cadence and this process of omission is used again in the next song, *There is a lady sweet and kind.*

Here the undeniable B flat centre is strengthened by moves to the dominant in the fourth bar of each verse. The voice uses the raised 4th on two out of the three occasions but, otherwise, avoids the 4th altogether, amending the melody in the second verse to do so. The result is a vocal line based, effectively, on a Lydian mode, although it is very difficult to hear it as other than in B flat with modulations, especially as the harmonies are structured so uncompromisingly, even exaggeratedly, to effect the change of centre. The lack of subtlety in this respect, especially in the context of contemporary treatments of note-centres, is out of character unless the key-change has some symbolic importance. In its mild-mannered way it looks towards the more extreme manifestations of *Whenas the rye reach to the chin.* It is worth indicating that, in this strophic work, Warlock retains modal purity throughout, even should the ascription of the Lydian be considered remote.

Lullaby is also strophic but with only two verses; as in the previous song there is much repetition of material, small changes being made to accommodate differences in syllabic stress. There is no modulation or other shift of centre; melodic construction relies entirely on a technique hinted at in these pieces so far but, until this one, not fully exploited. The two lines of the verse employ D-centred Aeolian and Dorian modes respectively and, as in *As ever I saw*, these evoke musica ficta. The refrain also employs a D mode, Mixolydian this time. Thus the melodic basis is strictly tailored to allow for a degree of change and development while denying strict, tonal considerations. *Lullaby* is the first example in

Warlock's output of a tightly controlled melody that bears repetition being used as a foil for diverse, coincident harmonic material.

The same cannot be said of *Whenas the rye reach to the chin*. The ABB structure (verse with repeated refrain) is melodically distorted (but with a retained motif) to fit the chordal progress. In this respect it demonstrates little change from earlier, heavily chord-oriented songs although the verse section does start with an unmodified pentatone that supports the G-centre. From the limited evidence so far, Warlock can often associate the pentatone with a (pseudo-) folksong environment. As well as in the *Preludes*, he has used the device for the rustic philosophy of *Bright is the ring of words* and now it marks the high summer frolics of *Whenas the rye reach to the chin*; its limited note range in the verse contrasts with the wayward chromaticism of the refrain sections.

The four verses of *Dedication* declare a self-conscious melody that is, once again, heavily dependent on the piano-part, a bombastic and self-indulgent affair the possible motivation behind which has already been discussed.[23] It is initially in B flat, to which it eventually returns,[24] and it contains none of the modal 'characteristics noticed in contemporary pieces. Altogether it is a curious song that is out of character for Warlock in many ways. It does not fit easily into the compositional style as it has been noted and contains other aesthetic and attitudinal inconsistencies. In contrast, *Love for love* employs a more carefully controlled melody which, despite the E-centre of the piano part, is written in a Dorian mode with an F sharp final harmonically disguised as a constituent of a dominant chord. However, the last verse is altered to end on E.

In fact, the tune is subject to other modifications too; they correspond to the harmonic alterations outlined above, but Warlock retains the modal basis throughout. In verses 3 and 4 he alters the chord relationships to favour F sharp in the second half of each verse, substantiating the melody's modal essence. All five verses are associated by the shared material that is their basis and, as a consequence, create something of a strophic structure, but Warlock has not yet succeeded in sustaining a credible melody line for more than a couple of verses; the remaining three of these Rogers songs are all through-composed.

My little sweet darling exhibits the relationship between centres that has become familiar in previous songs: the F-centred opening uses a limited note range a 5th which conceals the nature of material that could be major or modal. The passage is replaced by a similarly limited statement, minor or modal this time and again encompassing a 5th,

Ex. 5.21: *My little sweet darling* – bars 6-8

(In) beau - ty sur-pass-ing the prin - ces of Troy, (Sing lul - laby, lul - la!)

centred on D; F natural (the initial centre) is semitonally adjusted to F
sharp to create another D-centred motif (major or modal – see Ex. 5.21).
So, the familiar relationship of tonic to relative minor is again amended
to incorporate a different D-based content. The original note-range is
restored only to be replaced by an immediately adjacent section, still
dependent upon F, that could be either Dorian or Aeolian (there are E
and A flats but there is no 6th present). This persists for several bars
before a sudden, and none too subtle, modulation to C; the new
reference point has obvious, tonal associations with F but it also
suggests the 7th of the D-centred mode that is about to ensue. The
relationship between the F- and D-centres is strengthened by the vocal
line in the remainder of the song as the two 5ths that were aligned on
them are merged to form an Aeolian on D. This, in turn, is directly
replaced by an F-centred passage that completes the song and includes
A flat, a reminder of the earlier F mode.

The key-signature (or lack of one) and the last chord of *Mourn no
moe* suggest C major; but the melody, while it achieves C briefly in the
middle of the song, employs F minor for most of the time with
occasional major references, features that are similar to those in *My
gostly fader* and elsewhere. There is also a brief G minor passage. The
break with the F minor of the opening bars of the melody is made by the
appearance of A natural in bar 8, the first that it makes in the piece (Ex.
5.17);[25] its relevance has been discussed above. It heralds a period of 8
bars (11-18) in which, after just one further appearance of A flat (bar
10), the natural form is preferred. The orientation of this passage is
ambiguous; it could be considered as depending on F with a move to C
after four bars before shifting to G. Conversely, it can be considered as

being derived from two C-based sources, Mixolydian and then minor the coincident harmonies neither confirm nor deny one or the other. The B flat that is usually employed (there is just one melodic B natural in the whole piece) is responsible for the G minor quality of bars 15-18. The passage is another juxtaposition prior to the return of the F-centred material that will wind up the song although, significantly, the only F it possesses is sharpened (bar 16). The several sections into which the song is divided correspond to lines of verse; there is no change of material while any one line is in progress.

The through-composition of *Sweet content* incorporates some limited repetition and, as in many of Warlock's songs, the melody – the whole piece, indeed – is regulated by the lines of the text. There are points of similarity between the two verses but to describe it as employing even a modified strophic form would be incorrect. Despite the G Mixolydian/ musica ficta piano introduction, the voice employs a D Mixolydian before settling momentarily on to a G-based figure that is associated throughout with the words of the title (Ex. 5.22). This pattern employs

Ex. 5.22: *Sweet content* – bars 1-8

four notes of a pentatone, a device that is extended to its complete form in the two appearances of the refrain. D Mixolydian returns but incomplete; D itself is not sounded so that it transmutes into the E Aeolian that ensues. Ambiguity persists in the next section: this offers, in addition to C sharp, alternative G/G sharp and D/D sharp that imply D and E bases butted one against the other without any genuine modulation. The piano at this point has alternative notes and pseudo-sequences that merge one centre into another. Nonetheless, the return to G for the refrain is effected by means of a circle-of-5ths which prompts a more settled, tonal, passage in G major; once this is established it reverts to the G Mixolydian suggested by the piano's introductory statement.

In the second verse the D Mixolydian shape which had opened the first is relinquished to a D major figure, nearly pentatonic itself, although the brief G-pentatone pattern that ensues is retained. Warlock re-uses much of his piano part from the first verse but alters the vocal line, further evidence that he considers the aggregate sounds from the keyboard to be the element that projects the music forwards, an observation that applies to the overwhelming majority of his output. The melody is disadvantaged as a result: the approach to the A sharp in bar 41 (that signifies the B-centre) is ugly and, while the remainder of the verse conforms to an Aeolian on B, the melody has no individuality. The refrain, melodically more distinctive, is substantially the same as at its first appearance with some chordal thickening; however there are a few changes in the choice of chords to indicate the composer's intention to maintain harmonic interest and variety even where the vocal line has a greater strength of character.

The constructional complexities of these songs, often apparent in the foregoing analyses, are frequently a result of Warlock's developing style but it is significant that, with very few exceptions, they can be described in modal terms. Before moving to an assessment of their compositional elements, especially those aspects that pertain to the vocal lines, it is worth recalling a work discussed earlier. In case the impression has been created that the assumption of modal material is a phenomenon that only occurs after the Irish sojourn and, to follow the biographical fallacy once again, after he had had the opportunity to contemplate at greater length his knowledge of early music, a close examination of *The cloths of Heaven* reveals a melody based upon a Dorian mode. The centre in this case is C and, while there are a few notes that diverge, especially the whole-tone-derived final figure, the substance of the line is Dorian. It dates from March 1916[26] when his earliest delvings into the Renaissance could have yielded little of compositional substance.

In addition to the increasing incidence of modal material, it is also apparent that Warlock juxtaposes his linear material in much the same way that he handles his chords. The latter, chosen for their individual rather than their corporately functional qualities, are placed next to one another in such a way that motion within implied parts is limited and usually of a stepwise nature. Modal (or tonal) material within the voice-line is similarly positioned, there being one or two notes, usually semitonal alterations, different between adjacent uses. In these circumstances it is worth investigating whether there are any further similarities between chordal and linear devices.

It has been shown that Warlock's chordal usage depends on a small group of chords that have been collectively described as a family. These shapes – unremarkable in that, while dissonant or chromatic, they figure to a greater or lesser extent in tonal, functional harmony – relate to themselves only in that they are semitonal adjustments of each other. The exception is the pentatone, already shown to be an extension of the minor 7th shape. The chords are set out again in Ex. 5.23a. But they can also represent the frameworks of several modes. In view of Warlock's habit of writing melodies that rely on stepwise progress, it is not difficult to see the modes as linear manifestations of vertical units. A brief, further explanation of specific relationships is, however, also useful. This analysis validates the appearance of an increased frequency of diatonic material in Warlock's songs. But the use of these modes is an extension of what had happened in *Saudades*, not a denial of it. He orders his vertically inspired material in a linear manner to integrate vertical and horizontal shapes. This does not compromise the freedom of forward motion prompted by van Dieren's music. Some of the more curious juxtapositions of modes with different centres echoes his adjacent positioning of immediately attractive chords in some earlier songs; success there was limited and the practice abandoned or modified.

So far, there has been little evidence of Warlock's use of the Ionian mode. This is not regarded here as the same as the major scale. A small number of songs will be seen to utilise the Ionian in that they retain the notes throughout, without accidental alteration, even while the piano harmonies effect a modulation. In Ex. 5.23b the Ionian mode can be seen to relate to the major 7th chord. Similarly, the Mixolydian is associated with the dominant 7th/German 6th shape and the Aeolian with the *Curlew*-chord. The minor 7th is of interest because it can suggest either

Dorian or Aeolian modes, depending upon which of the two possible 6ths is employed. But a few songs actually oscillate between the two and it will be recalled that there was a brief passage in *My little sweet darling* that avoided the 6th and consequently produced a Dorian/ Aeolian ambiguity. It is noticeable that none of the chords relates to either the Phrygian or Lydian modes; Warlock's use of these is extremely limited: only one song uses the Lydian (*There is a lady sweet and kind,* mentioned above) and, while a couple of others have fleeting references to it, no song employs the Phrygian mode exclusively.

This link between chords and modes is of the greatest importance when examining Warlock's music; it represents a credible relationship between the vertical components that are the essence of his music and linear progress. These are what his compositions to this point have been striving for. This survey is principally concerned with that important, chordal inspiration, but references to horizontal derivations should not be seen as a substantial and irrelevant aside; rather they are a linear deployment of the same commodity. The degree of experimentation in these songs has been shown by the diversity of techniques that has been employed and, in some senses, the experimenting will continue. But the Winthrop Rogers songs also suggest a certain consolidation in that, although there will extensive, further development, Warlock's musical vocabulary is now established. Much of what follows chronicles the different ways that Warlock employs it.

Ex. 5.23: The relationship between Warlock's chordal and melodic families
(The pentatone is excluded; the pitch at which these examples are given is arbitrary)

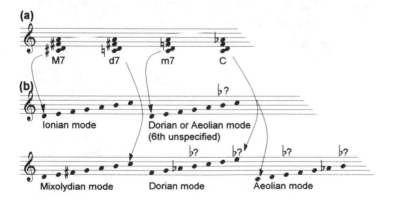

Notes

1 T; it is also in T(i).
2 By A; The early version is in T(ii).
3 See FT's preface to T(ii). The precise chronology is difficult to calculate without more information that is now unlikely to appear.
4 In CG mainly (the term "Irish Year" is his coining) pp. 158-199, but see also IC pp. 12-15 and FT1 p. 42. Why PW went to Ireland has never been made fully clear. Received opinion is that he was evading military service (he was a conscientious objector) although poor health would probably have prevented his call-up (IC loc. cit.). He was fascinated by matters Celtic, but he eschewed the ultra-Romanticism of the Celtic Twilight and, despite his championing of W. B. Yeats, there was no political motivation. He appears to have seen in Celticism an alternative to Englishness which, in his mind, stood for misguided and bigoted authority and, hence, both the antipathy of the musical establishment and those responsible for the War. His marriage had proved unsuccessful – it was less than a year old when he left England – and he may have needed the solitude that he apparently found on his lonely island. He had married Minnie Channing at her insistence (a letter, BL Add. Ms. 57794, to Phyl Crocker, the wife of a friend, Boris de Croustchoff, confirms this fact and states his distaste for the institution) after the birth of their son. CG discreetly mentions nothing of this but is equally reticent about William Ballet and his Lute Book, the Eynsford period and other important aspects of PW's life and work.
5 PW's delving into the English Renaissance dates from 1915 when he was examining keyboard music in the BM (FT1 p. 42).
6 FT preface to T(ii). See also CG p. 159.
7 See IC p. 66.
8 The spelling was modernised in some editions to "The Bailey beareth the bell away" .
9 See note 5.
10 The later setting (*Passing by*, 1928) employs more of the original poem than this one, restoring the three verses omitted here.
11 The sequences are not literal although the technique is familiar.
12 It has the same earnestness as Quilter's *Love's philosophy* (as does *Dedication*, in fact). PW sent a copy of *The singer* to Quilter inscribed "To RQ without whom there could have been no PW" (Ba p. 360). A letter to CT (9/8/1919) describes Quilter in glowing

terms (". . . the best lyrics . . . remain the sole examples of modern English music that one can hear over and over again with enriched pleasure.") but any influence was more spiritual than material.

13 Could this be considered as another autobiographical statement?

14 See note 10.

15 The text is of the early XVI century (time of Henry VIII) and is to be found in Harleian Ms 3362. PW's source was Ritson (1829).

16 FT: Preface to T(ii).

17 T(ii) includes it in the piano part. The version for string quartet is unpublished at the time of writing but will be published by T.

18 IC p. 76. His statement ("Those . . . who have regarded Warlock as no more than an ingenious pasticheur might find some grounds for their contention in *Sweet content*") suggests he misses the point.

19 For further information on the relationship between PW and Rogers see IC pp. 15 and 66-7.

20 PW's famous letter to CT of Thursday, August 22nd 1918 states that he had written ten songs in the last fortnight as a direct result of having rid himself of the psychological pressures of the preceding three years. PW could work extremely quickly but it is likely that these unidentified songs (". . . they are probably more fizz than actual stuff . . ." the letter continues) were conceived earlier. See note 6.

21 Ironically, some of his most truly melodic material is to be found in the tiny *Candlelight* nursery songs (1923).

22 *Songs of travel* (pub. 1905).

23 pp. 95 et seq.

24 In T(ii); originally (W 1919) a minor 3rd higher.

25 See pp. 101-102.

26 FT: preface to T(i).

CHAPTER 6

Experiment and consolidation (2)
The early choral songs

The handful of carols that Warlock wrote in 1918-19 (and which are therefore contemporary with the Rogers songs) were not his first essays in a choral medium. As well as the unsuccessful pieces of 1916 referred to above[1] Tomlinson also lists another partsong, *Liadain and Curithir* (1917), and, although now lost, this seems to have been envisaged on a much grander scale than any of the other choral works.[2] *The full heart* too was begun in 1916 but only the revised version of 1920 has survived so it will be considered later. Four extant pieces date from 1918 viz. *As dew in Aprylle*, *Benedicamus Domino* and settings of two poems in the Cornish tongue. *Corpus Christi* was written in 1919; Warlock's own arrangement of it for two solo voices and string quartet (which introduces no new material) was made in 1927.

As dew in Aprylle[3] exhibits many of the characteristics of its contemporary solo songs in terms of chordal choice and deployment. The sopranos sing what is effectively a melody although, as is the case with the other songs, the line is bound to the other parts not just harmonically but rhythmically too. This soprano part possesses features that are noteworthy in themselves and it is possible to draw parallels between procedures here and those encountered in the songs with piano. For the first twelve bars (a setting of the first four text-lines twice, the melodic outline being retained) it avoids any reference to a 7th; for another seven bars – the next four lines of verse – the Mixolydian 7th, F natural, is preferred (although there are only two soundings). In the subsequent 14 bars – the next eight lines – all 7th degrees are avoided until the cadence at which point Warlock declares the major 7th. But it does not rise, leading-notewise, to the tonic; rather there is a progression, a juxtaposition, really, of tonally confusing chords to obfuscate the issue (Ex. 6.1). In the last section, F sharp is first of all reinstated to prepare for the pseudo-modulation that draws attention to the climactic tenet "Moder and maydyn/Was never non but che"; however, in the four bars that answer it, the 7th is again abandoned altogether as the chromaticism of the coincident harmony intensifies to expand and reflect upon the implications of the statement. There is no perfect cadence (Ex. 6.2).

Ex. 6.1: *As dew in Aprylle* **– bars 31-33**

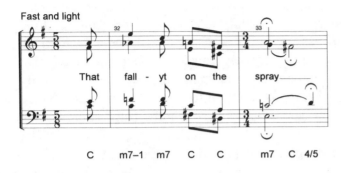

Ex. 6.2: *As dew in Aprylle* **– bars 38-41**

The harmony, only occasionally functional, relies for its impact mostly on family chords and the manner of their disposition: smoothness of passage from note to note in each vocal part is achieved largely by stepwise motion, particularly important in a choral piece that is suitable for amateur performance, and this is how the progress is justified. As in the Rogers songs, the proportion of major and minor chords is larger than in preceding material; together they make up about a third of the piece but this is still a minority in a work that purports, by virtue of its key-signature and opening and closing chords, to be in G major. There are references to this tonic at strategic points throughout the piece, at beginnings and ends of phrases mostly, but even these are not particularly prominent. The repeated lines of the first verse ("I syng of a mayden . . . To here sone che ches") are treated this way, as are the next four ("He cam al so stylle . . . That fallyt on the gras"); but thereafter, by means of interrupted cadences or other substitutions and interpolations, precise references are avoided – just as the absent melodic 7ths were – until the final chord, achieved unconventionally.

Adherence to the chordal family is observed even where the aggregate effect might be considered incidental, such as where motion or drive depends on the use of passing-notes or suspensions. Pentatone-derived chords (there are 17 of them) usually consist of four out of the five notes, a result of the number of voice-parts available and generally employed;[4] chordal thickening is reserved for climactic moments. There is an occasional sense of centre that results from repeated chords. They contain the impetus and are explicable as word-painting of "stylle". The effect is also declamatory, in the nature of a liturgical chant.

Benedicamus Domino is, in contrast with much of Warlock's output, noticeably lacking in accidentals. This is not just because of its averred note-centre ("Key C" conveniently announces the tonic sol-fa edition); Warlock extends the linear use of modes to his harmonic vocabulary but in a more rigorous manner than in the solo songs. The mode announced by the exposed, seven-note alto figure which opens the carol is pentatonic. While it does not provide an exclusive basis for chordal note-distribution, it does persist with very little modification in the soprano line which, as before, has a melodic function. The note-focus is ambiguous; the alto figure begins on C and the first four notes delineate a C triad. The remaining three have an element of A (minor?), descending from the tonic to the dominant through a modal (lowered) 7th although they could be thought of as suggesting the added 6th (Ex. 6.3). In the rest of the first verse – and the second and third that are repeats in essence if not detail – the notes not used by the pentatone, B and F (assuming a C major/Ionian scenario) each appear only once in the highest, quasi-melodic part (usually the soprano but, on one

Ex. 6.3: *Benedicamus Domino* – bars 1-4

occasion, the alto). In the final, fourth verse the soprano eschews the F altogether and only employs the B once. These appearances of what is supposed to be the leading-note do not occur melodically at the end-of-verse cadences but one bar (which means about eight notes) earlier.

Its most frequently occurring chord, like *As dew in Aprylle*, is the minor 7th although usage is less discriminatory in the use of Fs and Bs than the soprano line. No accidentals at all appear in the first verse and the only one in the second is an isolated F sharp (bar 15, altos) that attempts, unsuccessfully, to move to the dominant but is thwarted in the following bar by a minor 7th chord on E. While this does contain the notes of a G chord, it disorients the proposed modulation by inter-ruption. The F is immediately naturalised. F sharps are more evident in the third verse. There are significantly more harmonic changes here, effected at first by short, two-bar, two-note drones from divided basses. As in the previous piece and elsewhere, it is not only the chords at principal points that conform to the family; the incidence of the drone basses does not affect the general situation for all chords in these four bars can be described in terms of Warlockian practice. But the F sharps (bar 25) are again transitory and, while they may once more hold the promise of a dominant move, this does not materialise even though the A minor orientation of the preceding bars has the feel, if only by association, of an extended pivot.

The whole piece is penetonal: it pretends to manifest tonal procedures, getting as close to the brink as seems exciting, but declines to take the plunge. It makes more sense to view the F sharps, like the B flats of the last verse, as linear devices, semitonal manipulation of the notes that were absent from the expositional pentatonic phrase for, apart from a short and, in this exuberant piece, relatively extravagant, pre-cadential, chromatic bass-line (Ex. 6.4), they are the only accidentals. Warlock has

Ex. 6.4: *Benedicamus Domino* – bars 36-7

demonstrated the importance of the semitone in his compositional philosophy by using it as the regulating element that shapes his chordal family. But he has also used it in other ways in earlier pieces, vocal and instrumental, where it was used to amend chords that were otherwise family shapes by adjusting one note from the grouping. This is an inappropriate technique for the more diatonic environment in which he has now chosen to work; his semitonal manipulations in the Rogers songs (that effect movement between modes) and the relationships he establishes here indicate technical changes to his methodology that are an essential part of this stylistic development. But further to this, it must be recognised that the C-centre and the limited use of accidentals reflect the naïve faith of the words: "Glory! Praise! God is made both man and immortal". And the homophonic deployment, testimony to Warlock's chordal methodology, suggests a corporate statement of belief. These are remarkable and perceptive sentiments from a self-proclaimed atheist who felt uncomfortable at Christmas.

Warlock wrote two carols that set the ancient and, to all intents and purposes, dead Cornish language.[5] He had learned to speak Gaelic during his Irish sojourn and this had sparked off an interest in other Celtic languages including Breton and Manx as well as Cornish. But he had already encountered Welsh as a result of his mother's remarriage and their move to Montgomeryshire. It is typical of Warlock that, in his espousal of Celtic culture, he took his interest further and more practically than most of the English romantics of the Celtic Twilight. His learning Welsh was, in one way, provocative as the Welsh squirearchy, into which he had been thrust, eschewed the local tongue; and his use of Cornish, unknown to all but a small number of revivalists, necessitated a pronunciation guide upon publication. When *Kan Nadelik* was printed, Warlock gave in and allowed an English (metrical) translation alongside the original words; inevitably this has meant that the Cornish version has hardly ever been sung.[6]

Like *As dew in Aprylle* and *Benedicamus Domino*, the second of the two, *A Cornish Christmas Carol* (*Kan Nadelik* – "A Christmas song"), was published in 1924;[7] the first, *Kan Kernow* ("Cornish song") had to wait until 1973.[8] Warlock's own preference was for the longer, second carol;[9] although it is a powerful piece and emotionally richer than its companion (in the cumulative effect of the range of material employed) both pieces look back rather than maintain the tendency towards the refinement of detail that has been demonstrated in the other two choral works already discussed.

The chief difficulty in assessing *Kan Kernow* (and *Kan Nadelik* too) is the lack of consistency that pervades the harmonic distribution. The situation noted in *As dew in Aprylle* and *Benedicamus Domino*, where even incidental detail conforms to the chordal family, deteriorates here. Devices used for their own sake rather than as components within an encompassing logic, a criticism levelled at the earliest pieces, are not necessarily unsuitable, especially at the brisk pace demanded, but they do sound out of character. The situation is compounded by a busy texture that attempts to justify the fussy, falling-quaver motif sung by the sopranos (bar 2, Ex. 6.5). The choice of centres (and the means whereby they are achieved) is also disappointing when compared with contemporary practice. The move from E flat to F may be explicable in terms of modifying the original tonic to manufacture the new leading note but it is not convincing: the pivot chord at 3iv is unfortunate for it lies outside the family (which, nevertheless, still predominates in the matter of harmonic allocation).

Ex. 6.5: *Kan Kernow* – bars 1-4

Translation by Fred Tomlinson:
"Christ, Michael and Mary, send thy blessings now we pray."

In the context of two other pieces where modulation was virtually abandoned, the key-changes in this one sound forced. The move to A flat (bar 8) follows one chromatic and two Mixolydian D flats and lacks subtlety; the reversion to E flat, while it uses the pseudo-sequence technique already observed, is laboured. The rationale behind the F flat achieved at 15i may well be the raised tonic (E natural) of bar 4; a similar circumstance is about to reoccur when F is once again reached (in bar 16 – the move corresponds to a verbal reprise). It re-establishes the tonic, the relationship established in the first four bars but executed in reverse. So, while there is a logic to the choice of centres, it is tortuous. The piece is only 25 bars long and marked "con brio"; viewed alongside contemporary pieces, it is particularly unsatisfying.

The backwards glance in *Kan Nadelik* results not from the inclusion of the 8-bar quotation from *The first Nowell* – after all, the tune sets the message of the angels – but from Warlock's idiosyncratic harmonisation, sent as a Christmas greeting to Bernard van Dieren the previous year.[10] Although less than six months elapsed between the dedication and, at the least, some advanced stage of the composition of the carols (so much can be gleaned from the date and content of the letter to Colin Taylor)[11] the attitude and content of Warlock's compositions in general would appear, from the evidence already presented, to have progressed beyond the stage recalled here.

There are two surprising features about the choice of chords in *Kan Nadelik*, Warlock's preferred title on his original fair-copy manuscript.[12] The first of these is the prevalence of major chords. Although there is still a reliance upon family chords (but see below) the proportion of major (and minor) chords is much more akin to that discovered in the Winthrop Rogers songs. In addition, the percentage of chords not conforming to the family increases and ancillary material (appoggiaturas, passing-notes, suspensions and the like) fit less well into the vertical logic than had been the case. Most of the miscellaneous chords can be accounted for in terms of passing-notes and the other features mentioned, and it may seem unnecessary to include them as separate entities, especially as most of them occur off the beat and as the result of activity within a single part. But, given past experience and the knowledge that, in this very piece, other similar incidents do produce pure family-aggregations, it is appropriate to categorise them separately and draw attention to the fact.

Melodic material emanates from the pentatone. The soprano part (or the upper line where the part is divided) depends on the shape given in Ex. 6.6; this contains no Gs or Ds, flat or natural. In bars 1-15, (the first

Ex. 6.6: *Kan Nadelik* – melodic material (1)

verse) only one note does not derive from this note-pattern, a G passing-note in bar 7. Pentatones are unstable in terms of note-centre references; Warlock interprets the current shape as having focus-points on A flat (the principal centre) and F, which can produce either a major or a minor harmonic response. He makes this clear by employing a figure in

five of the six verses that depends on five A flats with an interpolated F
(Ex. 6.7). This shape is usually employed at the outset of the verse as a
point of familiarity; the material that supersedes it is, in all cases,
different.

Ex. 6.7: *Kan Nadelik* – melodic material (2)

These features appear in the first verse. The homophonic material
continues into the second where, although the melodic outline is
retained, the associated chord-choice is altered in the first few bars. The
new harmonic emphasis is in keeping with the developing strophic
practices already considered in relation to the piano-songs. The new
chordal perspective is characterised by the G flat (second soprano, bar
16, Ex. 6.8) that contrasts with the G natural of the first verse – yet
another example of the semitonal manipulation of notes absent from the
melodic pentatone. In this way the Ionian implications of the first verse

Ex. 6.8: *Kan Nadelik* – bars 15-17

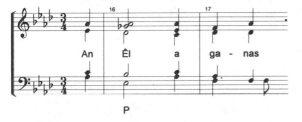

("To watching shepherds")
This translation and the remaining ones are those made by Trelawney Dayrell Reed
for the publication of this piece.

are transformed to suggest the Mixolydian. The tune of the first verse is
then abandoned but the stepwise nature of the substitute is transmuted
from an A flat Mixolydian (which therefore includes the G flat
presented in the chordally modified passage) via a D natural (also a
pentatonic absentee) that results in an F Dorian figure (Ex. 6.9).

It is these small melodic chromaticisms (that also appear briefly in a
harmonic context) which announce the more intense use of accidentals
in the *First Nowell* quotation that immediately ensues. The opening

Ex. 6.9: *Kan Nadelik* – bars 20-23

The - ra'n can - ma___ pur lo - wen - ek dho whêl;

"This was their song and lustily it rang")

semitone dissonance, E natural against E flat (tenors and basses), is explicable only in terms of the original version of six months earlier. In that case the higher part was moving upwards from an established E while the lower was descending in an F minor context (Ex. 3.23 again). Here, the musica ficta/melodic minor scenario still stands, but the relationship between the extract and the new material that precedes it is more strained. The quotation represents a stage of Warlock's compositional development that had largely passed and contains material which – like that of the *Folk-song preludes* – possesses undeniable note-centre attributes of its own. As a result, it fits the instructions at the start of the carol more aptly than might at first be discerned.[13] Consequently, the decorated and extended dominant feel that he cannot avoid (bars 28-9, Ex. 6.10) prepares for an A flat reorientation in time for the start of the next verse. But he has already cadenced in F minor, however loosely, and thereby confirmed the duality of centre already noted as a feature of the piece. An additional aspect of this section is the new textural effect created, first of all, by the reduction to semichorus in bar 28 and, then, by the wordless-chorus device in all parts but the soprano. This is not so much a Delian hangover as a new characteristic in a piece that has as its raison d'être a constantly fluctuating emotional emphasis. Its importance as a mood-generating stratagem apart, it also anticipates the use of melisma that will be important in bars 63-5 and the last verse.

The third verse, meanwhile, starts with the same static melodic figure that begins its predecessors (and its successor) although, on this occasion, it serves as *dux* to a potential *comes* that, while it picks up the repeated-note figure of its model, fails to materialise. It is another textural ploy; like the ensuing material (new in each verse), it suggests that, while strophism is the intent, ways of maintaining it as a force have

Ex. 6.10: *Kan Nadelik* – bars 23-31

Gor - dhyans—— dho—— Dhew— es— en— Nêv brâs.

soprani: Crês war an tîr—— dho dîs— bodh mâs
others: Ah ——

("All glory to God who in Heaven is King
And peace on earth to everything.")

not yet fully presented themselves. The attempted counterpoint is not
polyphonic at all but layered homophony and the device is quickly
abandoned (although it paves the way for later, more sustained efforts).

Alternative Gs flat and natural (contraltos bars 31-32) are kept a
respectable bar's distance from one another but, by the time bars 35-6
and 37-8 are reached they have become, effectively, chromatic passing
notes (contraltos once again) and prompt similar gestures elsewhere so
that, in the fourth verse, the intense chromaticism that relates the
mystery of the Eucharist is prepared for (Ex. 6.11). Warlock prefaces
this passage with, at nine bars, his most extended use of a bass pedal so
far. The device is related to the repeated notes that are a feature of the
motif that has opened all of the verses to this point (including this one,
although it is made less apparent by its positioning in a contralto line
that has soprano activity above it). The pedal produces a number of
dissonances that, while loosely related to the family, create tensions that
the intensity of the semichorus's Eucharist-chords do not resolve until
the F major chord in bar 66, only reached after the chant-like repeated
chords of 58-61 and the uncharacteristic melisma of 63-65. This
chromatically demanding section is related to earlier material not so
much by substance as technique. The tendency for textural change noted
in earlier verses is here represented by the use of a semichorus.

Ex. 6.11: *Kan Nadelik* – **bars 55-66**

semichorus
ppp
En ter - men Of - fer-ten ny vedn ê wê-las, Pan wrâ ê dhis -

kenn-ya rag dho gan——— whê——— las.

(basses) whê——————— las.

("At Holy Eucharist we shall behold Him,
Bread and wine made flesh in our hearts we shall enfold Him.")

Likewise, the chromaticism recalls that of the *First Nowell* harmonisation without actually duplicating material.

Hywel Davies states[14] that "The influence of van Dieren's music . . . reveals itself . . . in such devices as parallel 3rds or 6ths moving between pedal notes in the upper and lower parts" and refers specifically to *Kan Nadelik* and its companion. In this respect, the idiosyncratic harmonisation lifted from the *Christmas hommage to Bernard van Dieren* makes a statement as much about the compositional inspiration of the piece as the angelic association. However, another glance at the opening of *A lake and a fairy boat* reveals a manifestation of a similar device several years pre-van Dieren.

The fifth verse commences homophonically (and tutti); the motif of earlier verses is abandoned. But the link between A flat and F, a feature of the first two verses which had fallen into disuse in the third and fourth, is here reinstated. This duality of centre is achieved, in a manner very similar to that used in the second verse, by a pivotal, Mixolydian G flat (at 69i). In this instance, the descent to F in the melody involves the D flat of the key-signature so the result is Aeolian rather than the Dorian of the earlier appearance. While repeated-note figures do recall those of the preceding verses, Warlock relies on repetitions of technique – textural change, cyclical variation of the intensity of chromaticism and pre-cadential melisma – to maintain his forward progress rather than restating or reworking material.

Verse 5 concludes on the family chord of a dominant 7th; it has a B flat root and resolves on to an E flat figure, the subject of a short-lived polyphonic passage, that observes the demands of the key-signature and, consequently, possesses a Mixolydian quality. The choice of an E flat centre is curious after the predominance of A flat (and, to a lesser extent, F) in the song so far. It is, of course, the dominant and, like the B flat chord that heralds it, is based on a constituent note of the initial pentatone, but its appearance at this comparatively late stage in the piece comes as a surprise. Although a conventionally related centre it is achieved in an unusual place. It soon reverts to A flat. The polyphonic passage (which is undeveloped – there is no significant counter-subject material) proves to be a false start to the true final verse which recommences with a verbal repeat and the reinstated verse-opening figure. This re-establishes A flat although, as in the fourth verse, the figure is given to the contraltos so that it becomes submerged, another textural variant.

The piece proclaims a rustic ruggedness, a deliberate lack of sophistication that makes the continued rejection of its performance in the more guttural Cornish[15] to be the more regretted. The "sudden alternations of hardness and sweetness, of rude heartiness and tenderness touched with awe" required by Warlock's parenthetical directions at the beginning of the piece[141] are difficult to achieve without degenerating into bathos, but the composer's verbal demands are, nevertheless, substantiated by the sectional nature of his construction. The route between related textural devices and the rejection, for the most part, of motivic repetition is a continuous expression of the diverse sentiments of the text. These range from celebrating the transubstantiation of the bread and wine to a proto-nationalistic entreaty for Divine succour and they are the song's strength. The principally homorhythmic, chord-based texture is an essential ingredient both in terms of Warlock's methodology and the corporate identity inherent in the text.

There are some differences between the published version of *Kan Nadelik* discussed above and the holograph held in the British Library. There is no doubt that the amendments were made by Warlock himself prior to publication in 1924 and, since six years of compositional development elapsed between conception and print, they should come as

Ex. 6.12: *Kan Nadelik* **– discarded section**

* "I have substituted this word for the words 'Dew ny' in the original poem, on account of the difficulty of the 'ew' sound on a high note." [Warlock's own note on the holograph.]

No translation of these words is currently available. The gist is a series of requests for a Christmas blessing ("Bennath Nadelik") from the Lord ("Arleth") and "God's mother the Virgin" ("Dama Dew an Vahteth").

no surprise. Some of the alterations, such as those to spellings of the Cornish text (in line with contemporary research and practice), modifications to rhythms and inversions or note-redistributions of some chords are of little importance. Others are more extensive: there are some wholesale substitutions within the verbal text and the original eight bars that preceded the final, climactic statement ("Hebma yu dewedh dho oll ow hân" – "This is the end of all my song") are replaced in the printed edition, perhaps because of the chromatic excesses of the earlier writing (Ex. 6.12) or, possibly, to heighten the ending by delaying it longer. The *Curlew*-chord that concludes the statement leads neatly to the sostenuto conclusion but it lacks the drama and the dominant quality of the eventual choice. This passage apart, there is little significant, musical difference between the manuscript and printed versions. (What is of greater interest, perhaps, is Warlock's verbal substitution. It has not proved possible at the time of writing to fully explain this factor.)

Pedal-points, used with varying degrees of frequency and intensity in *Kan Nadelik*, and observed in smaller quantities in *As dew in Aprylle*, become the most important structural device of *Corpus Christi*. The chorus generates a continuum of pedal-based, seamless and wordless ostinati, a restless adjunct to two solo voices (contralto and tenor) that proclaim the text. Warlock's later (1927) arrangement of the carol has a string quartet in place of the chorus; in that version the two short passages where the choral voices had sung the text ("And in that bed there lithe a knight/His woundès bleeding day and night" and the more declamatory "By that bedside there standeth a stone: CORPUS CHRISTI written thereon") have a timbrally less unified power than in the choral original, although the exposed quality and consequent vulnerability inherent in the solo voices is given greater emphasis. In all other respects the two versions are identical and further discussion of the later format is unnecessary.

The opening figure encapsulates much of Warlock's current compositional thinking. All of the pitches employed conform to an A-centred Dorian mode and the harmony consists of four family chords, viz. two different minor 7ths, a *Curlew*-chord and a pentatone (Ex. 6.13). In this highly condensed device, F sharp, the Dorian mode signifier, possesses the quality of an added 6th (because of the note-distribution) that recalls the earliest songs. Solo-voice material is more enigmatic. While the setting of the refrain line is indisputably A-centred it lacks a 6th and so (a rare but not unobserved phenomenon in Warlock's output) could suggest either the Aeolian or the Dorian mode. The pair of chords at 5iii adds to this lack of clarity, not by the nature of their construction (both the main chord and its associated ancillary are pentatone-based) but in the matter of their content. They draw attention to themselves by breaking the run of the A pedal that otherwise regulates the first 23 bars. The secondary chord – and the weaker by virtue of its unessential elements – introduces C sharp. In this context C sharp is a Mixolydian signifier and the chordal complex consequently assumes a pivotal rôle by suggesting the potential of other, A-centred modes. The C is immediately naturalised (in bar 6) giving the preceding sharpened form a transitory, chromatic quality. However, with its F naturals, this bar employs an A-Aeolian that itself turns out to be pivotal. The naturalised C, incorporated into the pedal-become-drone, now assumes the status of a multi-modal final that suggests (in bar 7) first Mixolydian and then (by means of a Bartókian false relation) the Dorian. In bar 8 the A flat Aeolian signifier creates a dissonance against

Ex. 6.13: *Corpus Christi* **(choral version) – bars 1-9**

the A pedal harsher than any other already heard in the piece (and the pedal creates other shapes that are dissonant and do not conform to the family) but, by sounding it at this stage, Warlock has presented all 12 pitches logically in a diatonic scenario. Significantly, the tonal 7th (G sharp, presented as A flat) is the last to be unveiled.

But this expositional statement does not immediately let slip unbridled chromaticism. The only accidentals in bars 10-11 are the F sharp Dorian signifiers already familiar from the opening. In the next bar, chromatic occurrences proliferate, sometimes as passing-notes, but a tenor G sharp has a more functional quality than was the case on its previous appearance. The ostinato, modified in bars 8-9 (the point at which the A flat/G sharp had first been sounded), is now briefly suspended altogether in favour of a simple, triple-pulse backcloth for the first-verse motif. This is short and unsustained, servicing only two lines of text broken by a longer note at the end of the first. The essentially pentatonic outline concedes a discrepant F natural, delayed until the end of the figure where it is sounded twice. It cancels the Dorian signifier reintroduced by the chorus and substitutes an Aeolian one. The chorus counters immediately with the former and also presents the middle-C sharp momentarily referred to in bar 5. This note (which only appears at this pitch) alternates with its naturalised version and both notes dictate the next block, constantly shifting the emphasis against which the refrain is restated. The shape of this restatement differs from, but is motivically based upon, the initial form and it also employs the ambiguous Dorian/Aeolian note distribution of before. The melody of the ensuing verse maintains the same pitch choice until an F natural, the Aeolian signifier, just before the end. Chromatic, falling-semitone-motion dominates bar 20; it is a more intense statement than its related predecessor of bar 12 and here it is more exposed to punctuate the two text-lines of the verse. It contains eleven of the twelve available pitches; little significance need be attached to the omitted note (D sharp/E flat) although it could be tenuously associated with a rejected dominant modulation. This chromatic bar also serves to separate Dorian (bar 19) from Aeolian material (bars 21-3).

Apart from the momentary bass B (bar 5), Warlock has maintained his A pedal to this point. Now, as a preface to the third verse, he relinquishes it, quitting it semitonally. The chromaticism of verse 3, lessened in intensity by the chorus's reversion to the three beats/chords to the bar (bar 10 et seq.), is tightly controlled. Its reliance on G sharp, the note to which the pedal was abandoned, creates a stronger tonal feel than has hitherto been the case although the G natural from the solo tenor deliberately (and deliciously) maintains a status quo. The harmonic D sharp at this moment may make delayed amends for its absence in bar 20; it could be construed as having a functional responsibility in that it half-heartedly effects something of a dominant modulation. In fact, the two chords of the abstracted perfect cadence are a *Curlew*-chord (with B in the bass) and a 7th on E, but in the last inversion so, while the illusion and the allusion are both present, there is no unequivocal move. And although bar 28 has affinities with bars 12 and 20, it really serves to announce the false relations of bar 29 (F sharp in the soprano and F natural in the contralto chorus parts – the F natural at 29ii creates an indefinable, non-family chord) that continue and then prompt G sharp/natural discrepancies. Such false relations hark back to those of bars 8-9 and constitute the "gloom" motif.

The presence of G sharp in the last chord of this section (a dominant) provides a degree of stability, confirmed by the repeated, unison As that open the più lento fourth verse and its associated chromaticisms. Much of what happens here is an extension of what has already occurred earlier and, as in *Kan Nadelik*, Warlock employs a textural change, in this case homophony, to herald the new verse. Other verses too exhibit textural changes that separate them from surrounding material although not in as extreme a way as experienced in the Cornish carol. Here they are largely variants on the melody-with-accompaniment that has been the norm so far, bound together by the ostinato or its derivatives.

The chromaticism that shapes verse 4 is linked with, and can be considered a development of, the chromatic bars 12, 20 and 28: descending lines, first from sopranos and basses (bars 37-8), then sopranos and contraltos (39-40) follow earlier precedents, utilising all twelve pitches in the course of its unfolding. In this piece, then, Warlock's use of chromatic procedures, although still bearing the mark of Delius via van Dieren, is achieved logically, justified by the semitonal differences that exist between modes that have the same final. As if to prove this last point there is an immediate restatement of a device that initially appeared in bar 26 where the G natural of the soloist's melody had clashed with the G sharp of the harmonic underlay (Ex. 6.14). Now the momentary nature of the earlier manifestation is made more prominent. First there is a G sharp bass pedal against which a G natural can oscillate within the ostinato figure; then – and more blatantly – the ostinato, in coincident motion with its own inversion, has G naturals and sharps occurring simultaneously. Indeed, G sharp, rejected in the opening figure in preference to the G natural of the pentatone and its modal associations, asserts itself more and more. It is used as the long, sustained climax of the melody in verse 5 and systematically cuts through the sixth, final verse as an astringent component of the ostinato, this despite (or because of) the reinstatement of the A pedal/drone.

Ex. 6.14: *Corpus Christi* – bars 25-29

The textural device that characterises this last verse is the monotonous chanting of the text by contraltos (singing E) and basses (A, a 5th below). This dramatises and gives a quasi-ritualistic element to the text but is also derived from the drones and pedals that permeate the entire work. There is no tonal movement or other shift of centre and the general effect is consequently one of pulsating stasis, *The lover mourns for the loss of love* in an extended form, appropriate to the mystically religious atmosphere of the verse. The *Curlew*-chord at the end states that the carol, though diatonic and centred on A, is not tonal but modal; the chord stands as a distillation of the Dorian mode.

Corpus Christi is strophic in that it divides up into verses. But the melodic basis of these relies on common material rather than accurately duplicated figures. Transition between stanzas is marked by changes to the texture – so much has been noted – but the main compositional intent is a shift of the harmonic emphasis. Changes are effected by the differences between modes that have the same final but which necessitate melodic alterations.

Notes

1   See note 4, Chapter 4.

2   FT1 pp. 15 & 32

3   The source for the poem is usually given as Chambers and Sidgewick (1907). However, the spellings in this volume are at variance with those employed by PW ("Aprylle" in the song is "Aprille" in the book, "stylle" is "stille", etc.) so he either had another source or indulged in a little enhancement of the text.

4   Of 17 pentatone-based shapes, 3 use all five notes and 14 use four of the five. The miscellaneous chords comprise two diminished chords and 13 others that are less readily definable; they include chords based on clusters and family chords modified by the addition or adjustment of notes as well as two that appear to have no diatonic basis at all.

5   The carols are known collectively as *Kanow Kernow* ("Cornish songs") although they were never published as a pair.

6   *Kan Nadelik* was sung in Cornish by the choir of the University of Wales, Aberystwyth, under Ian Parrott in the 1960s (IC p. 213); the Cornish version of *Kan Kernow* was first performed by the Leicester University Singers directed by Anthony Pither on 4th November, 1994, as part of the celebrations of the Peter Warlock Centenary. These are thought to be the only times they have been given in the language Warlock intended.

7   By B as *Can Nedelek*; the alternative spellings are valid.

8   Its publication by T under the title *Two carols* (not Warlock's designation) is confusing because its companion is *The rich cavalcade* (1928). The pieces are otherwise unconnected.

9   A letter to CT of 13th June 1918 expresses this and, with typical force, his views on the chances of their being performed as a result of the linguistic demands. See IC pp. 186-7.

10   This was published *facsimile* as *Hommages* (T 1974) alongside BvD's *The long barrow* (a tribute written after PW's death).

11   See note 9.

12   BL Add. Ms. 52905. The published version was slightly amended (see p. 131).

13   See p. 131.

14   Notes to Abacus recording ABA 604-2; see note 2, Chapter 8.

15   On the autograph (see note 12) this instruction is in brackets although the published version omits them.

CHAPTER 7

Experiment and consolidation (3)
Three more songs

From a purely chronological standpoint[1] – and because it is primarily a solo song despite its various guises[2] – *Balulalow* (1919) could be discussed alongside the Winthrop Rogers songs. But, because of its affinities with *Corpus Christi*, it is more sensible to consider it nearer to that piece. Like *Sweet content*, other, preceding songs and *Corpus Christi* itself, *Balulalow* employs juxtaposed, multi-modal material; several E flat-centred modes are placed in close proximity to one another, creating false relations and dissonances while pedals and drones assert the centre, another feature already observed in the choral model. Most of the material, melodic and harmonic, is derived from Mixolydian, Dorian and Aeolian modes although, occasionally, the raised 7th (D natural) is preferred (by no means always in a ficta context). Other accidentals, like those of bars 14-16 and employed for momentary gratification, are comparatively few. There is nothing resembling the chromatic proliferation that was periodically witnessed in the other carol.

While strophic it has only two verses. The harmony is identical in both although, in the second, the ostinato drone-figure creates some additional tensions. There is no modulation but A naturals in bars 12 and 16 (and corresponding points in the second verse) issue an unful-filled promise. Melodic note-choice changes at the midpoint of each verse. The first halves (of eight bars) depend on an unmodified Ionian mode; in the second halves, the melody sits in the upper part of the vocal range and contains no mediants of any shade. It introduces the C flat of the Aeolian mode in addition to the C natural of the Mixolydian and Dorian and it uses the D flat associated with all three alongside the D natural of the Ionian/ major resulting in chromatic shapes like those in bars 13-15 and 18-19 (Ex. 7.1). In some respects this chromaticism is an extension of inner part-motion at bar 11 which, in turn, can be viewed as related to the F flat passing-note of bar 3, an unusually early aberration in the song given Warlock's practice to date and one that is given an increased element of surprise by the quaver chord that precedes it, interrupting the chromatic flow (Ex. 7.2). Like the harmony, the melody

Ex. 7.1: *Balulalow* – bars 13-15 & 18-19

Ex. 7.2: *Balulalow* – bars 2-3

is unchanged in the second verse except for a tiny rhythmic modification to compensate for a change of syllabic stress.

The intent is made clear in the first couple of bars. The E flat-centre is stated, speedily followed by the simultaneous modal (flattened) 7th and Dorian/Aeolian (minor) 3rd; the latter is immediately contradicted. The expositional rôle accorded to the piano is presented harmonically rather than – the assumption given the linear attributes of the modal usage – horizontally. For, while the melody possesses a logic of its own as outlined above, it is itself a constituent (the upper component) of the primarily chordal rationale. The logic is not so much that the piano duplicates the vocal line throughout, rather it is the other way about: *Balulalow* is essentially a piece conceived at the keyboard with the voice as a textural rather than a constructional entity. These are readily explicable features in a piece which, appropriately for a cradle song, is simple and even naïve in what it expresses.

The contemporary *Romance* has a robust character; its strong, dotted rhythms and common-chord harmonies anticipate later songs such as *Captain Stratton's fancy* or *The cricketers of Hambledon*. The vocal line, based on a pentatone like that of the other Stevenson setting (*Bright is the ring of words*/*To the memory of a great singer*) seeks to be contrivedly rustic but the result is more suitable for the drawing room than the open road (and the same can be said of Vaughan Williams's setting[3] too). The composer's paronomastic title (the poet gives it none) recognises the poem's idealised image of the romantic traveller motivated by the natural world, a view as close to reality as Warlock's song is to musical ethnicity.

It promises to be uncomplicatedly strophic. An interpolated Mixolydian 7th (A flat) invades an otherwise pentatonic melody, all of which is retained, with a single, added E flat passing-note (another pitch foreign to the pentatone) to serve the second of the three verses. The ending of the third, final verse is altered to make for a grander, more climactic and, it must be said, more conventionally romantic finish. It not only includes the previously encountered E flat, now more prominent, but uses A natural, the tonal leading-note. Indeed, there is a more overtly tonal aspect to this piece than to *Balulalow* or *Corpus Christi*. B flat pedals that contain the introduction and the opening two bars of each verse; they mirror the stasis-inducing devices of these other two pieces, the effect does not last; the brief tonic pedal becomes an even more brief dominant before being abandoned altogether until the start of the next stanza. The ensuing circle-of-5ths – it appears in all the verses – confirms the tonal bias without going all the way to a shift of centre. In fact, the E flats (a passing-note at first, then an essential) symbolise the reluctance to modulate to the dominant. There is no sustained move at all; the transitory reference to the relative minor (in bar 8 and equivalent places) is the starting point for the aforementioned circle-of-5ths.

The family-based, harmonic underlay of the first verse is recycled in the second and, apart from a little harmonic thickening (a textural marker) it continues effectively unchanged into verse 3. Here, though, a chromatic alteration to a passing-note (F sharp for F natural in bar 24), heralds the more extensive modifications that necessitate a reshaped melody. Unfortunately this sort of overt tonalism has got Warlock into trouble and prevented his being taken seriously. The result is not so different from Vaughan Williams's setting[4] but Warlock lacks the body of other compositions that excuses the older composer's lapses.

It should be coming clear that one must be wary of too readily ascribing features of Warlock's composition to his interest in the music of the Renaissance. However, he was attracted by the timbral possibilities of a solo voice accompanied by viols and this may have prompted him to arrange some of his solo songs for performance with string quartet (the same forces for which he had transcribed some old material). *My lady is a pretty one* (1919) is a rare example of a solo song written, rather than arranged, for the medium. It resets the text used in *As ever I saw* but the sedate, rhythmical restraint of the earlier song is exchanged for a more exuberant statement characterised by syncopation, moto perpetuo quavers in the string parts and, occasionally, vocal melisma. Likewise, the homorhythms of 1918 are replaced by a more linearly aware, even contrapuntal, treatment that is made audibly clearer by an instrumental contingent of four players rather than one. A partsong version has, unfortunately, been lost[5] and a comparison with the wordless-chorus technique of *Corpus Christi*, with which it is contemporary (and which itself would rematerialise in an arrangement for string quartet) provokes a tantalisingly attractive conjecture.

My lady is a pretty one is significant because it is the first of Warlock's songs to combine a strong, horizontal quality (attributable to the *Saudades*/van Dieren experience) and his modal assumption. Because it is was written about the same time as the second group of Rogers songs it shares features with them. The melody uses G-centred material with a raised, ficta 7th (F sharp) in the lower octave and a Mixolydian (F natural) in the upper (although a non-ficta F natural creeps into the lower octave in bar 36). There are pentatonic hints which fail to materialise fully. Of interest, though, is the subsequent insertion of some pentatonically derived motifs into other melodic passages.

Later accidental usage (from about two-thirds of the way through) is more complex. Immediately beforehand, viola and cello had been vigorously asserting the song's G-centre; but a shift at bar 59 stabilises a few bars later on A after starting from a chord of E. It is, actually, more consistent to think in terms of E or, rather, E-based modes as all ensuing accidentals conform to these and, at the start of the passage, the voice briefly appears to suggest an E centre. Ex. 7.3 shows bars 59-72 in which – chromatic notes apart – E is the regulating, if not actually the proclaimed, centre before the reversion to G. It could be acceptable to think of the assumption of E as a vestigial tonal practice, a move (however much it is abstracted) to the relative minor from a G major beginning. This may well be the point of familiarity from which

Warlock departs but, in the context of his output as a whole, it is also necessary to consider the use of the G sharp (which is also allowed to become the leading-note of A in bars 60-64) as a semitonal disturbance to the centre that begins and concludes the song. The horizontally deployed instrumental parts assert these prevailing centres and, apart from some good-natured counterpoint (original melody in the second

Ex. 7.3: *My lady is a pretty one* – bars 59-72

violin, new counter-melody in the voice) there is no real motivic
significance. The introductory figure in the first violin is a horizontalised minor 7th, a figure one semitone different from the opening of
The curlew with which, in mood or use, it has no more affinities.

Notes

1   The song was written in 1919 and is, therefore, contemporary with the later Rogers songs.
2   It was published in a number of forms, as a unison song, as a carol for soprano solo, SATB chorus and strings and as a song with string quartet. See FT1 p. 10 and FT's preface to T(ii).
3   Ralph Vaughan Williams: *The roadside fire*, one of the *Songs of travel*. See note 22 in Chapter 5.
4   idem.
5   FT1 p. 24.

CHAPTER 8

Delius revisited and Warlock rediscovered

Examination of *The full heart* (1916-21) produces much the same kind of reaction as a lot of *The curlew*, the mixed elements of *déjà vu* and retrospection. For, although completed in 1920,[1] it contains stylistic detail familiar from earlier songs like *The water lily* and *Saudades*. Here, chromaticism is a dramatic and formative element in both vertical and horizontal presentations, and chords are thickened to a point rarely encountered in later material: six- or seven-note aggregations are not at all unusual. Other choral items considered so far have all, to a greater or lesser extent, represented the emergent, more diatonic and often modally derived style that developed during and after the Irish sojourn. But now Warlock employs the sustaining potential of choral voices in a harmonic texture regulated by uncompromisingly semitonal motion – chromaticism extended into linear statements – that makes this outstanding example of post-Delian writing difficult to perform.[2]

In addition to the details referred to above, the song is characterised by the limited frequency of those major and minor chords recognised as a regular feature of the post-1917 compositions. There is a heavy reliance on *Curlew* and semitonally adjusted family chords. Such factors, along with the linearity of the separate vocal parts, place this piece firmly in the van Dieren era, and this in spite of any modifications that might have taken place prior to publication. However, there is a strong sense of the Delius of *On Craig Ddu*,[3] the piece reputed to have launched the young Philip Heseltine on his quest for all things Delian in 1910.[4] Some of the similarities between the pieces are slight and of little real consequence, such as the repeated-note anacruses of their respective openings; others are more significant.

Both use falling semitones to decorate a sustained chord – the soprano lines at bar 9 (Delius) and bar 1 (Warlock) are single instances among many (Ex. 8.1a-b). Likewise, both rely on multiple appoggiaturas as a means of decorating vertical shapes: Exx. 8.2a-b have the device in the contralto and bass parts at bar 28 (Delius) and soprano, upper contralto and tenor parts at bar 20 (Warlock). The former resolves on to a German 6th configuration and the latter on to a minor 7th; both of these, along with chords such as the *Curlew* shape, are concords in a Delius/Warlock

Ex. 8.1:
(a) Delius: *On Craig Ddu* **– bars 8-10**
(b) Warlock: *The full heart* **– bars 1-2**

Ex. 8.2: *On Craig Ddu* **– bars 27-28 &** *The full heart* **– bars 18-21**

environment. But for Delius the semitone is an incidental unit used to colour existing chords; Warlock turns it into an integral device. His intent is stated from the very beginning of *The full heart* where the initial *Curlew*-chord is immediately semitone-modified. This could be viewed in terms of Delian harmonic colouration but not only is the resulting dissonance sounded by the upper tenors, it is also assumed by the sopranos; they compound both the semitonal array and the dissonance in a chromatic, falling figure. The relationship between the two composers' use of the interval can be further epitomised by any sense of inherent note-centre. Delius, although he modulates freely, begins and ends in G (major at the beginning, minor at the end); Warlock makes veiled references to note-centres in the course of the piece but begins and ends with (different) *Curlew*-chords.

Thus, the initial colouration-device is stretched into a motif that turns semitonal decoration into semitone-dependency and hence, philo-logically and musically, colour (chromaticism) into form. Reuse of the procedure in bar 2 confirms and substantiates the practice although resolution is not fully achieved (despite momentary stabilisation at the end of bar 3) until 4iv/5i (on to a *Curlew*-chord). Warlock's technique is superficially akin to that of Delius, although it has a greater intensity. But similarity of detail, as in the respective openings, does not imply a common philosophy. Warlock's attitude towards the semitone suggests an essential rather than a decorative element and his chromatic flourishes are justified by the exposition of the interval at the outset. (This is not the last time that Warlock will seek to validate a familiar, even a clichéd, figure before or after the event.) He uses dissonance as a device for enhancing harmony. Had it been more crucial to his methodology one would have expected that he might have been more inclined to give it a higher profile in the post-1917 songs. As it was, and as the Rogers songs and their successors attest, the semitone was retained not so much as a device but as a unit (which is, after all, how it is used here) even though its precise deployment and the environment within which it worked were to change.

Since the immediate stylistic language emanates from Delius and, to a less obvious extent (in the autonomy of individual lines) from van Dieren, it must be recognised that this song becomes a tribute to Gesualdo only as an afterthought,[5] especially as Warlock and Gray appear to have encountered Gesualdo's work after the piece in question was begun. If Gesualdo was an influence, then his inspiration was akin to that of Quilter[6] although the distinctive parallel between the semitone-dependent technique witnessed in *The full heart* and the step-chromatic lines of Gesualdo's *Dolcissima mia vita* (or, to use an example that Warlock himself employed,[7] *Moro lasso al mio duolo*) is undeniable. And, while it owes a great deal to *On Craig Ddu* both formally and inspirationally, it cannot be regarded as Delian pastiche for it both transcends and transfigures Delius's style and methodology by presenting a fresh approach to chromaticism.

Likewise, whether or not the *Serenade* (1921-22) for string orchestra was actually conceived, as its dedication states, as a tribute "To Frederick Delius on his sixtieth birthday" or developed into one is not for consideration here. That it has a strong Delian quality about it is indubitable; the similarity is so strong that, like the beginning of *A lake and a fairy boat*, its eclecticism borders on parody. The restless, unbroken 12/8 metre that drives the piece may have something to do with van Dieren, too, but there is a similarly prevalent animation in *Consider* and *Dedication* as well as Delius's *A song before sunrise*, written four years before "For Philip Heseltine". Indeed, marked similarities between this and the *Serenade* can be found not only in the general sound of the music but in the construction and deployment of the lines, the extended ternary form, the shapes that delineate it and the blatancy of the chromaticism. Christopher Palmer goes further and claims that Warlock's piece is "clearly modelled" on that of Delius.[8]

The beginning of the *Serenade* provides more evidence of the link between pentatonicism and the other modes as well as the nature of Warlock's peculiar diatonicism. The first-violin figure dips and soars – it is not really a melody but, as Copley suggests,[9] an aggregation, linear this time, of motivic blocks. It is a busy statement, a textural rather than a structural melody, and this observation was also made about some vocal shapes in the piano-songs. Its pentatonic line is stated over a precarious, held B (cellos and basses) that affirm the centre while the divided violas play parallel 6ths; these, with the second violin, announce a modal 7th in uncompromising terms unacceptable to textbook harmonisers (Ex. 8.3). Only when this network of relationships is

Ex. 8.3: *Serenade* – bars 1-3

established does Warlock feel able to embark upon a chromatic journey. Delius's, in *A song before sunrise*, begins earlier, in fact from the *Curlew*-chord that begins the first bar (Ex. 8.4). What the beginning of the *Serenade* conveys, then, is that Warlock's methodology has not relinquished the Delian ethic; rather, it has created a new vocabulary from it that can recall its antecedent but, more importantly, that has its own pre-eminent criteria that must be reconfirmed before the appearance of other phenomena.

Ex. 8.4: *A song before sunrise* (Delius) – bars 1-4 (wind parts omitted)

The G sharp at the end of bar 2 is not just the Dorian signifier sounded by the violas in the previous bar, but a note that has associations with the chord of A (the chord on the modal 7th), an important constituent of the harmony. The E-based shapes of bar 3 relate to both the B of the opening and the modal A; they use the outline of the pentatonic figure from bar 1 but, in spite of the chords with which they are associated, are now modified to create an ambiguous B mode that has no 6th. These gestures become the signal for chords that suggest chromatic lines. After the G sharps of the first bar, the frequency of accidentals increases considerably. But that particular note does not break with anything already established; it is itself a delineator. The chromaticism that follows is sudden and difficult to justify except retrospectively for, from rehearsal letter A (bar 5), there develops the – by now – familiar dispute between modal signifiers. The G natural (second violin) asserts the Aeolian mode but this is peremptorily contradicted, not just by a G sharp but by a chord of the 7th built on it (see Ex. 8.5). This single gesture introduces other pitches that lie outside the original material. In this way, pentatonic content is extended to the Aeolian and, thence, to the chromatic; once chromaticism is established, it is quickly extended to incorporate all 12 notes.

Ex. 8.5: *Serenade* – bars A1-3

(basses rest)

It is difficult to divide up a piece like this into convenient sections for it all grows out of what is heard in the early bars and the same ideas swirl throughout the continuum. A semiquaver figure emerges for the first time in what could be considered a "second subject" area. Although this is pentatonic to begin with (Ex. 8.6 – it is an extension of the rising first violin figure of bar 2), at times it relinquishes this association and serves largely as a textural decoration to the prevailing chord progression. However, at J, the pentatones reassert themselves and, two bars later, a version of the figure (transmuted into a diminished 7th) overflows into the recapitulation. But this return of the pentatone is chordal as well as linear; it presents the most extended vertical pentatone to date which, when combined with the horizontal form and given such a critical, even pivotal position (it ends the first half of the piece at bar 46 out of 93), makes a statement about the place of the pentatone as a précis of the other modes.

And then the piece starts all over again but, like a Warlockian strophic song, incorporates harmonic modifications that, in this case, also lead to

Ex. 8.6: *Serenade* – bars D4-5, G3, G5 J1-3

motivic changes; they terminate any further strophic allusions. Thus the first-violin figure of the opening bars evokes a more chromatic harmonic response the second time around, prompting new material in only the third bar of this recapitulatory statement. But it is not immediately followed up so that bars 51-62 correspond exactly to 5-16. Likewise, bars 68-70 are identical to 25-27 (with the addition of motifs based upon the rising semiquavers) and 72-79 repeat 29-36. One way or another there is a considerable amount of repetition in the *Serenade*. It is developmental in that it offers Warlock the opportunity to find alternative harmonies, except that such a statement implies a melodic, or a motivic, importance. In fact, as has been observed elsewhere, it is the chord-choice that is the driving force behind the music. The motifs, as in many a song's melody, are a convenient, structural vehicle, a contrivance that very often puts a gloss on the chordal progress enhancing it and possessing a peculiar quality the while. But, in this case at least, while the result is attractive, the real substance is small. Homer nods occasionally and he will do the same in *Fair and true*!

To say that these two pieces mark the end of the impact of Delius on Warlock's output would be an overstatement but there will be no further, sustained, overt manifestation of the older man's influence. It is difficult to put fully into perspective the effect that Delius had on Warlock – and not just in a musical way. Delius's letters to his young friend contain news and encouragement but, also, opinion. Indeed, he wrote on one occasion that "On any subject or question whatever I will tell you what I really think" and this in March 1912, only nine months after their first encounter. Thereafter, Warlock's views on religion, militarism, philosophy, politics and aesthetics come to sound remarkably like Delius's. And the manner in which Warlock described his contemporary composers, especially his compatriots, has its foundation in Delius's linguistic style. It would not be an exaggeration to claim that, in particular respects, Delius was a surrogate parent who was able to tell Philip what his real father never had the opportunity to demonstrate or his stepfather, despite his virtues, the emotional expertise to convey. The mark made by this strong personality was hard to shake off and it is not surprising that it surfaces strongly in Warlock's compositions. But, through the chordal family and the transmutation of chords into modes, Warlock personalised it. The next song, roughly contemporary with the two pieces discussed above, makes this point.

Play-acting (1920) possesses such striking qualities both dramatically and compositionally that it is difficult to understand why so much time elapsed between its composition and publication.[10] It represents both the chromatic, post-Delian linearity of the van Dieren era and the modally inspired structuralism of the Rogers songs. Some aspects of the song are easily dealt with; its modality is stated directly in the autograph where, sans key-signature, it proclaims a D-centred Dorian. Unfortunately, upon publication, in a well-intentioned attempt to make the piece more accessible to a "medium voice", compromise defeated reason: in the process of transposing the whole thing up a tone, editing imposed not the two-sharp signature that would have implied an E Dorian but the single F sharp that proclaims E minor. This music has been subjected to a lack of sympathy even by those who seek to promote it.

Modal practice here is more complex than has been seen elsewhere. The Dorian melody that predominates gives way, for three of the 13 bars, to a pentatone-derived passage. The C sharp, Dorian signifiers (in the transposed, printed version) are ignored – there are, in fact, no Cs of any kind – and the piano harmonies become less easy to define in comparison with the family-dominated shapes of the Dorian majority. But the melodic content, actually two superimposed pentatones, creates a Dorian/Aeolian ambiguity (the absent C, sharp or natural, leaves the issue unresolved) with an F-basis. This focus is referred or alluded to between bars 9ii-11i in particular, a semitonal shift of centre from the original E; indeed, F natural was the first note to break from the original E Dorian outline (bar 9ii). This change of melodic basis coincides with a shift in the text from narrative to personal identification (Ex. 8.7).

Ex. 8.7: *Play-acting* – **bars 8-11**

Ex. 8.8: *Play-acting* – **bars 7-11 (chordal summary)**

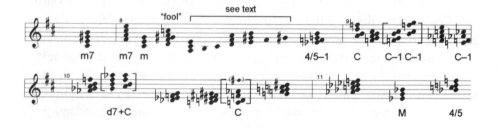

While chordal material is family-dependent in the section where the voice is regulated by the pentatone, it becomes more individualistic. The result is a group of aggregations which can consistently be described as spread clusters. These first occur in the chord at 8iii which prefaces the pentatone-based passage and climaxes at the line "An' the big mun tricks the fool aht", the point at which the mood of the words begins to alter, highlighting the word "fool". The chord is otherwise difficult to analyse satisfactorily; it is a dominant 7th shape on D on to which an E major chord has been grafted, although that is to imply a function which does not exist; its resolution, on to another big chord, is also problematical. It can also be thought of as an A melodic minor scale raised to the vertical but with D and E polarisations, a whole family of primary triads within a single chord. Other cluster-derived chords in the passage under discussion are based on whole tones to a greater or lesser extent, as is this one, and they are shown in the summary (Ex. 8.8).

Notes

1   FT1 (p. 13) gives the composition dates as 1916-21 but, later (p. 34), as being complete in 1920. Either way, the stylistic content is consistent with the material that predates the Winthrop Rogers songs. *The full heart* was eventually published in 1923 by O.

2   Rarely heard, it has, miraculously, been recorded twice by the Finzi Singers/Paul Spicer (Abacus ABA 604-2 and Chandos CHAN 9182).

3   In CG this is referred to as "On Craig Dhu", another of Gr's aberrations. However, PW also spells it thus in PH (September 1922) pp. 5-10 – it was to form part of his joint venture with Gr on Gesualdo – see note 5).

4   According to CT it was he who introduced PH to the music of Delius via this particular piece (CT 1964). CG says (p. 37) that it was encountered at a concert ("the performance of the unaccompanied part-song . . .") but perhaps neither is accurate; in a letter to his mother of 28th June 1910, PH wrote that he "would give anything to hear it sung". Presumably, he had only read the score. See FT (1976) for more on this matter.

5   It is dedicated "To the immortal memory of the Prince of Venosa". If this piece was begun in 1916 (FT1 p. 13) then the book that PW wrote in collaboration with Gr was nearly a decade in the future. And if, as Stravinsky wrote in 1968 – preface to Watkins (1973) – Gesualdo was "academically unrespectable, still the crank of chromaticism, still rarely sung" how much more so must this have been the case in 1920 which, from PW's articles in *The Sackbut*, marks the beginnings of his interest? (Gr (1948) is imprecise about when their first encounter occurred but implies that it was after 1917 and, hence, after PW's composition of the piece had started.) The quality of the music aside, Gesualdo's controversial uniqueness was as likely to attract PW as was van Dieren's. Watkins's bibliography lists no work in English before the Gr/PW joint venture (Gr and PW (1926)) a fact the authors themselves relate (p. xiii). Not only was this the first study in English but the first substantial one in any language.

6   See note 12, Chapter 6.

7   On p. 121 of the book about Gesualdo, PW cites three instances of linear chromaticism having shaped chordal choice. As well as *Moro lasso . . .* he cites Wagner (*Die Walküre*) and *On Craig Ddu*.

8   CP p. 160; other movements may have been planned (IC p. 233).

9   IC p. 243

10   It was written on the 27th January 1920 (FT1 p. 18). It was first published in 1972 by T.

CHAPTER 9

Rum, beer, good ale and other frolics

Warlock has been criticised to the point of ostracism for writing "all those songs about beer"[1] and *Captain Stratton's fancy* (1920), "a bellicose bellowing if ever there was",[2] is the obvious and most infamous example (although – a minor point – the words are really about rum). It certainly appears incongruous when placed alongside *The curlew* or *The full heart* and even *Play-acting* but, once any aesthetic problem of approaching what is, unequivocally, a drinking song has been set aside, the piece can be seen to exhibit many aspects of Warlock's style that, in other circumstances, must be deemed perfectly respectable. It will become clear that Warlock viewed the categorisation of songs this way as snobbery; in his view, "sociable" (lighter) and "artistic" (more philosophical) songs were equally valid.

The melodic outline, superficially in F, is actually – by virtue of the recurring E flats – Mixolydian. Even this is an oversimplification for the real basis is a pentatone into which Mixolydian detail has been spliced. The compass of a 6th that defines the opening phrase conforms to a pentatone (Ex. 9.1); it is approached by an idiomatically obligatory, rising-4th anacrusis but then includes a B flat semiquaver passing-note. This pitch is given greater credibility during the sequence that begins the following phrase but some of the motifs here are already familiar from *The curlew*, and this state of affairs continues into the beginning of the refrain line. The melody that results from these procedures has, consequently, great strength although the Mixolydian 7th is made too obvious. Doing without any reference to a 7th at the start of the refrain line produces a better shape: what would have been a contradictory, tonal leading-note is avoided and the pentatonic element in the process is

Ex. 9.1: *Captain Stratton's fancy* – bars 4-8 (summary of vocal melody)

re-enforced. The E flat/natural interchange is less successful here than the equivalent use in *Sweet content*. There, the dichotomy was dependent on musica ficta; there are more overt, tonal implications here. This is particularly so in bars 9-10 where the harmonic E flat effects a move to the subdominant only for the E natural to produce a reversion to F.

This is Warlock's first attempt at an extended, strophic form. Earlier attempts had fewer verses or resorted to melodic compromises, even wholesale changes. There are alterations here too, in fact, in the last two verses, but they are largely occasioned by syllabic or emphatic irregularities in the text. They confirm further the pentatonic basis by ignoring the rogue B flat of the first halves of the preceding verses. The main weakness of the song lies, surprisingly, in the chordal writing. The harmonic scheme remains much the same for all the verses and is varied only by thickening or reduction of shapes from one to the next, by alterations to the pitch-range or by some combination of these factors. Like that of *Good ale*,[3] the piano-part is largely superfluous, a rare and uncharacteristic feature within the Warlockian canon. Over ten years, then, the composer has gone from one extreme to another: the juxtaposed chords from which perfunctory melodies were extracted in the 1911 songs have evolved into this piece. A strong melody with no real need for a chordal underlay (ironic, this, from the composer of the *Folk-song preludes*), marks a song for singing unaccompanied in public places, even if these turn out to be bars and tap-rooms. (And the ritornello, while motivically derived, is too much like Purcell's familiar trumpet tune for comfort, even in jest.)

Its companion piece is *Mr Belloc's fancy*, a frivolously unremarkable song, Squire's text being a joke in itself.[4] It is important to consider Warlock's motivation for writing pieces such as this for they are as significant within his oeuvre as the informal songs of Purcell or Ravel; nor do we preserve *The beggar's opera* solely for its historical importance. Warlock had a genuine interest in popular musical styles:

> . . . a great deal of it is really very good – far better, quite immeasurably above a great deal of the high-art stuff that is turned out. Stravinsky himself is not nearly as good as Irving Berlin[5] . . . the latter [is] more clean, direct and sincere, and also . . . more important.[6]

Elsewhere he writes that:

> Pot-boilers – the best of them – are full of genuine emotion – not perhaps the highest we are capable of feeling but genuine for all that. You know

what I think about the priggish and artificial distinction between popular music and 'art' music.[7]

It is, then, important to recognise in both *Captain Stratton* and *Mr Belloc* that Warlock knew what he was doing. They are conscious digressions; those that would use them as a stick with which to beat him erroneously assume that they typify his outlook as well as his output.

As is the case with some other songs, two versions of *Mr Belloc's fancy* exist, an original one (1921)[8] and a revision (1930).[9] Some differences in the later one are cosmetic, mostly thinnings-out of the dense chords in the earlier form, although there are more significant modifications. The original has a preference for heavily stated dissonances; many of these were edited down and appropriately so. Warlock tended to work slowly at the piano ("strumming" to use his own expression)[10] and his big chords create technical as well as aesthetic problems at the tempi he subsequently imposed upon them. So, while the harmonic intent remains, it is not so weightily – or aggressively – stated. A similar comment can be made about some of the rhythmic figures in the piano part; quavers, often with their associated chromaticisms, give way to crotchet chords that, from a metrical standpoint, state the pulse and nothing more. Examples of this process can be found in bars 7, 30-31, 46-7, 48 and 53; some of these are shown in Ex. 9.2. There are occasional differences of chord-choice in the revision but these are comparatively unimportant; the exception is an extended passage, in bars 54-7, where not only has the number of notes been reduced, as elsewhere, but the chordal progression is completely changed. There is a similarity of approach: in each one the bass parallels the melody, in 3rds (1921) or 6ths (1930). Both passages employ family chords but the earlier edition has a stronger diatonic sense and flat-side moves that, in other songs, are effected by a circle-of-5ths. The heavy reliance on the *Curlew*-chord and, to a lesser extent, pentatone shapes in the revision denies even the limited allusions of the earlier form. The spread clusters of *Play-acting* are here manifest in a closer formation. The penultimate chord, an innocent enough dominant 11th (in the versions of both 1921 and 1930) is presented as a tight and arresting dissonance that will find echoes later in *Jillian of Berry* (1926).

Melodically, the voice adheres to an unmodified major scale. But it would not be stretching a point too far to refer to this as an Ionian mode for, although the piano part modulates, no corresponding move is suggested by accidentals in the vocal part. Such a statement begs a

Ex. 9.2: *Mr Belloc's fancy* – bars 30-31 and 53-54 (versions of 1921 and 1930)

question about the relationship between the two sound-sources in Warlock's music: his melodies, while they are vehicles for words with which he had either sympathy or affection, serve largely to decorate – timbrally and linearly – a progression of piano chords on which the principal musical interest of the piece is focused. Strophism creates an opportunity for harmonic invention over (or under) what comes across as a vocal cantus firmus. But this is to imply a melodic hegemony; in reality, the harmony changes in spite of the melody, not to suit it, which is why there can be a dichotomy (in this case a mild one) between the two parts. The problem of binding vertical and horizontal components is solved in that the convention of melody-with-accompaniment is retained but the traditional hierarchy is reversed. The construction of vocal lines suitable for this kind of treatment was subject to degrees of refinement over a period of time as his imagination developed but one should never lose sight of just where the principal interest lies. It is not surprising, then, if voice and piano material can, at times, appear to emanate from different bases.

Good ale (1922) is another drinking song although with an antique rather than a contemporary text. It exhibits the multi-modality of *Play-acting* writ large and includes some rhythmic gestures that imbue it with a greater degree of credibility than otherwise might be the case. As Copley points out,[11] it aspires to the Aeolian mode before resorting to the Mixolydian. But this is only part of the story; the modal exposition is initially ambiguous because the first four bars of melody, doubled in octaves by the piano, employ no 6th. Although B flat is specified in the signature it does not become an audible phenomenon until bar 7 and then only once as part of a falling-3rds motif prior to the refrain. This demands a modal shift anyway: the centre moves from D in the verse (with aspects of the minor) to F in the refrain (with major associations) – a common enough tonal procedure even if effected, as here, without a formal modulation. The Mixolydian 7th, E flat, has been anticipated by omission rather than presentation at the end of the verse where the melody skips E before sounding the final D (Ex. 9.3). As with the B flat of the Aeolian, the E flat Mixolydian signifier occurs but once before being replaced by E natural (itself destined for a single sounding). This is not so much a reversion to tonal practice but, rather, a combination of semitonal adjustment (there is no ficta situation) and restatement of

Ex. 9.3: *Good ale* – bars 55-62 (vocal melody with chordal summary)

material heard at the beginning, again with sequentially stated B flats. F is still the final.

The emphasis has shifted markedly towards the melody. This attitude, fully intended by the composer,[12] is reinforced by the accompanimental devices, especially in the first three of the four verses – octaves in the first and (mostly) one chord to a bar in the second and third. The refrain is always homorhythmically harmonised, though. Second- and third-verse harmonies grow from the 3rd-less chords that preface the song – they are hardly an introduction beyond setting the singer's pitch. The D major chord at the end of verse 2 lacks the preparation noted in similar circumstances elsewhere although it provides a semitonal shock to the F-centred melody that ensues. B natural – a Dorian signifier – in the next chord harks back to the absent Aeolian signifier of the verse openings but, even more importantly, it delays the sounding of an F chord after the preceding D shape. When, in the third verse, the time comes to fill out the empty 5ths, the additional notes are not, as might be assumed, the missing 3rds but 6ths and 2nds; the resultant chords, rather than being triadic, favour the pentatone.

The relationship between fixed melodic line and harmonic variation is more developed in this piece than hitherto. Modification of the voice-part is minimal: there is a climactic, metrical change to the last appearance of the refrain but other alterations to accommodate syllabic fluctuations can be ignored in this context. And, while the chord-choice is less remarkable than elsewhere, there is a sense of growth and progress between the settings of successive stanzas: the melodic hemiola that closes the refrain to each one is treated simply in the first and allocated a circle-of-5ths in the second; it reverts to the original harmonisation in the third (to counteract the richer chords that have preceded it) and recycles the circle-of-5ths in the last but with thicker chords that, given the faster tempo and changed metre, have a much closer proximity one to another. The pentatonic aggregations that underlie the third verse are summarised, also in Ex. 9.3.

The last verse mixes practices already encountered; the rhythmic placement of the chords is increased, though, and the end of the verse, where the absent E had cleared the way for a Mixolydian E flat, is modified to produce a conventional, imperfect cadence which emphasises both the F-centre and the tonal potential of the refrain. A charitable assessment of this move would stress that, because it is so obvious, the tongue must be firmly in the cheek. There are other overindulgences too that provide fuel for critics such as the chromatic progression (bars

78-80) that prefaces the last verse; but even this may be self-mockery, a throwaway gesture immediately neutralised by the directness of the melody that it seeks to introduce. Archaisms like the piano figure in bar 90 are decorative, not essential; they reflect the antiquity of the words but have no other importance. The rationale continues, in this song, to be the fitting together of chordal and melodic material – and this despite the composer's apparent disregard for the accompaniment.

Three little *Peterisms*,[13] inconsequential to the point of frivolity, are quickly dealt with. They add little to an understanding of Warlock's output and are included as much for completeness as anything else. For the most part, they are testimony to a continuing craftsmanship and, if their triviality suggests bad taste, it should not imply poor workmanship.

Some of *Hey troly loly lo* (1922) reverts to the declamation that is a feature of Warlock's output after *The cloths of Heaven* and *Saudades*. Its main interest again lies in the modal diversity that shapes the vocal line; this is mainly consistent with an F-centred Aeolian mode although there are two distinct deviations. One of these keeps the notes but changes the centre, creating thereby a Mixolydian mode with an E flat final. The other keeps the centre but changes some of the notes; D flat is naturalised to create a Dorian mode and, in combination with D natural, A flat is naturalised to produce an F-centred Mixolydian. The exposition of the available pitches is as restrained as in the case of *Good ale*: the Aeolian or Dorian signifier is avoided in both the first and second phrases and the D flat, sounded once only in bar 5 is immediately naturalised in bar 6, the signal for the A natural. Given the earlier propensity of E flats this suggests the Mixolydian; however, and characteristically, Warlock avoids sounding the 7th so there must be an element of doubt. The next phrase (bars 7-9) implies an E flat centre with restored A and D flats, although it ends on F. The whole piece progresses in such a manner and it is curious, given the plethora of accidentals which suggest particular modes and centres, that it is all written without a key-signature.

This phenomenon may arise from the fact that not only do the modal foci shift but the piano part also is very fluid in the matter of note-centres. The only accidental in the first two (admittedly sparse) bars is a B flat associated with the F-centre; the As in the opening flourish remain natural. But, after concessions to flattened notes in the melody (bar 3) and an insistence on A natural again (bar 4), the situation is weakened further by the circle-of-5ths that ends on a D flat chord (bar 5) that seeks to harmonically justify the Mixolydian 7th of the E flat-centred vocal phrase. Accidentals outside the established centres are rare, being chromatic rather than formative, although the D flat major-scale flourish (bar 24) relates back to bar 5. Ex. 9.4 shows bars 21-27 which are a modified version of bars 1-7.

The whole song is a compromise between strophism and through-composition, the two formal structures associated with Warlock. It is a

Ex. 9.4: *Hey troly loly lo* **– bars 21-27**

relatively short song but by no means as brief as *Play-acting*. In fact it has a ternary shape: material associated with the first six text-lines returns for the last six, leaving six more in the middle, some of which derive from those already heard.[14] While these repetitions present opportunities for alternative chord-choices they are not exploited as fully as might be, a D flat scale apart; the final text-line, for example, employs no more than a doubled-melody version of more sparse (and more enigmatic) figures already encountered twice.

The bachelor (1922) is centred on F sharp – a Dorian with a consistent D sharp. The E sharp in bar 17 suggests the minor, even though the melody descends at that point. The rising 4th anacrusis at the start of the vocal-line is more appropriate to an A centre confirmed in bar 4 (Ex. 9.5) despite the F sharp oriented chords. The parallel-5th harmonies produce a neo-Renaissance dance atmosphere and the 30 bars are, like *Hey troly loly lo*, in a ternary formation. This time, variation in the passages to which the melody is common is achieved not so much by changes to the chordal choice (A major is preferred to F sharp-centred chords as at the start) but by textural and rhythmic means. For all its inconsequence it is, like *Captain Stratton*, well written with some pleasant countermelodic touches in the piano part that assist the harmonic flow.

The same cannot be said, alas, of *Piggesnie* (1922). The specified "very lightly" is difficult to achieve because Warlock insists on sounding the vocal line in the piano, a weakness exacerbated by the predictability of the rising 3rds – played on the piano alone the song has all the vitality of a keyboard-harmony exercise – and the breakdown of what had promised to be a strophic structure after two verses; the relentless quaver motion is not sufficiently strong per se to prolong the piece (Ex. 9.6). The melodic C sharps in bars 7, 17 and 27 are tonal, associated with modulations to the dominant. To begin with there is actually a sense of D as a final despite the single sharp of the key signature – the first G in the melody (bar 5) is harmonised with a minor 7th on A and the C natural evokes the Mixolydian before being superseded by the sharpened form – but is not sustained. The G Mixolydian that manifests itself at bar 34-5 (F natural in the upper octave of the voice) echoes the D-centre suggested earlier but neither statement has any conviction. The harmony is conventional and repetitive; exactly the same vocal and instrumental shapes are employed in each of the first two verses (where the strophic form is still intact).

Chopcherry has the same text as *Whenas the rye reach to the chin*

Ex. 9.5: *The bachelor* – bars 1-4

Ex. 9.6: *Piggesnie* – bars 1-8

but, this time, Warlock retains throughout the melodic idea that sets "Then, o . . . She could not live a maid", changing the harmonic bias rather than, as before, altering chords so that the melody too needed modification. It is safe to say that this piece is in A major and its modulatory scheme follows other recent examples by moving to the mediant major at bar 8 (the plagal cadence allows a sharpening of the tonic in the melody) and, thence, to the dominant at bar 11, maintained until bar 15. The settings of the repeated text reflect the fact that, on the first occasion, the harmony is quitting the modulation and, on the second, can decorate the dominant chord, converting it into a G sharp minor 7th. The differences in treatment only last some four bars; thereafter, both versions are the same, give or take some countermelodic embellishments. The harmony is essentially triadic and functional and, although the song is adequately put together, like some of the other *Peterisms*[15] it contains little of compositional interest. It should be said that, apart from the A sharp already mentioned, the vocal line remains true to the notes of A major, even at the modulation to the dominant. As a result, this could be another case for classification as an Ionian mode.

The format of *A sad song* is horizontal rather than vertical and this emphasis on line has harmonic implications considerably distant from those of songs like *Chopcherry* or *Roister doister*. The A-centre[16] is unstable because, as will also be the case in *Tyrley tyrlow*, it contains Dorian references in the form of F sharps. But, there, the pentatone will substantiate the A-centre; here the combination of a minor 3rd (C) and a major chord on the fourth degree results in insecurity if a tonal context is evoked, the more so as the major 3rd (C sharp) in bar 4 creates not so much an impression of modulation as a sense of D having been the real centre all the time. Add the fact that Warlock's developmental technique of harmonic substitution, usually reserved for the later stages of a song, now occurs in the introduction – based on three statements of the same short linear motif to anticipate the entry of the voice – and the fragility of the intended note-centre becomes more apparent. The situation is not really resolved at the end, either. A rogue sense of D is still evident three bars from the end and the 3rd-less chord on A that follows is as surprising as the G chord that will mark the end of *Sleep*.

The chromaticism has family-chord implications to begin with; these become less apparent in the middle of the song, returning along with triadic shapes in the latter half. While there are exceptions, the majority of the accidentals employed have tonal or modal implications within A-centred material, hence the frequent F, C and G sharps and their corresponding naturalisations. These apart, there are six D sharps (sometimes written as E flat) which can suggest the leading-note of the dominant, and two B flats, used adjacent to D minor and F major chords respectively. Once again the linearity favours instrumental resources other than a piano and it is a pity that the versions that Warlock made for other combinations[17] remain in manuscript.

Rutterkin contains features alluded to elsewhere but not in such an overt fashion and they make it virtually unique in Warlock's output. Copley remarks[18] on the Bartókian quality of the metrical deployment – largely in 7/8 with a few bars of different lengths – and other associations with Bartók have been noted in this survey.[19] The blatant whole-tone scale at the end of the refrains relates to some of the spread, whole-tone clusters that have been a fleeting and rare feature of his harmonic armoury (dominant 7ths with added 9ths and no 5ths). Additionally, there are polymodal implications which go beyond anything witnessed so far.

The introduction appears to herald C[20] as the centre, a fact assumed by the voice which, the refrain apart, utilises a Dorian mode in keeping with the signature of two flats. But the piano, at the outset of the verse, has a chord – and it lasts for most of five bars – that is rooted on F. An F-centred mode with the same restrictions would be Mixolydian and the A flat in the second bar therefore has Dorian implications. The end of the refrain also suggests F as a focus but the whole-tone scale, preceded by G and D flats, clouds the issue; in the end this instance must be counted amongst an increasing number of pieces in which vocal and instrumental components have different bases: the situation will recur in *Rest sweet nymphs*.

The 3rd-less F chord with an added 2nd that opens and then occupies all of the first verse gives way at the start of the refrain to chords of C and then G, once again without 3rds and with added 2nds; the fusion of F- and G-centred elements at bar 8iii is a pentatone. If ever there was a real case for sustained bitonality in Warlock's music here it is in this song: centres vie with one another and chords of different derivations get squeezed together. But the striking feature of the chords that characterise *Rutterkin* is their dependence upon 4ths and 5ths. Nor is it just the chords which are subject to these intervals for they both regulate the horizontal motifs that are a feature of the piano writing and shape the vocal melody. The 5th is becoming an important harmonic feature; it was remarked on as a neo-Renaissance device in *The bachelor*. It also featured in *Chopcherry* and *A sad song*, often in parallel (consecutive) formations, the way that it frequently turns up here. Some of the chordal aggregations, either as a result of their 4ths/5ths basis, their different note-centre bases, or both, create pentatonic shapes and culminate in the

Ex. 9.7: *Rutterkin* – bars 29–31

close-position formation (shades of *Tyrley tyrlow*) in the penultimate bar (Ex. 9.7).

Rutterkin's verses all follow much the same linear shape; there are rhythmical differences between them which sometimes demand modifications to the line, as in the last verse. But, as the opening of *Sleep* will also attest, this is not a weakness; the essential feature is the harmonic variation sounded with it and it is this way that the two components justify their existence one to another. However, in *Roister doister* the melody is subject to continual change even, at one stage, being replaced by one that is new to the song but recognisably familiar otherwise. Its essential strophism is greeted by a diversity of piano techniques that characterise the different verses. The big chords – eight notes or more is not unusual – favour pentatone-derived shapes (with some rather heavy chromaticism from time to time). The first-verse melody continues into the second on the piano while the voice has a new, countermelodic line, an unusual occurrence in the output (but see *Passing by* as well). Whether or not this change of material warrants the use of the *Mulberry bush/Nuts in May*[21] tune in verse 5 is open to debate; perhaps Warlock was aware that no end of chordal dressing would sustain his rather trite little tune for six consecutive manifestations. The melody sticks to F major all the way through except for three Mixolydian 7ths but, as one of these occurs in the very first bar, it creates expectations. Other soundings of the 7th are largely avoided in verse 1; E natural is used only once and that right at the end as a perfect cadence constituent although it had been immediately preceded by E flat from the piano. In verse 2, Warlock uses the major-2nd-plus-minor-3rd shape to get around it.

These features aside, *Roister doister* is not a very successful song and, in comparison with the energy and abandon of *Rutterkin*, the relentless 6/8 is perfunctory. Warlock's musical vocabulary was, by this stage, fairly well defined. What he needed to embark upon from this point forward was a process of refinement.

The predetermined jolliness of *Spring* evokes a similar response. It is possible to comment upon its pentatonic, harmonic references, its G-based[22] modes and its melodic accidentals – F natural denoting Mixolydian, E flat and B flat implying Aeolian, F sharp for Ionian/major – but after all is said, these sorts of things have already been encountered. What is given represents nothing unheard before; there is no new format, but then the verse is similarly uninspiring[23] and Warlock responded to his texts! One must look at songs such as this and see them as representing the consolidation of a technique rather than pieces remarkable for some other innovatory property. Alongside the best of Warlock's output they sound mundane and lack even the visceral vitality of *Captain Stratton's fancy*.

With its pentatonically derived melody and harmonically varied strophism, *Lusty Juventus* represents what might be termed a state-of-the-art, 1922 Warlock song – although this is meant in a technical rather than an aesthetic sense. The parallel 6ths, a variant of the 3rds in other songs, become laboured and no single device has the strength to sustain the song. The melody possesses increasingly familiar qualities, essentially based upon a single pentatone that then introduces a new note from another one a 5th away (a modulation substitute), the absent note of the resulting hexatone being the one subject to semitonal interchange within the piano part. This chromaticism triggers other alterations that vary the harmonies in successive verses. The melody ultimately sheds its modality and accepts the note previously omitted in time for the introductory device to serve as an interlude for the next verse.

That one can reduce Warlock's compositional technique to such a readily explicable formula stems partly from the fact that, at this time anyway, he wrote so many songs in such a relatively short period of time. Although his stylistic development had reached a formal maturity, he had not always found quite the right verbal vehicle to inspire a substantial song. *Lusty Juventus*, like *Roister doister* before it, is too earnest for what is really an expression of trivial sentiments. *In an arbour green*, another setting of the same words, is more successful for it has greater energy and lighter figurations. Although it may have been written later,[24] it is dated 1922 and will be discussed at this point.

It shares several features with the previous setting – pentatonic melody (at least to start with), strophic shape with harmonic changes, ritornello usage of the introductory figure – but also contains other

Ex. 9.8: *In an arbour green* – bars 8-10, 19-21 & 30-32

details that keep the song moving. The repetition of the melodic component is literal apart from amendments to suit changes in syllabic stress. (There is also an unfortunate pre-cadential pitch-change, complete with fermata, in the last verse). The resulting stability helps to offset the extreme flat-side move that is a characteristic of the second half of each verse; it is effected in the first verse by a decorated circle-of-5ths; the leap back to the original centre at the end of bar 10 (the dominant 7th comes out of the blue) is reminiscent of the more extended device in *Rest sweet nymphs*, even to the point of a sequential melody line (Ex. 9.8a). But, contrary to his approach in that song, Warlock is here prepared to vary his harmonies. The effects are similar – in that there are lurches in the same direction – but the processes change: in the second verse the falling, then rising, semitones in the bass come to rest on a chord with a C flat root, a tritone away from the original tonic (Ex. 9.8b); in the third, there is a combination of techniques from the preceding verses that conclude with a chord that is a fusion of A flat and E flat (Ex. 9.8c); the minor 7th added to the former creates minor implications in the latter.

This is a more tonally regulated song than many that have been discussed so far. The flat-side plunge may be a case of deliberate excess, a technique taken (almost) ad absurdum, especially as, in the first verse, it settles on the flattened mediant minor (see Ex. 9.8a again). The destabilisation – it is hardly a modulation – may emanate from the Mixolydian 7th in bar 2; it returns, another link with *Rest sweet nymphs*, in bar 9 to prompt the move. The ritornello contains some familiar chordal derivations but it is important to point out that the chord at bar 5i, though pentatonic in origin, is employed as a dominant 11th.

Notes

1   *Captain Stratton's fancy* is subtitled "RUM" while *Mr Belloc's fancy* has the subtitle "BEER". The pair were entitled (by PW) "Two True Toper's Tunes to Troll with Trulls and Trollops in a Tavern". Cockshott (July 1940) is one of the first to dispel the myth that Warlock's lighter songs are ipso facto bad. He sums up the attitude of those who would adopt such a viewpoint by attributing to them the generalised complaint, "What a pity he wrote only one *Frostbound wood* and all those songs about beer!"

2   Hold (1975).

3   See note 12 below.

4   FT preface to T(iii).

5   Irving Berlin performed in London in 1917 as the "King of rag-time". *Alexander's ragtime band* had been written in 1911, as had another popular song *Everybody's doing it now*. But how much of Berlin's output was familiar to PW must be a matter of conjecture.

6   In a letter to CT dated January 18th 1917.

7   In the letter to CT of 24th September 1917. See note 35, Chapter 3.

8   Published by A (1922).

9   Published by A.

10 In a letter to CT dated 24/1/12.

11 IC p. 88.

12 PW said of this song that ". . . for roaring unaccompanied [the pitch at which it is performed] doesn't matter." FT: preface to T(iii).

13 "Peterisms" was a favourite, derogatory term of PW's to describe his own lighter pieces. Six other songs were later published, in two sets, using this title although the "Little Peterisms" (which did not appear under the name) include *Good ale*, the three songs discussed at this stage and a speculative number of others. See MP pp. 126-7 for a summary of the details.

14 See MP p. 128 for information on the text.

15 "Peterisms": unlike the Little Peterisms referred to above, these six songs of 1922 appeared in print under the title: first set (*Chopcherry*, *A sad song* and *Rutterkin*) Ch (1923); second set (*Roister doister*, *Spring* and *Lusty Juventus*) O (1924).

16 A is the centre in T(iv), currently the most accessible source. The string quartet version (unpublished) is centred on C, the Ch edition on B.

17 There are arrangements for voice and string quartet (contemporary

with the piano version) and soprano and small orchestra (BL Add. Ms. 52910) dating from about five years later.

18 IC p. 93.

19 See pp. 9, 23, 37, 65 and passim.

20 This is based on the transposition in T(iv). The original (Ch) was a minor 3rd higher.

21 This tune exists in variant forms to a host of different words. See Iona and Peter Opie (1985).

22 The centre of the original version (O) was A flat.

23 Compare the content, rhyme-scheme, metre and poetic depth of Nashe's text with PW's drinkmat doggerel that extols the virtues of Pimm's No. 1 cup ("Pimm's number one/We have just begun/it's as good as John Donne/you son of a gun" etc.) in BL Add. Ms. 57794!

24 FT: preface to T(iv).

CHAPTER 10

Refinements

1922 would prove to be something of an annus mirabilis. London had become financially and socially over-demanding so, in the autumn of 1921, Warlock had gone to live at Cefn-Bryntalch, the home of his mother and stepfather in mid-Wales. The security and stability this visit afforded came to be responsible for some of his most positive and best music. In 1922 he wrote 14 extant songs (including the five *Lillygay* movements), completed *The curlew*, produced numerous transcriptions, published several articles and finished his book on Delius.[1] His walks through the Welsh countryside (which he loved) gave him numerous opportunities to experience that refreshing solitude which can be so conducive to creativity.

The innocent charm of John Clare's words in *Little trotty wagtail*, like those of a nursery rhyme, elicit some familiar, multi-modal responses. The voice's rising, D-modal figure eschews the 6th at first (although it is provided by the piano) and, despite the D minor implied by the signature, all melodic Bs are natural except for the last one. In the instrumental introduction, though, much is made of the discrepancy in a welter of pentatone-derived chords; in these, parallel 5ths assume a more interesting, almost pandiatonic, function than was the case in *The*

Ex. 10.1: *Little trotty wagtail* **– bars 6-8**

bachelor. The chords, which allude to a diversity of centres, reappear in verse harmonies, once again as decorations of semitonal motion, as in bar 7 (Ex. 10.1). The pentatone-chords also reappear, not just as part of the introductory figure (which later assumes the rôle of interlude) but, occasionally, as a verse-harmony chord.

Yet it is in the attitude towards strophism that the piece achieves the most success. Although the song is only three verses long, there is just sufficient variation in the piano part to maintain the interest without becoming either exaggerated or precious. There are a couple of moments of descending chromaticism (such as in bar 26) but these are brief and isolated and do not take the piece over. The short play-out figure echoes the ascending opening of the verses (sans a 6th) and is uncharacteristically monophonic.

In contrast to *Little trotty wagtail* is the chordal opulence of *Late summer*; in the relationship between centres, the sensuality of the harmony and the chromaticism of line, it chimes exactly with the verbal content – in Shanks's words, "More sweetness than the sense can bear". This is the counter to *The lover mourns for the loss of love*: there the stark desolation of the restricted chord-choice paralleled Yeats's picture of dejection – limited motion to the point of stasis. Now, to match Shanks's image of autumnal achievement epitomised by a fulfilled human relationship, a modulation to the mediant minor is transfigured into the mediant major. These unusual, even distant relationships are the stuff of late-romanticism and, were the material not controlled as strictly as it is, Warlock could be open to a charge of pastiche.

Like those of other Warlock songs with bucolic subjects, this melody grows (via an appropriate rising 5th this time, tonic-dominant) from what is basically a pentatone; the only extraneous pitch (the A at the end of bar 4) is heard as a quaver passing-note. A has a little more presence (at 7ii) in the second phrase but then becomes the note sharpened to effect the modulation in bar 10. A pentatonic outline is retained at the start of the second stanza, a restatement of the opening of the first but now centred on G sharp rather than E. It creates thereby a pseudo-strophic quality but, this apart, there is more a sense of through-composition, unsurprising in a song of only 25 bars. The chordal content of the song is emphasised by the fact that nine of these bars – more than a third of the total – are given to the piano alone.

The harmonic language, despite its richness, is simpler than has often been the case. Many dissonances can be explained as appoggiaturas (which resolve on to triadic chords) rather than chord-shapes that are inherently dissonant. In this respect they recall *The full heart* and, consequently, Delius's *On Craig Ddu*. But their appearance in what is a very short song, combined with the key-scheme (the repetition of the opening phrase allied to the new centre emphasises this), suggests that technique has been used as imagery. As Copley points out[2] the use of the mediant major is not unknown to Warlock and cites *My little sweet darling* as a precedent. But, in this earlier example, the A flat chord (in relation to an initial F-centre) is transitory; there is no modulation and the fact that the chord and illusion are immediately quitted negates any claim that it might be dramatically significant. In *Late summer*, providing that the prescribed "Lento – molto tranquillo" is adhered to, there should be no sense of the piano part being "overloaded".[3]

The singer, another Shanks setting, is not so much short as truncated. The ternary shape has strophic implications as the introductory piano figure recurs (bars 21-4) to announce the last eight bars (four lines of text) from the voice. But, earlier in the song, the voice had 17 unbroken bars (eight lines of text) that had given the impression of a single verse, an illusion increased by the interruption at the final cadence. The new chords that greet the (apparently) new verse are chromatic and clichéd but, that apart, are consistent with the harmonic revitalisation that has become a feature of recent strophic manifestations.

This song has a strong pentatonic basis too; the piano chord that opens it is a vertical pentatone and the monophonic figure heard against it contains the notes of a pentatone that lies a 5th higher than the chord. As in figures encountered in *Late summer* and elsewhere, passing-notes from outside the strict shape are introduced and form hexatonic modes. But here (and, as closer scrutiny confirms, in *Late summer* also) the hexatones are those that would result from combining two pentatones a 5th apart. This relationship, anticipated at the beginning, is only referred to here rather than exploited although it is worth stating that, as examination of Warlock's output continues, the pentatone is, for Warlock, a shape with several constructional origins and possibilities.

The melody commences with a variant of the rising-4th anacrusis (which is restored in bars 24-5), the ascending major-2nd-plus-minor-3rd motif that was so prominent in *The curlew* and is a common derivation of so much of the modal/chordal material that Warlock employs (Ex. 10.2). The voice remains true to the piano's horizontal pentatone, sans E, until bar 10 when it appears in the figure used instrumentally in the introduction. That it was avoided for five bars – and will be for another four – prepares for the appearance of E flat, in

Ex. 10.2: *The singer* **– bars 1-8**

the lower octave, at bar 15 (anticipated by the piano in the previous bar). The centre has shifted by now from the original F to G (there are D major chords in bar 12) and the pentatone has given way to an Aeolian mode. What ensues is less easy to define for the melody, as a result of harmonic chromaticism, is subject to semitonal adjustment. These involve A flat, B natural and D flat (written as C sharp in the piano part, which also retains the F sharp from the D major chords). The vocal line at this point becomes contorted in comparison with the directness of associated material, and its coming to rest on C – a dominant to anticipate the lower C that will restart the verse-melody in bar 24 – sounds contrived.

So do the chromatic chords of bar 26 that were referred to earlier (Ex. 10.3). But, significantly, the only accidentals employed are the F sharps

Ex. 10.3: *The singer* – bars 24-27

(from bar 12 and elsewhere) E flat (from bars 14-15) and B natural (from bars 17-19). There is no reappearance of either A flat or D flat, suggesting an incomplete technique, but chromatic relationships of this sort will surface once again in other pieces. It is, however, worth pointing out that, in the process of chordal thickening associated with the return of earlier verse material – a technique already discovered elsewhere – the pentatone chord that opened the song is undistorted although it now contains eight notes compared with the original six.

Because of its seasonal association, *Adam lay ybounden* has become one of Warlock's better known pieces, due in no small part to its inclusion in *The Oxford book of carols*.[4] Although the C-centre is never in doubt, a precise modal character is not immediately revealed – a situation which is already familiar; voice and piano (especially the latter which has more to do) hold back the sixth degree until bar 9 when an Aeolian signifier (A flat) occurs in both parts. Bar 11 (piano) contains both this Aeolian and a Dorian (A natural) signifier while bar 12 (piano) introduces E natural, associated with a Mixolydian – or the major – on C (but see below). The major (etc.) reference is perpetuated by the voice; it may be thought that the melody modulates, as does the piano (to the dominant) but, except for a chromatic D flat in bar 23 (that is harmony dependent) no notes are brought into the voice-line that are not consistent with C-centred modes or scales. In this way, although the strophism is heavily modified – only the four-quaver figure that opens the first verse is common to all of them – Warlock manages to perpetuate the principle of chordal variation without compromising the tune. He may not retain the literal identity of his verse-melody but he substitutes the reliance on a fixed centre. In this circumstance it is possible to consider the latter half of verse 2 as conforming to an Ionian mode rather than a major scale.

There are many points of harmonic interest too. The alternating C minor/G minor 7th chords of the introduction contain all the notes of the first mode to be used (excluding the sixth degree, of course) so that the minor 7th, as well as having the harmonic significance of being a family chord, is also linearly important through its inclusion of F. And the juxtaposition of minor 7th chords on C and B in bar 13 is curious within a strictly tonal context – until it is realised that Warlock is not actually working within one; the same can be said of the adjacent C minor/B minor chords two bars later, a brief parallelism that, in a different guise, will dominate the last bars. The harmonies that open verse 3 (bars 21-3) echo the past, a chain of five *Curlew*-chords only heard previously in the most tonally evasive pieces. The vocal D flat at the beginning of bar 23, though melodically chromatic, is forced by the minor 7th chord that underlies it, a not unusual state of affairs and one that was also evident in *The singer*. What is of greater interest in the context of the piece as a whole is that, although the other eleven notes are used often (depending on circumstances and, obviously, some more than others) this is actually the only appearance of the note in the entire piece; it is as though, in this more chromatic passage, D flat had to appear for the sake of completeness.

It is just before and during the verbally climactic final phrase ("Therefore we moun singen: Deo gratias!") that some of the most extraordinary chords are to be heard. The two chords in bar 33 and the first in bar 34 are all pentatones that form a short, circle-of-5ths statement (as the summary – Ex. 10.4 – explains). The deployment of the remaining chords is as much a linear procedure as a harmonic one: three pairs of parallel chords in the right hand in conjunction with two pairs in the left (the C in the bass at bar 34iii is a vestigial tonic pedal).

Ex. 10.4: *Adam lay ybounden* – bars 33-38 (chordal summary)

The aggregate chords thereby manufactured can be described as 9ths but that misses the point. What the chords are doing transcends individual identification; it is a true melody-of-chords that declares all the C-centred modes employed in the vocal line but, once again, harmonically rather than melodically. This is a much more satisfactory situation than the attempted integration observed towards the end of *The singer*. It is noteworthy as much for what is not there as for what is – had there been a C sharp or an F sharp present the point would have been lost.

Parallelism also a feature of the opening of *Rest sweet nymphs*. The resultant chords, major and minor 7ths to begin with (Ex. 10.5), conform to the family. The progression is broken after only four chords

Ex. 10.5: *Rest sweet nymphs* – bars 1-3

by the aggregation that end bar 1. The left-hand shape that would have been sequentially correct is that which appears at 2i, a constituent of the pentatone chord that arrests the chordal motion in favour of the monophonic arpeggio at the top of the texture. Warlock substitutes a chromatic appoggiatura-chord that, in combination with the right-hand shape, produces an exquisite dissonance. Apart from a concealed *Curlew*-chord content, this is a chord in itself. Although made up of two inverted triads, C flat in the lower part, D minor in the upper, there is no suggestion of bitonality. Indeed, the chromaticism of this chord should not be considered arbitrary, a momentary frisson of transient sensuousness, even if that is how it comes across; as will be explained shortly, the notes it contains are anticipatory.

The importance of the opening, chordal descent is that it establishes no stable centre. Apart from the chromatic chord to which reference has already been made, the pitches employed are consistent with F-centred modes (Ionian and Mixolydian) without actually stating them and, while bar 2 has an F/C 5th in the bass, the pentatonic remainder of the chord is sufficiently ambiguous to maintain the status quo, however briefly established. The harmony's F-focus is supported by a pedal for most of three consecutive bars; there is a swerve on to an A major chord in bar 6, another mediant major move although one not effected with the same reverence displayed in *Late summer*. The chord of A is achieved not via its dominant but from a pentatonic chord that contains B natural and F sharp. These correspond to the C flat and G flat of the chromatic chord in bar 1, the third constituent of which was the E flat Mixolydian signifier presented, at the same pitch, two chords previously.

Melodically the picture is less clear. The voice does not interfere with the sense of F in the piano (bars 3-6) but the note distribution suggests that its peculiar centre is elsewhere. The absence of B flat is reminiscent of those occasions in other songs when modal 6ths have been avoided; if this is the case here the vocal focus is D and the move to A in the piano – which is substantiated by the voice in the next phrase – fits into and consolidates such a scenario.

In the ensuing material (bars 7-10) the voice maintains the A-centre (B natural in bar 7 quickly followed by a G sharp). The piano, meanwhile, uses no chords that substantiate the voice's centre apart from a dominant 7th at the end of bar 7 (with the melodic G sharp) preferring, instead, ambiguous chords (*Curlew* and pentatone-based); at bar 10 it moves to C, the dominant of its own initial centre. Given this diversity of centres the noncommittal nature of the introduction becomes clear although, once more, there is no real bitonality. The temporary allegiances to A can be construed as a pivotal gesture but the suggestion of the mediant major in bar 6 is a reminder of earlier practices.

What has been described so far relates to half of the verse, the remainder of which ("Lullaby, lullaby . . .") is in the nature of a refrain. It affords a remarkable example of the chordal family in operation. Motivically it picks up the E flat of the opening which is turned into a 7th to create a flat-side move. This is developed sequentially and extended into a circle-of-5ths that reaches a D flat chord (with an added minor 7th) in the middle of bar 14. The semitone bass shift that follows converts this chord, retrospectively, into a real German 6th, plunging the harmony back into F again. The melody too has picked up the E flat but its own assumption of D flat, although linked with the coincident harmonies, recalls the semitonal adjustments of earlier songs and substantiates therein the claim for a D-centre at the beginning. The harmony never achieves F at the end of the verse as pentatonic and other ambiguous chords prevent a conventional cadence.

The second verse is substantially the same as the first apart from a few rhythmic adjustments and only a couple of alternative chords. F finally prevails as the principal centre, at least as far as the harmony is concerned, but the little piano coda is based on the introduction and holds back the unequivocal chord until the last possible moment, especially as the end of the melody is, like that of the first verse, sounded against pentatonic chords. When the perfect (in both senses) cadential moment arrives, the dominant 7th that precedes the tonic is fused with a *Curlew*-chord to create a complex and audacious added 9th/11th aggregation. Otherwise, the richness of the harmony – it has the ability to surprise even after numerous hearings – does not warrant wholesale change. Warlock omitted the middle verse of the text, a musically sensible move; a third verse with the same harmony would have weakened it by overexposure; a third verse with alternative chords would have distracted from the balance between fleeting sensuousness and constructional credibility that is achieved as it stands.

Rest sweet nymphs demands a vocal tessitura of just an octave, one of the narrowest that Warlock writes. *Sleep*, perhaps Warlock's best-known song, requires only a semitone more. Its contrapuntal intricacies make the string quartet version (with which it is contemporary) more appropriate. Although Tomlinson is unsure whether piano or strings formed the original instrumental component,[5] some of the writing (bar 19, for example) is very pianistic. The autonomy of line, vocal and instrumental, the rhythmic fluidity and the occasional intensity of the chromaticism mark this piece as one in which the van Dieren influence is still strongly evident. Although barred, mostly in triple time, the composer demands metrical freedom in performance including a flexibility of the length of the tactus (between crotchet and quaver); a performance note at the outset requires phrasing "according to the natural accentuation of the words", a feature common to both van Dieren's and Renaissance practice. (Bar 5 has a vocal line in 6/8 against an instrumental 3/4 à la Morley and others.) As if to emphasise the point, the second of the two verses of this strophic structure is rhythmically as well as harmonically altered. On several occasions the voice appears to be metrically separate from the instrumental part – that the instrumental lines are more conjoined in this respect suggests that, whichever version was written first, some of it at least was conceived at the keyboard.

The falling 5th at the start proclaims G as the centre although the first inversion minor chord means that the full recognition of the fact, at the beginning of bar 3, has greater impact. The E natural/F sharp in the first bar followed by F natural/E flat suggest a melodic minor or musica ficta practice (the tonic is never reached) but the D flat is purely chromatic, as are most of the accidentals in the second bar, by the end of which all twelve pitches have been used. In fact, during the first verse, much of the content is biased towards G minor and, apart from a B natural in bar 5, the only accidentals are the E natural and F sharp already referred to; musica ficta does not always apply, however. The melody exhibits similar characteristics: E flat, a 6th above the tonic, is set as its upper limit and is inviolable. In the lower octave, E natural is preferred but it is only sounded once, along with F sharp, in an ascending figure.

If the first bar of the introduction anticipates the first verse then its inter-verse successor prophesies the second. The level of chromaticism increases markedly, firstly as word-painting triggered by "sliding". It prompts a descending sequence (bar 14) which, though only two crotchets long, utilises all twelve notes – in fact, the last twelve instrumental notes of the bar are all different (Ex. 10.6) although this is achieved in a tonally uncontentious way that is partly the result of parallel, diminished-triad chords. Chromaticism is more freely employed throughout the instrumental component of the second verse and it is so different, in places, from the setting of the first that it gives the

Ex. 10.6: *Sleep* – bar 14

impression of being unrelated. Only the vocal line, itself subject to modification, maintains the unity of the piece at such points.

In spite of all these exciting details, the most striking feature of this song is the ending, three bars of van Dierenesque instrumental writing that grows from the G major chord at bar 23iii (Ex. 10.7). This sounds like a *tierce de Picardie* but its origins really lie in that early B natural in bar 2. The passage remains sporadically faithful to G: there is a tonic

Ex. 10.7: *Sleep* **– bars 22-28**

pedal in bars 24-5 that culminates in a momentary tonic chord at 24iii and, after some more chromaticism, a dominant at 26i. But none of this prepares fully for the convolutions and dissonances of the remainder of bar 26 and the curious chord upon which it comes to rest. It contains elements of *Curlew* and 7th shapes but really stands as a unique and distant entity. The G major chords that follow it in order to close the song are almost out of place; indeed, two of them are needed, the second to confirm the first. There are two contemporary comparisons, though, which have already been examined; the pentatone chord that precedes the A chord in bars 5-6 of *Rest sweet nymphs* and, in the same piece, the chord at the end of bar 40 that precedes the F major chord. Neither of these has the boldness of the example in *Sleep* as they both have a dominant quality that aids progress to the next chord, but they do represent a tendency on Warlock's part to approach cadential chords in unusual and dissonant ways.

While it displays some familiar technical characteristics, there is nothing quite like *Autumn twilight* anywhere else in Warlock's output. In places, this ravishing song recalls Delius far more than has been the case in recent works and the Romantic derivation of the material, much as was observed in *Late summer*, is a continuous device that matches the imagery of Symons's poem where day, year and life are drawing to an obvious close, a backcloth to the "wandering" couple. Its declamatory through-composition, again unusual for a song of this duration and at this stage of Warlock's development, is reminiscent in intent, if not in content, of *Saudades*, although with a more limited palette and a tighter level of control as a result of the use of motifs and other linear techniques developed in the intervening years.

The first eight bars depend on a modified pentatone, constant repetition of which creates a sense of stasis. The piano figure substantiates the C-centre by avoiding the note itself as much as possible although it does appear at strategic moments; there is no reference at all to a seventh degree. The vocal line, restricted to only three pitches to start with, employs an inverted variant of the *And wilt thou*-shape, the three-note figure heard in *The curlew*. The same motif, in both prime and inverted forms, is the means whereby it grows and accumulates new pitches (Ex. 10.8). The first accidental is an A natural that not only converts the sense of Aeolian mode (given the situation

Ex. 10.8: *Autumn twilight* – bars 4-10 (voice only)

created by the absent 7th) to a Dorian but also represents a "correction" of the opening pentatone. One accidental prompts another and only this procedure is a cue for the appearance of B natural, the leading-note.

Discussion of songs written after 1917 has tended to concentrate on their linear qualities, the sublimation of van Dieren's horizontally motivated methods into Warlockian melody. But, as has been pointed out, the assumption of these characteristics (including modality) is chordally inspired. *Autumn twilight* contains reminders of the fact for, although imbued with a sense of linear progress, some of its content can only be explained harmonically, a situation emphasised by Warlock's continual demand for the sustaining pedal. The G flats of bar 15 come as something of a horizontal surprise although their *Curlew*-chord associations are unmistakable; they prepare the upper part of the next bar where they are joined by parallel 6ths, a device Warlock employs many times elsewhere although not quite in this fashion (Ex. 10.9).

Ex. 10.9: *Autumn twilight* – bars 13-16

The introductory figure returns to suggest the start of a second verse and, hence, a strophic outline. This does not actually materialise. Instead, there is a succession of disguised pedals; they are based on falling semitones, first on C, then C flat, then B flat, but they also include one other note a 5th above or below the principal one. The C-Dorian material of the opening is reinstated, although this too is subject to semitonal manipulation, first to a D flat Dorian (bars 27-8) then to less easily specified shapes until a black-key pentatone (anticipating *Rantum tantum*) is replaced, in another semitone shift, by one on white keys only (bars 34-6, summarised in Ex. 10.10).

Ex. 10.10: *Autumn twilight* – bars 13-16

Thereafter, *Curlew*-chords predominate before these also break down to become chromatically indefinable in the piano coda. The abstracted dissonance of this ending may be compared with that of *Sleep* but the brilliant incongruity of the final chord there is replaced here by a chord that could have been written by Messiaen (second inversion major with an added 11th at the top) against which an arpeggiated pentatone is sounded.

Thus, in *Autumn twilight*, Warlock can be seen to utilise ideas that have already been witnessed in other songs. But the result is, taken as a whole, atypical. It nevertheless bears testimony to a composer whose methodology does not always result in the same sort of song. It is possible to see similar processes at work here to those of the *Peterisms*, a comparison that, on the face of it, could be considered unlikely or even inappropriate.

The Oxford book of carols contains versions of *Balulalow* and *Tyrley tyrlow*[6] as well as *Adam lay ybounden*. *Tyrley tyrlow* has an A-based Dorian melody introduced and broken up by pentatone-derived material. The introductory figure, played in the piano original through a pedal-sustained chord, is clearer in the later, orchestral arrangement where a shape held by violas and horns provides a firmer manifestation of the composer's intentions.

The opening phrase adheres strictly to Dorian characteristics (G natural and F sharp) in both vocal and instrumental parts over an A pedal; in fact, the voice is Dorian throughout. It has not been a feature of Warlock's music to this point to have chordal material conform so faithfully to the modal tendency of its coincident melody. Even when it begins to diverge, during the remaining two bars of the verse and beyond, the modifications are relatively slight, F is naturalised (once, in bar 10) and G is sharpened (once, in bar 12) before a return to the modal status quo by the end of the refrain. The second verse of this strophic – and quite strictly so – piece recycles the material of the first with some small rhythmic modifications in the refrain. Chordal amendments begin in the next verse. Even these are conformist and move little beyond those pitch variants already noted. This is very much the nature of the whole piece: the melody is subject to a minimal amount of purely rhythmic amendment and the harmony utilises for the most part the Dorian restrictions established at the outset. The pentatonic references also continue and not only in the form of the introductory motif, as some close position formations in bars 63-4 attest.

Tyrley tyrlow is, in many respects, unspectacular. Rhythmic interest is generated by displacing the first beat of the bar in some figures but, otherwise, it contains no stimulating dissonance, for example, or extreme, if accountable, chromaticism. What it does demonstrate is a relationship between pentatonicism and other kinds of modality in Warlock's output, a feature which is worth a small digression at this juncture.

On several occasions, mention has been made of Warlock's deliberate tendency to conceal material, particularly notes – referred to as signifiers – that make the difference in identification of one modal derivation as opposed to another. This has been especially true of the 6th degree of modes containing minor 3rds which possess, in all other respects, the same shape (i.e. Dorian and Aeolian configurations). At other times there has been noted a discrepancy that has developed between major and minor 3rds. If the common features of those particular modes that Warlock has been seen to favour (Dorian, Aeolian and Mixolydian) are retained – that is the final, 2nd, 4th, 5th and 7th – the result is a pentatone (Ex. 10.11a). Other pentatonic associations have been mentioned but it appears that another important attribute of this device is as a universal shape that relates to all the others; the first

Ex. 10.11: pentatonic derivatives

of the *Folk-song preludes* expresses just this phenomenon. It is noteworthy that, in *Tyrley tyrlow*, pentatonicism is retained, albeit sporadically, as a harmonic feature when the melody favours the Aeolian. So often it is the vocal line that is left to proclaim the modality, of whatever kind, while the piano has greater note-choice freedom.

Also, at this stage, it is worth pointing out another pentatone-related phenomenon. Warlock occasionally employs two pentatones a 5th apart. When combined they produce the hexatone shown in Ex. 10.11b. At the pitch shown this can either be considered as a C Mixolydian/major, depending on which 7th is employed or, assuming a D final, another Aeolian/ Dorian ambiguity where the 6th is subject to modification. The most spectacular example of the phenomenon is to be found in *The curlew* at the words "I know of the sleepy country . . ." (bars U8-V7 – see Ex. 4.14).

The situation described above does not include the Ionian mode. If it is to be counted, the 7th must also be left out of the reckoning. The remaining four notes constitute the *Frostbound wood*-chord, a device that can also be explained in terms of two pentatones, although further description and comment on this particular shape will be left until discussion of the eponymous song.

All of these manifestations suggest that, in Warlock's methodology, pentatonicism is more than simply an adjunct to other processes or a stylistic convenience acquired as a result of contact with folk-music or its promulgators. On the contrary, it is an essential element that can, in different ways, demonstrate or even stand for the common ground between other uses of modal material.

Notes

1   i.e. D.
2   IC p. 80.
3   idem.
4   First published (by O) in 1928. One of the editors was Ralph
     Vaughan Williams for whom PW wrote the *Three carols*. See note
     6 below.
5   FT: preface to T(iii). But see also IC p. 159, note 43.
6   With *The sycamore tree*, they make up the *Three carols* PW
     compiled for Vaughan Williams and the (London) Bach Choir. See
     note 3, Chapter 13.

CHAPTER 11

The way forward (1)
Lillygay

The cycle *Lillygay*[1] has not hitherto been considered with the same respect given to its immediate predecessor *The curlew*. The more modernist style of the latter and its treatment of Yeats's introspective angst is considered to be of greater significance than what is interpreted as the frivolous hedonism of these songs, particularly *The shoemaker* (misplaced) and *Rantum tantum* (justified). In fact, Warlock wrote it quickly in the summer of 1922 shortly after he had completed *The curlew*, a work which, it has been noted, took something like seven years to compose, on and off. *Lillygay* is a work that, because of its stylistic variety, advertises its differences and even its incongruity within the Warlockian canon. It is the only work in which Warlock uses what could be considered elements of folksong in anything like an extensive way and this in a contemporary, national context that includes many examples of the type, real or fabricated, simple or abstracted, by Vaughan Williams, Gurney, Rebecca Clarke, Butterworth, Finzi,et al. It may be coincidental, of course, but *Lillygay* appeared only a few months after Warlock had renewed his acquaintance with and been visited by Bartók who stayed with him at Cefn-Bryntalch en route from a concert engagement at University College, Aberystwyth.

Warlock's title for the cycle is the same as that of an "anthology of anonymous verse" devised by his friend Victor Neuberg.[2] The anthology was the source of his five poems. Speculation about the origins of the words, once thought to be by Neuberg himself, has now been largely resolved.[3] Although Warlock indulged in a degree of contrived rusticity in producing these settings it should not be assumed that his use of pseudo-folksong is the result of his admiration for Harry Cox[4] or (however flexibly) Vaughan Williams. Warlock's use of modality transcends any ride on a stylistic bandwagon but, given the contemporary awareness of folksong and the folk-movement in general, it could be considered a response to it. It is more sensible, though, from the compositional train of thought so far, to see a folksong style as a result of his assumption of modality rather than the other way about. It is significant that, when modality gives way to tonality (in *Rantum tantum*, the last song of the cycle) the new format is used not so much to evoke functional chord- and centre-relationships as a linear device in its own right.

Until now, songs have been dealt with as separate entities even when collected together in sets. Such sets are convenient aggregations of material and the choice of songs that make them up should not be thought to suggest structurally integrated relationships between the constituents. A similar view could apply to *The curlew* too; although given a sense of unity by the use of common material, chordal and motivic, it is, nevertheless – perhaps because of the timespan over which it was put together – an accumulation of essentially separate items. In *Lillygay*, however, the first four songs of the cycle (*The distracted maid, Johnnie wi' the tye, The shoemaker* and *Burd Ellen and young Tamlane*) have to be considered as a whole. And although *Rantum tantum* will be mostly discussed afterwards it is no unrelated afterthought. It is a fact that its tonal considerations characterise it but it differs in other respects from the four songs that precede it, not least in its rejection of the strophic form that prevails in them. In the first four songs of the cycle Warlock continues to employ repeated melody as a constant and readily assimilable reference point against which the piano can suggest, through alterations to the harmonic and motivic emphasis, emotional and onomatopoeic changes that follow an expositional first verse. But, even when this fact is understood, the folksong context notwithstanding, it has to be recognised that the place of the form in the composer's methodology demands the stylistic ambience, not vice versa. And any isolation of *Rantum tantum* from the others on this count should not be taken to indicate that it does not lie easily within the cycle. It is a deliberate contrast to the other four, a foil to their inherent melancholy.

The first song, *The distracted maid*, actually takes on an expositional function in terms of the whole cycle. The 4ths – and 5ths – that have been an increasingly common harmonic feature of recent songs derive from both modal and tonal practices; they will be seen, as the whole piece unfolds, to have an important rôle here too. Warlock's intent is clear at the start of this first song: the 5th is both the limit of the scalic piano motif that pervades it and the regulating interval in melodic construction. The rising-4th anacrusis is, in this case, a gesture related by inversion rather than just a dominant-tonic statement (Ex. 11.1). As with strophism, Warlock likes to validate such well known procedures structurally, choosing not simply to rely upon their familiarity.

Although he extends the emphasis on the 5th in the piano part (in bars 7-8 initially), these are preparations as much for the rest of the set as for

Ex. 11.1: *The distracted maid (Lillygay)* – bars 1-10: use of 4ths & 5ths

the opening song. The opening of *Johnnie wi' the tye* confirms the process: rising 4ths on the piano (F sharp-B) give way to a rising 5th (B-F sharp) in the voice – a reversal of the process encountered in the previous song. Another manifestation of this intervallic relationship occurs in *The distracted maid* (bar 39 et seq.) where the major 2nds of the relentless quaver figure (that characterises the maid's pacing up and down and also symbolises her obsession with her estranged lover) are transformed into stylised birdsong ("Oh if I were a little bird to build upon his breast"). The understanding that these appearances are expositional is important for, in the ensuing songs, Warlock's extended use of the 4th in particular becomes bound up with other linear material, especially pentatones.

Warlock uses modal material in all of these songs (including *Rantum tantum*) but rarely in a pure state. However, the significance of the first two bars of *The distracted maid* cannot be overemphasised. The repeated B flats, in combination with the Fs that occur on the secondary beat of the bar, produce a decorated drone – a pedal, even – that is entirely pianistic and, more importantly, anticipates the non-modulatory character of the first four songs. To draw greater attention to this fact the first song is the longest of the five. Modality in this (and the second) song is less extended than in those that succeed them although, here, the flattened 7th is always preferred to the raised (tonal) leading note in the melody, and the absence of G, either flat or natural, in the first half of each verse briefly creates that Dorian/Aeolian ambiguity already witnessed several times elsewhere. Yet at no stage can the piece be said to be "in" B flat minor; there is no other reference point against which its B flatness can be measured.

Likewise, *Johnnie wi' the tye* is not really in B minor. The piano has a few, incidental A sharps but all melodic As are natural. Furthermore, despite the undisputed B-centre of the opening and other passages, ten of the song's 21 bars (viz. 4-5, 7-8 and 13-18) contradict B, and – a statement of intent on Warlock's part – there is no key-signature. This phenomenon is an inaudible but fairly rare event in his output; one is reminded not only of the atonal leanings of *Saudades* but also the tonal and modal fluidity of *The curlew*. Even to describe *Johnnie wi' the tye* as a fusion of B minor and major would not be true; the first bar conforms to the Dorian mode and the second bar employs Mixolydian and Aeolian – an instance of concentrated polymodality. While these are fleeting references, their implications will enable other, sustained techniques to be developed to suit the words "And o as he kittl'd me . . . But I forgot to cry".

In *The shoemaker* the 4th emerges – indeed comes into its own – as a non-tonal unit. The song starts with a flurry of them (Ex. 11.2) and contains many chords in the piano that would appear, on the surface, to be built from them. A chord such as that at bar 5 (Ex. 11.3a) has been

Ex. 11.2: *The shoemaker (Lillygay)* **– bars 1-3**

Ex. 11.3: *The shoemaker* **– bar 5**

related to Warlock's knowledge of lute tunings.[5] But the same chord can also be reduced to a vertical pentatone (Ex. 11.3b), the shape that defines the vocal melody and the piano introduction. The function of this introduction, then, is neither to promote the note-centre nor to reveal significant motif but to establish the principal of pentatonicism, a procedure utilised in the past but not previously validated by Warlock in such a strongly integrated manner. This interpretation does not necessarily negate the "lute-tuning" theory: this is not the first time that multiple derivations of material or devices have been encountered.

The pentatones of the introduction and the melody are different: that given to the voice is higher – by a 4th. Such a relationship between pentatones has already been encountered but not even *The curlew* presents as tightly controlled an environment as this. Four notes are common to both shapes; the C, heard in the piano, is not initially included in the vocal line, although it does appear towards the end of the verse. The process of exposition by concealment (rather than revelation) is a Warlockian trait that has come to fruition in *Lillygay*; it will be encountered again.

Nor is pentatonicism abandoned in *Burd Ellen and young Tamlane*. The melody is yet another example of Warlock's simultaneous use of different techniques. A is prominent and it would be convenient to assume that he employs the Aeolian implied by the signature, but the presence of F sharp in the introduction (there is no F, sharp or natural in the vocal line) creates a sense of the Dorian. Moreover, the last phrase of the melody (bars 8iv-10iv) conforms to a pentatone which has already been alluded to. The interpolated B is a constituent of the pentatone a 5th (or a 4th) away from it – not the first time that this hexatonic shape (two interlocked pentatones that make a minor-3rd mode without a Dorian or Aeolian signifier) has been met with. The simultaneous use of different modes is a Bartókian technique, of course, although Warlock's method suggests not so much Magyar astringency (which, incidentally, he relished)[6] as inventive English compromise.

Given the absence of functional key-relationships in the cycle, harmonic tension depends on chords based on (Delian) falling semitones. Horizontal material also emanates from minor 2nds and these are presented in a number of ways. The absent G at the start of *The distracted maid*, another apophatic exposition, has already been mentioned; when it does occur (at bar 7 in both parts) it is the version given by the key-signature. At bar 11, G natural is preferred (producing a *Curlew*-chord in the process) and it nags its way into the second verse.

The dichotomous notes are kept at a distance from each other to start with, that distance becoming smaller as the song proceeds until their proximity to one another produces effects that are sometimes neo-Delian and sometimes, by virtue of their false-relationships and dissonances, more akin to Bartók, such as the "gloom" motif in bars 30-1.

Johnnie wi' the tye contains similar discrepancies: by cancelling the preceding G sharp, G natural at the end of bar 2 (piano introduction) characterises the Mixolydian/Aeolian conflict that has already been chronicled. The disparity is instantly developed within the piano part as G and G sharp (often written as A flat) vie with one another. The same sort of dispute explains the D and D sharp of the first two bars. Warlock refers to it momentarily in bars 4-5 but eschews lengthy development; perhaps this is because, given the A centre, it has tonal rather than modal implications. Nevertheless, this aural cubism, in which alternative solutions are presented adjacent to one another, continues throughout the song. Its most striking manifestation is a two-bar, A flat bass pedal (bars 7-8) that falls to G, not as a gesture of resolution but inevitability. It underpins the melodic wriggling – more semitonal displacements that distort any vestigial evidence of a tonal centre. The practice of using alternative notes from two modes that are, otherwise, transpositions of each other is substantially different from bitonality, which depends on simultaneous or adjacent polarisations of material. The linear format is brought to bear on the harmonic structure, creating not so much these bitonal polarisations but irritation and disorientation of the vertical effect. This is entirely at one with the quasi-mannerist, sexually implicit, pleasure/pain content of the words.

Material employed in *The shoemaker* is similar to that of *The distracted maid*, even down to the identical conflicting notes, G and G flat (Dorian and Aeolian signifiers once more). They appear in neither of the expositional pentatones. In this song, because he wants to give prominence to the 4th in his harmony, Warlock temporarily relinquishes the sort of chords already described but without abandoning his interest in the semitone. He creates a harmonic language[7] that fuses the pentatone (vertically deployed) and semitone displacement. This latter technique is not merely an abstract, compositional tool; its appropriateness to the verbal content has already been commented upon above and a further example is to be found at the climactic point in bars 29-30. The piano had favoured G natural initially but, in the last verse, Gs are flattened until the falling 3rd (G natural-E flat) – a huge, knowing wink that acknowledges the double entendre of "And there he has fitted his own pretty wench . . ." – far more effective a conclusion to the tale than the seven more verses of predictable content the poem provides.

In *The distracted maid* and *The shoemaker* the semitonal conflicts had arisen between signifiers that could imply tonal or modal structures, whereas in *Johnnie wi' the tye* the dichotomous notes characterise separate modes. In *Burd Ellen and young Tamlane* the process is slightly different. The F sharp of the introduction is, indeed, a Dorian signifier (given the A-centre); now it combines (in the first bar) with the G that precedes it creating thereby a falling semitone, an exposition for similar events later in the song. But it is only one of a number of intervallic motifs presented by the introduction to be given prominence later in the song (Ex. 11.4). Although presented horizontally, as before, the motifs have vertical implications.

Ex. 11.4: *Burd Ellen and young Tamlane (Lillygay)* – motifs in bars 1-3

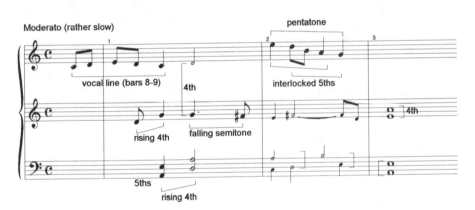

In the first two songs, the relationship between horizontal and vertical components, while important, is kept relatively simple. The 4ths and 5ths of *The distracted maid* and *Johnnie wi' the tye* do have a harmonic significance although their presence favours the melody, given the exceptions already cited. But it is in *The shoemaker* that the symbiosis between the two becomes indisputable not just through the 4ths for which the listener has been prepared but, also, in terms of the pentatone. The lute-tuning formation is superseded by a more complex set of chords derived from the pentatone shape but with semitonal displacements. A chord may be a fusion of two pentatones and, as is the case in triadic harmony, notes may be added or omitted. In bar 10 (Ex. 11.5), the "wrong" notes (G and D flats) are immediately "corrected" by

Ex. 11.5: *The shoemaker* **– bars 6-10**

a falling 5th in the bass. Such semitonal modification of family chords has long been a feature of Warlock's technique and, while it has not been as widespread a feature of works written after 1917, it continues to appear, as *The shrouding of the Duchess of Malfi* will attest inter alia.

Burd Ellen and young Tamlane contains a nice variant on the practice of semitone displacement. Warlock realises that, assuming the set of songs is performed complete, such disturbances to the harmony are by this stage fully validated; consequently, the B flat in bar 4, like the D and G sharps in bar 8, comes as no real surprise. But such is the economy of Warlock's writing that these little gestures, like the

conflicting notes in the previous songs, bear fruit later: so far, a purely
strophic form has been obligatory; now the climax necessitates an
alteration in the vocal line to heighten Ellen's angry outburst ("And a'
women's curse in his company's gane"). The modifications are
accordingly built around G sharp, D sharp (E flat) and B flat (Ex. 11.6).

Ex. 11.6: *Burd Ellen and young Tamlane* **– bars 4 & 8 (piano) & 43-47 (voice)**

In the same song, the harmony has become more intense. The density
of the *Shoemaker* chords – pentatones raised to the vertical then
extended or manipulated to thicken the texture – is here abstracted. The
process begins relatively early, halfway through the second verse; the
latter half of bar 13, a mixture of held chord and arpeggio, can be
reduced to Ex. 11.7a and the piano-part to the last two verses reveals a
similar harmonic consistency. The pentatone shape is not lost but is
often submerged in a welter of spread clusters (Ex. 11.7b).

It should now be clear that there is a cumulative relationship between
these songs, a formal interdependence that weakens the performance of
separate items. This is particularly true of the fifth song which, as an
isolated entity (an important qualification), is disjointed and, in view of
the sexual abandon implied by the words, even restrained. Yet *Rantum
tantum* clearly belongs to the other four, a truth made plain by quoting
the introduction to *The shoemaker* at bar 31. In some other respects it is
appreciably different from them.

First of all, it possesses a sense of the major whereas all the previous
songs, despite (or because of) their modal leanings, have embodied the
minor 3rd (mediant). Secondly, there is stronger sense of through-
composition in the structure of the piece; the strophism both of the

Ex. 11.7: *Burd Ellen and young Tamlane* – bars 11 & 30-48 (chordal summary)

preceding songs and the text is rejected. Lastly, and of the greatest interest, there is a definite sense of key provided by the modulation to the dominant in bars 5-6, a unique experience in the context of the set as a whole but one that is a further development – the apotheosis, even – of the opening 5ths of *The distracted maid*. All of these factors contribute to a loss of the folksong element that has hitherto been frequently present but which began to break down at the end of *Burd Ellen and young Tamlane*. Warlock's *Lillygay* tunes tend to be busier than their ethnic models anyway, but in *Rantum tantum* he comes closer to the idiom of his "sociable" songs.

Each of these differences has a structural relevance. A sense of the major at the start emerges from the otherwise pentatonic introduction in the form of the mediant F. This is similar to the way that Warlock has previously introduced material that is to become significant – by interpolating it into content to which it does not initially belong only to exploit it in the course of development. A major sound also instantly epitomises the contrast between this song and its companion-pieces. The loss of strophic form is inevitable because of the way Warlock develops his material, but such a move had to some extent been anticipated by the melodic aberrations at the end of *Burd Ellen and young Tamlane*. Such links between songs are an essential feature in the cycle and it is pertinent that Warlock not only maintains the pentatonicism established in *The shoemaker* but continues to develop it in *Rantum tantum*.

For the final sting in the linear tail is that, having founded the principle of moving the focus of the operational area (by modulation),

Warlock initiates exactly the same process with regard to the pentatone. He started the song with the notes of the black keys themselves; after the first verse, expositional as before, he sets out on a number of pseudo-sequences that propel the melody and its accompaniment through a diversity of terrains as if this new-found freedom of centres symbolises the act of – and attitude towards – "rantum tantum" itself. Even this gesture conforms to the grand plan, though, for the bass line that drives the harmony into the modulation is restating the 4ths and 5ths presented at the beginning of *The distracted maid*. Again, Warlock formally validates a familiar device and then exploits it: instead of developing the relationship between two key-centres a 5th apart he utilises similarly related pentatones. As was demonstrated in the early bars of *The shoemaker*, two pentatones a 5th (or a 4th) apart have notes in common and thereby form a parallel with other modal usage in the cycle.

Thus, the D flat pentatone (the black-key shape) predominates during the first verse, allowing for the modulation, and it also dictates the two-bar interlude before the second. At the outset of this verse (bars 12-13) the A flat shape (a 5th above the original) is prominent; after a transitional bar (14) the next four bars (15-18) use the F and C, then A flat and D flat shapes respectively, the last of them continuing into bar 19. Thereafter, the harmony is more freely based although bar 24 conforms to the E shape. The melody, meanwhile, tends to follow the pentatone instrumentally current; where the harmony relinquishes the pentatone the melody remains strict, settling on to the A flat configuration. In bar 31 the *Shoemaker* quotation re-establishes the harmonic procedure, this E flat form giving way to that on A flat (with some interpolations) before settling on the D flat version – a truncated circle-of-5ths that relates to the modulation.

After all this activity, it is to be the semitones that have the last word. Before the final low D flats there is a short volley of them, a reminder not just of their continual presence (Ex. 11.8) but of the sense of linear integration that pervades the set – an assertion of Warlock's own character as a composer that prevents *Lillygay* from degenerating into folksong pastiche. They serve to comment on the cycle as a whole: the first four songs are about lost love or troubled relationships. *Rantum tantum* is about more physical matters that can be pursued because of their very inconsequence. And if the song is insubstantial, here is the rationale for it.

The final semitones also emphasise their structural importance throughout the five songs and not just as the means for modifying

Ex. 11.8: *Rantum tantum (Lillygay)* **– bars 36-37**

material, even though that is the way that each song generally develops its own impetus. An examination of the note-centres shows how this particular aspect of the compositional logic is also semitone dependent. The first song in the cycle, *The distracted maid*, is centred on B flat; the subsequent note centres (of *Johnnie wi' the tye*, *The shoemaker* and *Burd Ellen and Young Tamlane* respectively) are B, B flat once more and then A. The last song, *Rantum tantum*, has D flat as its final despite some ambiguity at the beginning. Nevertheless, there is a clear modulation to the dominant, A flat, at bars 6-7 which completes the semitonal logic. Here is further proof – were it needed – that *Lillygay* is a cycle rather than a set and even, like *The curlew*, a single piece with a number of movements that both belong one to another and, therefore, discourage performances of individual songs. Given these circum-stances, it is distressing that the most recent edition of this piece[8] sees fit to transpose three of the songs.

Notes
1   This section is a heavily modified version of BC (August 1986/7).
2   Victor Neuburg (ed., 1920) *Lillygay: an anthology of anonymous poems*, The Vine Press, Steyning. PW took other texts from it too.
3   See articles by BC in PWSNL nos. 39, 43 & 44.
4   A folk-singer to be heard at, among other places, the Windmill Inn, Stalham in Norfolk. See Augustus John: foreword to CG. Cox is one of the best documented of English singers and his voice is preserved on a number of commercial recordings.
5   Parrott (May 1966).
6   ". . . the stimulating harshness and dissonance of Bartók . . ." in a letter to CT dated 19th January 1929.
7   See p. 201.
8   i.e. T(iv). The semitonal relationship between the note-centres of the constituent songs is sacrificed to the policy of providing material for the "medium voice". However, the reprint of T(iv) has a note by BC pointing out the relationship between the note-centres of the original.

CHAPTER 12

The way forward (2)
Candlelight and *Jenny Gray*

Candlelight (1923) is a set – indeed a cycle – of a dozen nursery rhymes written for his young son, Nigel. Their bagatelle-like qualities aside, they add a further dimension to an appraisal of Warlock the composer. These tiny songs, short even by his standards, are mostly monostrophic; in some, though, verbal repetition – not contained in the original text – extends them somewhat. Their brevity – and the relatively small amount that can be said about each of them – should not imply a lack of worth.

Ex. 12.1: *How many miles to Babylon* (*Candlelight*) – complete (bars 1-5)

The contrasts between individual songs (of mood, tempo, dynamic and duration) suggest that they be sung successively. Pilkington suggests[1] that sub-cycles be constructed but, since "the whole [cycle] only lasts just over six minutes"[2] it is parsimonious to reduce it.

The first song, *How many miles to Babylon?* (and hence the cycle), has a monophonic opening that flouts – and thereby draws attention to – the chord-based norm of the Warlockian oeuvre. It states B flat minor and is substantiated by the harmonised second phrase: minor 7ths both affirm the family precedents and anticipate the harmonic changes about to ensue. The chromaticism of bar 3 is pivotal rather than merely decorative – it heralds the B flat major of the last two bars. Again, this is not merely a *tierce de Picardie*, even an extended one, but a new mode (or scale) centred on the same note as before. At only five bars' duration this is Warlock's shortest song and is given in full at Ex. 12.1.

To exaggerate a contrast in duration between the first two songs, the quasi-refrain ("T'other little tune . . .") of *I won't be my father's Jack* is used twice in succession. The duality of *How many miles to Babylon* has become ambiguity, encapsulated in the E flat/natural dispute that shapes the first six bars, inspiring in the process some of the most extreme parallel, falling semitones that Warlock wrote (Ex.12.2). Despite the suggestions of the key-signature (and emphasised by the E flats), the centre seems to be G with the Es flat and natural as alternative modal signifiers. The vocal melody avoids both but does use F sharp, at least to begin with. E flat is suddenly sounded at bar 7 without any preparation other than that which has been referred to and, after a short chromatic passage (much as the pivotal chromaticism in the previous movement) is established as the new centre; this is harmonically maintained through the remainder of the song. The melody, on the other hand, while it accepts E flat between bars 7 and 10, thereafter hovers around G for the duration. G is the mediant of E flat, of course, and it may appear an unnecessary complication to suggest a duality of centre in this way. But, given the discrepancies presented at the beginning and Warlock's multimodal tendencies in the past, such a construction is not out of keeping. G is the last note to be sounded by the piano after the little pentatonic flourishes of the closing bars.

Robin and Richard is written in the Mixolydian mode (the E-centre is supported by a signature of three, rather than four, sharps). The E pedal is joined by another, on B, in the voice and the melodic component, hardly a fully-fledged tune, is played on the piano creating pentatonic chords in the process (Ex. 12.3). The vocal melody eventually has a

Ex. 12.2: *I won't be my father's Jack (Candlelight)* – bars 1-6

pentatonic tendency too and the Mixolydian basis sparks off a flat-side circle-of-5ths. From all these points of view the sudden appearance of D sharp at the end of the melody is startling. In this way Warlock can employ a tonally unremarkable device – a leading note – and turn it into something foreign and even exciting within an otherwise modal context.

The text of *O my kitten* is repeated in its entirety and the resulting 16 allegretto bars constitute the longest song (in time) of the twelve. Much of the musical material remains the same, too, although alterations to chordal choice of the sort witnessed in earlier songs are also apparent here (but not excessively so because of the reduced scale). Once again, both melody and harmony show a Mixolydian influence; this time, the key-signature suggests D major and Cs are naturalised or re-sharpened as appropriate. Melodic (and harmonic) Cs do vary according to musica ficta although there are stretches where they are ignored altogether. The whole ambience of the song is very gentle and easy-going. The limited

Ex. 12.3: *Robin and Richard (Candlelight)* **– bars 5-8**

Allegretto

Ro- bin and Rich- ard were two pret - ty men, They lay in bed till the

clock struck ten.

chromaticism of the second presentation only involves a G sharp so it has the air of an aborted modulation. It serves as a foil for the next song, *Little Tommy Tucker*, a presto outburst of vigorous pandiatonicism ostensibly within a framework of G major (or G Ionian – the voice has no accidentals despite the piano harmonies). The most extreme chords are reserved for the introduction and (Ex. 12.4) the coda while the sung portion depends for its harmonic effect on Fs sharp and natural (Ionian and Mixolydian signifiers).

The opening chordal material of *There was an old man* is first pentatonic and then, with the appearance of G natural, Dorian. This figure works as an ostinato for six of the twelve bars. The voice makes no reference to any sort of G at any stage, indeed does little beyond state the B flat-centre. Apart from the low F anacrusis, the range is restricted to a 5th from B flat up to F. The D natural in bar 8 could suggest the major on B flat or, in collaboration with the instrumental G naturals, Mixolydian once again. These characteristics return in the last four bars (9-12) after two others in which the chords break with the material

Ex. 12.4: *Little Tommy Tucker (Candlelight)* **– bars 10-13**

already established. The aggregations of these bars (8-9) have family associations and, although their non-functional nature maintains the methodology of the opening (and of *Little Tommy Tucker*), their blatant dissonances are startling. This applies particularly to the chord at 8ii, a fusion of *Curlew* and German 6th shapes (Ex.12.5).

Ex. 12.5: *There was an old man (Candlelight)* **– bar 8 (part)**

I had a little pony packs a relatively large amount of material into 20 presto bars. The piano introduction implies a C-centred, Dorian mode at the outset (all As naturalised) although an occasional A flat (demanded by the key-signature) creeps in later. The melody, meanwhile, favours a G-centred Aeolian that gravitates towards C in the middle. The 5ths-based chords and parallel motion that was becoming more and more a feature of the 1922 songs here becomes the essence of the writing as Ex. 12.6, the closing four bars, illustrates. The feature is extended to the point of excluding the 3rd from the final chord (hence denying a tonal cadence). The dissonances of bars 13-16 are prompted by the discrepant A natural/flat (the chord at 14ii contains both)

Ex. 12.6: *I had a little pony (Candlelight)* – bars 12-20

although they also qualify as fusions of semitonally modified family-chords that constitute a mock circle-of-5ths progression.

Little Jack Jingle contains the only genuine modulation of the cycle so far. Its F major diatonicism contrasts with the preceding three songs. Alongside them it sounds conventionally sweet to the point of tweeness for its hero has a similarly sickly, counter-Warlockian attitude to life. The semitonally shifted melodic sequence of bars 9-10 prompts a harmonic move to A major, the dominant of the relative that could have been anticipated by the chromatic C sharp in the piano introduction at the end of bar 2 and which is once again referred to in the coda at the end of bar 14. Whatever its origins, its suddenness is on a par with the dissonance and non-functional juxtapositions in preceding movements. It is appropriate to draw a parallel with *Rantum tantum*, the tonal properties of which only make sense when set against its companion pieces.

There was a man of Thessaly reinstates the energetic qualities set by *Little Tommy Tucker* and *I had a little pony*. Verbal material is once again repeated; the re-use of the last four (short) lines of text matches the melodic recycling of the first phrase and also extends the song to offer a durational statement (more content than the previous one but shorter, and shorter too than the next but with much the same amount of content); there is no alteration to the musical material such as has been experienced elsewhere. The introduction exhibits a number of representatives of the chordal family, *Curlew*, pentatonic (both four- and five-note) and German 6th chords, that reappear in the verse harmony. They mock the F sharp minor tonic-dominant bass-line that meanwhile endeavours to assert itself and which, during the verse, gives way to a Baroque passacaglia figure. This shape asserts itself again for the second half of the verse (in A). The B flat 7th chord that takes the place of a more conventional pivot arises from a semitonal displacement of the principal melodic motif and provides yet another example of Warlock's willingness to distort conventional tonal procedures.

Suky you shall be my wife contains the most extreme Warlockian circle-of-5ths of all. The song commences innocuously enough in E flat with some pretty and purely diatonic, dissonances. As in the past, the instability grows from a Mixolydian 7th, a D flat in the melody (which has previously evaded commitment to any kind of 7th) doubled in the piano. This extends as far as A major (B double-flat), the most distant centre from E flat, where it rests for the whole of bar 12 – it would appear that Suky's suitor is motivated by more than mere affection. The reversion to the initial tonality is sudden; the C sharp of the A major chord is retained as an enharmonic link and is added to the E flat chord that ensues to make a 7th, echoing the Mixolydian signifier that began the move four bars earlier (Ex. 12.7).

The chromaticism of *There was an old woman* stems, as has so often been the case, from the use of alternative modal signifiers – D naturals and flats denote Dorian and Aeolian modes respectively in an F context. The former is the more common but the situation is complicated and extended by the E and B naturals and G flat of bar 2, a situation given little credence by the succeeding material which reverts to the Dorian in both melody and harmony. It is only halfway through the song that these notes, or others derived from them, begin to assert themselves so that, in bars 10-12, the D flat (Aeolian) signifier re-establishes itself and acts as a trigger for the B double-flat chromatic passing note (Ex. 12.8). This, along with the earlier notes, provides the basis for the octatonic line

Ex. 12.7: *Suky you shall be my wife (Candlelight)* **– bars 9-13**

Ex. 12.8: *There was an old woman (Candlelight)* **– bars 9-12**

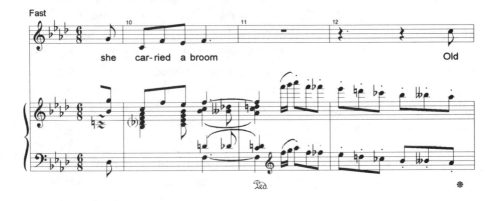

(actually Messiaen's Mode IV) that includes F flat (E natural) C flat (B natural) and B double-flat again, as well as the Aeolian D natural. This shape in turn provides the stimulus for more general chromaticism rich in family chords (although, by this stage all but one of the 12 pitches has been announced).

But none of this fully prepares for the pre-cadential chords in bar 22: the first of them is a spread whole-tone cluster, the second nearly is. So rich are they that the ensuing perfect cadence is reduced to the roots of the usual chords (Ex. 12.9).

Ex. 12.9: *There was an old woman* – bars 22-23

Most of the songs in this cycle are short and fast and *There was an old woman* is no exception. But for sheer busyness the last song, *Arthur o' Bower*, outdoes the rest by virtue of its climactic bravado. The rhythmic bluster conceals a contradiction between voice and piano: the key-signature suggests A flat major, a fact not disputed by the four bars of introduction although the broken, 3rd-less E flat chord of the first bar takes on the air of a tonic and the (broken, 3rd-less) A flat chord of the second sounds like a subdominant in consequence. The uncertainty is heightened when the voice enters. The vocal G flat suggests a Mixolydian 7th, especially in the light of received knowledge – the piano is non-committal and employs a pentatone-derived arpeggio. As the melody develops it assumes an outline determined by an Aeolian mode on E flat, though, thereby confirming the pose of the first introductory bar as the centre. Once more the keyboard avoids resolving the dichotomy, this time by employing chromatically confusing material – in this case there has been no careful presentation of semitonal adjustments earlier in the song, the technique employed elsewhere. And, when the time comes, there is no recognisable cadence; the conclusion is effected by a double A flat arpeggio (with 3rds this time) approached from a C flat 9th that further contributes towards the wayward impression. *Tumultuosissimamente* is more of an *affekt* than an indication of tempo.

Much of the constructional technique of *Candlelight* has already been encountered in other pieces but what Warlock demonstrates in this cycle is a conciseness of approach not previously seen. The concentration of devices and attitudes into such restricted areas results in settings that, in earlier songs, might have been reserved for the later, developed verses of a strophic structure. Indeed, any triviality inherent in the texts does not extend into the music; the strength of the melodic construction and the relationship between the constructional elements is the same as – or better than – that of longer songs and, had more substantial texts been employed, the material presented in the individual songs of this cycle would have been suitable for more extensive treatment. But it is in the distillation of procedures that these pieces demonstrate their effect. There are no more examples of this particular approach in Warlock's output although the *Candlelight* songs do suggest a changing attitude towards constructional procedures in general, something that will continue to be apparent through the remaining discussion.

Jenny Gray (1923) has much in common with the *Candlelight* songs; it is another monostrophic nursery rhyme which, despite its lack of any tempo direction, echoes the more lively constituents of the collection. If taken too slowly the harmonic richnesses become ponderous. The many dissonances are mostly appoggiaturas, often multiple and audacious, whose resolutions are not conventional. On the other hand, the dissonant aggregations can be explained in other ways, chiefly as pentatones.

The melody depends more heavily on the instrumental chords than had been the case in *Candlelight*. Although it initially uses an E-based Aeolian mode, this breaks down for four bars at the beginning of the second half. The piano has effected a pseudo-modulation to A at the beginning of bar 10 and the notes employed melodically, between bars 11-14 inclusive, do conform to A-centred modes and scales before the return to E in bars 15-18. This seems unnecessarily fussy when chordal juxtaposition is the most striking feature.

The harmonic intent is apparent from the start of bar 2; the pentatonic chord can be considered as a multiple appoggiatura that resolves on to a B chord, although this is reduced to only two notes, and the more complete version that follows is at the wrong pitch (Ex. 12.10a). There is a similar occurrence with motivically related material at the end: the pentatone is only achieved as the result of a resolution of the double appoggiatura that precedes it, and is itself resolved on to the final E major chord, again at the wrong pitch (Ex. 12.10b).

The modal instabilities of the melody in the second half of the song are anticipated to an extent by the piano. C sharp in the pentatonic chord of bar 2, referred to above, is also a Dorian mode signifier and it is used considerably throughout the song, alternating with (the Aeolian) C

Ex. 12.10: *Jenny Gray* – bars 2 & 19-20 (piano only)

natural. In this context, the G sharp that appears momentarily in bar 6, a portent of the same note at the very end of the piece, is a representative of another E-final mode. The C sharp is, of course, a constituent of the aforementioned A chord that is reached with such a lack of conviction in bar 10. This chord is not so much a modulatory achievement as a springboard for the subsequent D-chord, itself a point of departure for the ensuing material. Such a quantity of contradictory and wayward material in a short setting of a banal text appears to express Warlock's attitude to tonal references: by subjecting them to this degree of over-use he reduces their structural significance. It is as though the composer were equating the fluctuation of implied note-centres with the triviality of the verbal sense, an evaluation that can also be applied retro-spectively to *Rantum tantum*.

Lillygay and *Candlelight* mark the beginning of what can be seen as Warlock's mature style. The chordal origins have been refined to just a few and their horizontal manifestation has been achieved (in the use of a limited number of modes). Melody too has assumed its rôle as the means whereby chordal progress is smoothed. It is still dependent on the "melody of chords" with which it is coincident and is often shaped by chordal outlines but it has become a more self-assured and credible entity in itself, strong enough to bear repetition within strophic structures or to stand up for itself in shorter forms. In these little pieces where there is limited (or no) opportunity to develop material in the usual Warlockian way, the relationship between melody and harmony is heightened. Melodically the *Candlelight* tunes are among Warlock's most successful and his increased linear confidence is announced by the exposed vocal statement that opens the first song. The initial unease inherent in the minor qualities of the statement creates a faint echo of that other moment of unaccompanied insecurity, *He hears the cry of the sedge*, the last movement of *The curlew*.

Notes
1   MP p.140
2   idem.

CHAPTER 13

Three pseudonyms (1)
Amorous and pastoral

It has already been stated that, during his life, Philip Heseltine wrote under a variety of pseudonyms[1] of which only one has become well known. Gray, in his biography of 1934, imposed the sinister characteristics that have become so associated with "Peter Warlock" that rational assessment has been made more difficult than it should be. But Warlock's noms-de-plume simply delineate his numerous activities, musical and literary and, if they can be considered a comment on his character, draw attention to his wit, ingenuity, acumen and invention. The remainder of his output does the same. It can be conveniently subdivided into three categories of songs (or song texts – although Warlock is very capable of implying sentiments in his music that enlarge, not always in the most obvious way, those of his chosen words). It goes without saying that any credible composer will display a breadth of emotional statements in his music. If Warlock's methods lacked flexibility, he may have only been able to churn out clones of *Captain Stratton's fancy* or *The cricketers of Hambledon*. There would have been no *Shrouding of the Duchess of Malfi*, *The fox* or *The frostbound wood*, let alone *Heraclitus*, *The curlew* or *The distracted maid*.

For it is worth pointing out in advance that by far the largest of these groupings (31 songs) sets the more serious, philosophical sort of text. Those with which he may be more readily associated are smaller – pastoral and amorous (17 songs, not all of them light or otherwise frivolous in their intent); hearty and robust (14 songs, and not necessarily all of the drinking variety). These personae stand as alternative pseudonyms, then. They are as harmless as the others he used but are more conformist and have a greater cultural acceptability.

Milkmaids (1923) is another piece in a folksong style and its simple structure reflects the charms of its subject to produce a very satisfying result. A five-stanza[2] strophic song, it has an expansive, Mixolydian melody that sounds the 7th in the upper octave only. Such an idealistic image of these country girls requires only limited harmonic chromaticism that largely depends upon the Mixolydian/Ionian 7ths and the leading note of the dominant achieved in the middle of each verse (though not necessarily at precisely the same relative point each time); the climactic "For you have kisses plenty" economically incorporates these same notes, along with an A flat that prepares the subsequent E flat chord, to create an element of *double entendre* (Ex. 13.1). No doubt had "ladyes" been equally generous, the style would have been otherwise. The three-note motif (rising 2nd plus minor 3rd) is used here not so much as a means for melodic growth as a way of avoiding the 7th in the melody (also evident in Ex. 13.1) and imparting too serious an intent.

Ex. 13.1: *Milkmaids* – bars 45-47

The sycamore tree (1923) was added to *Tyrley tyrlow* and *Balulalow* to constitute the *Three carols*.[3] It was the only one of the three specifically written to be sung with an orchestra (the others were arranged). It may be thought appropriate for discussion alongside other quasi-religious songs (like *The birds* or *Carillon carilla*), but Warlock latches on to the rustic aspect of the text and gives it a skipping, compound metre and a straightforward, four-verse strophism that is in unison most of the time. Its most striking feature is the polymetrical treatment of the beginning of the third verse that briefly, though less spectacularly, recurs in the instrumental coda. Warlock writes in a mode rather than alluding to it by the use of accidentals – as in *Robin and Richard*, the Mixolydian is supported by the signature or, in this instance, the lack of one. A final G means that there is, inevitably, some F natural/sharp interplay but, for the greater part of the song, the latter is the only accidental in evidence and does not complicate the bucolic serenity. The only exceptions to this are a perfunctory dominant move in bar 30 (necessitating C sharps in one chord only), a similar occurrence in bar 45, and some flat-side contradictions of the rising 4ths and 5ths (D-G and G-D) that conclude the piece as mirrors of the beginning.

A sharpened F (in preference to the natural) is not always regulated by the conventions of musica ficta. This is particularly true in the vocal line but the perversity moderates after the first two verses. Thereafter, the melody is amended to conform but, in the second half of verse 3, it is abandoned altogether in favour of an unaccompanied chordal passage that has nothing to do with the line it replaces. The resulting chords are bland and conform to a strict G major. This assumption of a key arises not just from polymodal manifestations; it denies the attempt at modulation that precedes it, reasserting the G-centre without reverting completely to its modal origins (Ex. 13.2). Its textural simplicity also helps to recover the metre after four bars of instability and provides a contrast with the parallel, widely spread chords that precede it.

I have a garden (1924) may be a revision of a piece from 1910, called *A child's song*.[4] It is difficult to say just how much (if anything) of an earlier song survives for, while some aspects can be described in the same terms as, for example, the 1911 pieces, other details appear to belong to a post-1917 scenario. Triplet figures enhance the pulse in the way that they do in *Music when soft voices die* and arpeggios recall *The cloths of Heaven* – but the latter also look forwards to *Ha'nacker mill* (1927) and the number of modal references does not tie in with the authenticated first compositions. The D-centred modality is delivered in a way familiar from the Winthrop Rogers and later songs: the 6th is first omitted, then B flat (Aeolian) is introduced, only to give way to the Dorian B natural. The only other melodic accidental is the F sharp that suggests a shift of centre to G, although it is actually chromatic, momentarily obfuscating the eventual move to F. The modulation itself is clumsy and the dissonances too prominent. In a straightforward, mostly triadic, harmony that mirrors a pedestrian verbal imagery, procedures made interesting elsewhere deteriorate into the matter-of-fact.

Indeed, there is an absence of the sort of chords associated with the early songs. Some of the choice, similar to the opening of the contemporary *Twelve oxen* with its forced modal allusions and parallel (or nearly so) deployment, has a distinctly recent feel to it and there are other details that recall specific usages elsewhere: the flourish in bar 6 is similar in spirit to the beginning of *Hey troly loly lo* and a snatch of melody in bars 12-13 anticipates *And wilt thou leave me thus* (1928);

Ex. 13.2: *The sycamore tree* – bars 30-34

the phrase before it (bars 10-11) recalls *Love for love*. Add to these the references mentioned above and there emerges the picture of song pasted together from a diversity of components. This is not, of itself, a weakness but there is no single factor that binds it together. It appears to have more of the new than the old in it but some of the melody does sound about right for an early song, particularly in the way that material is chromatically adjusted from one appearance to another.

The carol *Chanson du jour de Noël* (1925), one of Warlock's rare settings of a language other than English, was the first solo-song written after his move to the Kent village of Eynsford.[5] Like *The sycamore tree* it is more plebeian, more artisan in this case, than religious in tone. The Ionian melody, centred on C, incorporates repetition not suggested by the words. The result is a strophic song of two relatively long verses, each with the form AABB. It is surprising that, given this amount of melodic re-use, there is no correspondingly alternative chord-choice – its manufacture is as unsophisticated as its "laboureur". Harmonic difference within and between verses is very small. Two pairs of isolated quavers in each verse (at the starts of the B sections) are foci for harmonic variation and enhance the verbal and rhythmic drive but, on the last occasion, further change is difficult and the ensuing bar is altered instead (Ex. 13.3). Otherwise the differences – and, hence, in a Warlockian context, structural growth – only result from chordal inversion or thickening.

By contrast, *Pretty ring time* (1925) is a song in the classic Warlock mould. Mixolydian tendencies in the melody are anticipated by the

Ex. 13.3: *Chanson du jour de Noël* – bars 8-10, 13-15, 25-27 & 30-32

chords of the introduction although both parts are tempered by the alternative, raised 7th. In the course of each verse, the lowered 7th initiates a number of references to flat-side centres. Another characteristic, met with before, is the limitation to the piano of modulatory accidentals; each verse moves to the dominant at the end of the third line of the text but it is important to consider this sort of gesture not so much in terms of conventional, unquestioned practice as a necessity, a counter to the Mixolydian-generated, flat-side chords that follow. In other words, this Warlockian technique needs a sharp-side modulation beforehand and the key-change does not occur as a formal inevitability.

The circle-of-5ths, a frequent route to the flat side, is not as extended as was the case in *Suky you shall be my wife* even though it promises otherwise. Instead it is interrupted; it reaches D flat (the chord on the Mixolydian 7th) only after resorting to sequence and then lurches back towards the tonic. Halfway through this progression it momentarily restates the tonic via the dominant chord of B flat. As a variant on this in later verses the progress is amended, once more by a Mixolydian signifier, to incorporate a B flat minor chord (Ex. 13.4a-b).

The countryman (1926) is a pleasantly unexceptional piece that romanticises the rustic worker. The F-centred, Ionian melody has, like other songs with similar verbal sentiments, a pentatonic component and it spills into the harmony. Harmonic difference between verses is negligible; it relies chiefly on redistributions of individual chords or the addition of more notes for climactic effect. The only occasion where the harmony substantially differs (there are a few isolated chords) is towards the end of the second verse, necessitating an alteration to the vocal melody. Because it is a single instance, it sounds incongruous.

Fair and true (1926) has little to commend it either; a melody, stagnant in both shape and intent, is enhanced in vain by chromatic harmonies that have little allegiance either to a centre or the family. To reverse the expression, Warlock's chords only have limited melodic potential. A descending quaver motif fails to impose order. The melodic evasion of the 7th in the first verse (an established and creative technique in other songs) is readily given up in the second and third and the chromaticism lacks the modal ordering (or any other sort) found elsewhere. Copley is equally dismissive but less charitable and quotes the excesses![6]

Walking the woods (1927) uses perpetual quavers, matched by the piano, in a folksong melody and the homorhythmic result has a marked horizontal flow that does not follow the triple-time metre

Ex. 13.4: *Pretty ring time* – bars 7-11 & 31-35

unquestioningly. This quality alone is sufficient to make the song work over its three verses. The Mixolydian 7ths are not as exploited as elsewhere and the chromaticism in the last verse tries too hard. These shortcomings aside, it is unfortunate that a string-quartet version of this song has not materialised.[7] It should be easy to reconstruct.

Passing by (1928),[8] the other, fuller setting of the same anonymous text as *There is a lady sweet and kind*, presents something of a problem

when analysing Warlock's oeuvre; it fails to conform to the received –
particularly the contemporary – archetype on several counts. It is overtly
tonal – in G – and modulates to the dominant, but its change of centre
stops short of the sort of paratonal instability that will be seen to arise in
Cradle song and *Mockery* (both 1927) and which was prophesied in
such songs as *Whenas the rye* and *Suky you shall be my wife*. It exhibits
no real modal tendencies, the sense of the tonal G being too strong to
claim even a theoretical D-based Ionian/Mixolydian in the voice. And,
although family chords are in evidence, there are many others that do
not belong. Their apt, if ephemeral, sensuousness counters a text that
proclaims chaste longing. The structural rationale of the song is
becoming reliant on motif, more than has been the case; although there
are pentatonic references, the logic depends largely on a four-note,
rising figure, heard most strongly at the vocal entry but also elsewhere
in both parts, sometimes as an inversion/retrograde (as in *Sigh no more
ladies* (1927), another motif-dependent song). Ex. 13.5 reduces the first
verse to show the principal references.

Ex. 13.5: *Passing by* – use of 2nds in the first verse

The basic shape can also be considered as two pairs of seconds, heard in isolated, falling forms in the introduction (though complete in an inner part) and occasionally contracted to three notes (two overlapping pairs of 2nds) thereby relating it even more to *Sigh no more ladies*. While pentatonicism is a device used mainly in the introduction, vertically and horizontally, and it is a lesser feature of the melody too, its rôle in the piece as a whole is limited. The song is difficult to assess in terms of Warlock's developed compositional procedures. But, even if many of the more familiar features are not present, what remains is a continuing experimentation and concern with chordal progress. The motivic 2nds that bind the chords together are only tenuously derived from familiar material (in that 2nds of one sort or the other are constituents of linear versions of all the family chords – they convert chords into modes). Parallelism, a device that features in contemporary songs, is present here too; the consecutive 5ths of bars 4-5 and similar locations are motivically pertinent but their blatancy (as a tonally unacceptable procedure) questions the modulatory convention that succeeds them. It is of interest that, in the third verse, chordal choice at the modulation is modified to include an Italian 6th; the subsequent chromatic departure dilutes the change of centre by exaggerating the resultant instability (Ex. 13.6a-b).

Ex. 13.6: *Passing by* **– bars 21-23 & 25-27**

(a) Will make a law-yer burn his books;   (b) And yet I love her till I die.

Melodic change within what is really a strophic form is also motif-dependent. The introductory figure cannot fulfil the inter-verse function it has elsewhere without destroying the cumulative effect of the words but its countermelodic use in verse 3 is transferred to the voice in the next. These changes herald those of the concluding, sixth verse where both vocal and instrumental material is modified, the latter picking up the mediant-major interruption that closed verse 5. If *The curlew* is a precedent in the managing of longer structures, the scale of *Passing by* (compared with the earlier setting and many other songs) may also warrant a linear approach. The fact remains that, for all its qualities, it is problematical in terms of Warlock's compositional consistency.

The passionate shepherd is also concerned with changes of key and picks up the G-B relationship that appears towards the end of *Passing by*. By doing this it recalls earlier songs such as *My little sweet darling, Late summer* and *Rest sweet nymphs* where references to the mediant major also appear. The change of centre destroys the pentatonicism briefly promised at the start of the melody, but this tonal allusion initiates the circle-of-5ths. The device is used elsewhere to disorient but here, although subject to modification, it confirms the song's G-focus.

The passionate shepherd – and this is true of most of its companion pieces[9] – is a competent, if speedily written, piece[10] that, like other, more successful ventures[11] can only be considered to have been written with money in mind. Like *Passing by* it is dependent upon motifs based on 2nds. The first bar of the melody deploys these within a pentatonic environment and there are, consequently, some familiar shapes present (Ex. 13.7). But Warlock's melodies tend to be simple and scalic anyway – the use of 2nds has already been frequently encountered. This song is

Ex. 13.7: *The passionate shepherd* – bars 3-10 (vocal line only)

something of an exception in that respect: 2nds are used as isolated units, not aggregated to make longer runs, and arpeggios take over from them after only a few bars. As was the case too in the motivic nature of *Passing by*, there is a tendency towards an increased emphasis on autonomous melody rather than the linear but chordally derived emphasis prevalent since the Rogers songs.

One outcome, in *The passionate shepherd* at any rate, is a sense of a strong tune to which chords have been fitted. The modal element has all but disappeared and there is a stronger reliance on tonality; the circle-of-5ths in this situation strengthens such a state of affairs rather than producing the disorientation that has been the case elsewhere. The comments made earlier about the device in relation to *Dedication* still apply,[12] but that was a more experimental work that Warlock chose not to repeat.

Tom Tyler modulates from G to D although the sudden use of an A chord in bar 8 had been anticipated in bar 6. On both occasions it appears straight after a chord of G – the move is not smoothed by a conventional pivot. The C natural in bar 7 creates, within an overt tonal procedure, a passing sense of an A-centred Dorian after the Mixolydian implications of the C sharp. But the pre-eminence of a G-centred tonality is too strong for this oversubtle allusion and the reference is swamped. Even the parallel 5ths in the lower piano part cannot adequately mock the familiarity of the modulation. Parallel 5ths are a frequent, though not obsessive, device throughout the song and further examples can be found at bars 13-14, 15-16, 31, 39-40 and corresponding points in repetitions of the material. In this song, the essentially triadic nature of the chord-choice (there are some pentatone chords but they are few and far between) needs the piquancy of these moments. Its brisk, compound metre has an inevitability that mirrors the ironic fatalism of the words and this may be enough to deem it successful. Otherwise, it offers little to enhance Warlock's status as a serious composer; some of its failure can be ascribed to the fact that the melody preceded the choice of chords and was not, anyway, of Warlock's devising.[13]

Eloré lo also depends on the forward drive of its metrical – or, in this case, antimetrical[14] – melody and the piano part has a similar, linear tendency that often eschews chords for their own sake in favour of, for example, parallel motion between implied parts. While this can sometimes involve strings of 7ths, the family connection is limited and, in the allegretto con moto context, juxtapositions such as the chords of C sharp minor and F major (bar 11) pass by almost unnoticed, vertical frissons in a mainly horizontal texture. The melody is regulated by F-centred Mixolydian and Ionian modes and, if B flat is occasionally naturalised, this is chromatic rather than modulatory. Tonal movement, then, is avoided, and the song is a more successful venture than *Tom Tyler*, for example. Nevertheless, the reluctance to vary material, even in a quick piece, is disappointing given prior knowledge of Warlock's techniques.

The strophism of *Eloré lo* engenders no significant chordal modifications but the situation is remedied somewhat by *The contented lover*. Through-composition provides a more satisfactory solution in a short, intense song that recalls the romanticism of *Late summer*. But persistent quaver motion, chord-based despite its horizontal aspect, creates affinities with *Take o take those lips away* in *Saudades*. The texture here is less dense and uses very few vertical chord-shapes and, while the use of the same key- and time-signature in both songs may be only coincidental, four flats is fairly rare for Warlock.

A greater tonal confidence in this song makes it the most endearing of the seven. It teeters between F minor and A flat even if extended tonal usage results in other references too (F major, for example). The semitone is much in evidence as a modifying force although Warlock's peculiar use of it – to change modal signifiers – is not. Melodically the F minor/A flat relationship is maintained and the F major passage at the beginning of the second verse is also taken up by the voice. The choice of this particular scenario is curious; there is not the verbal justification evident in *Late summer* unless Warlock is using it again to symbolise a complete and rewarding relationship. The song is, nevertheless, striking within the set as a whole for it maintains the linearity of the others without assuming their corporately harmonic blandness.

The contented lover, then, recalls earlier work. But so does *The droll lover*: here the antecedent is *Sweet content*, not just motivically (in the way that the instrumental, falling semiquavers cut across the bar line) but in its use of alternative degrees, 7ths in the latter, 6ths in the former. This suggests a modal basis for some of the material of the later song and is, indeed, the case. There is a nice ambiguity in the vocal part not just as to whether the delineator is a G-based Aeolian (with an E flat) or a Dorian (with an E natural) but whether G is the final at all; there is, at times, also a sense of a Dorian with a C final or a Mixolydian with an F final: both of these employ the same notes as the first-named mode. Such dichotomies chime well with the verbal perversity.

Warlock divides the verbal material into two verses and exercises not a little ingenuity in creating differences of harmonic nuance between the two. The audacious setting of "I love thee for thy ugliness/And for thy foolery" is particularly appropriate, the parallelism being the only feature that holds it together (Ex. 13.8). But the song as a whole lacks the motivic strength of *Sweet content* and this despite the more naïve approach of the earlier song and the motivic awareness of the later one's contemporaries. However, it must be pointed out that, given the harmonic concentration in this piece, its brevity is essential. Or, put

Ex. 13.8: *The droll lover* **– bars 31-35**

another way, the brevity imposed by the words demands a concise, even brutally uncompromising, treatment.

The sweet o' the year, by contrast, offers little in the way of new material from verse to verse. This is particularly unfortunate for the melody includes an ambiguous modulation ripe for exploitation: the line, substantially F-Ionian, is broken in the fourth bar of each stanza by a motif which, by virtue of its B natural, could belong to a D or G mode. In fact, Warlock keeps to the latter and seems to make a statement about his own attitude to the relationship between F and G centres – also to be heard in *Capriol* (1926). This is the main interest within a song that, like the others in the set, is agreeable enough but does not want to take the sort of risks that characterised earlier material.

And much the same could be said about *Youth*, the third attempt at a text used in *Lusty Juventus* and *In an arbour green*. It is acceptably, if plainly, strophic with a tune dependent on single-line phrases and four-square rhythms. The melody is principally in an F-centred Ionian mode although there is a shift to the mediant major in the third line of each verse. The melody can, in fact, be broken down into a number of family-chord motifs: the first line is set to a broken major 6th (minor 7th) chord followed by a four-note shape derived from a pentatone; the second line is strictly pentatonic; the third, which incorporates the shift, is simply a transposition of the first; the last line, except for a rogue B flat quaver, is also pentatonic. The various pentatonic elements in the first, second and last lines utilise the same notes so the transposition in the respective third lines assumes an even greater importance.

The internal repetition of each verse extends into the piano writing. Pentatonic chords are in evidence here, too, but there is no real difference from one verse to the next. The octave transpositions in the last create, as elsewhere, a textural change but offer little contrast beyond this. The A major line, then, which utilises a chordal as well as a melodic transposition, must serve as the only diversion in the piece.

So, while these seven songs contain moments of Warlock at his most adroit, taken together, they fail to sustain his achievement in the way that the five songs of *Lillygay*, written during the security of his stay in Wales, had done. Indeed, they show him back-pedalling, relying on basic formulae and techniques long-established. The financial demise that was to take him from the comfortable companionships of Eynsford was imminent and it would be charitable to excuse the set for that reason. They do demonstrate, in a limited way, a continuing struggle for linear credibility; he endeavours to achieve this motivically, a technique that, while it is present to a greater or lesser extent in other pieces, has never been of paramount importance. *The frostbound wood* (1929) will be more positive, although it too stops short of a level of integration between vertical and horizontal components that is provocatively promised but never delivered.

On the surface, *The fairest may* (1930) is a new version of *As ever I saw*, written over a decade beforehand. The four-square rhythms of the latter, restrained in terms of the amorous nature of the words, are transmuted here into a much more appropriate compound metre that dances its way through the text. Most of the original chords and shapes reappear, albeit in a new metrical guise; the effect is very satisfactory, more so than before, and the rather staid young lady of 1918 becomes an altogether more interesting prospect. But what makes the piece striking is not the harmonic content which, after all, belongs to the experiments of the Rogers songs, but the injection of linear decorations. These, it cannot be denied, create something of a sense of the Renaissance or the early Baroque; they are similar to those in, for example, Morley's *First book of consort lessons* of 1599 or, more appropriate to Warlock's own interests, Italianate influences in Purcell's output. But Warlock has not fabricated a piece of pseudo-antique music. His own individual techniques are as evident as are Stravinsky's in *Pulcinella*; to see either work as emanating principally from its respective composer's musicological experiences is to miss the point.

Little more need be said about its chordal and melodic language beyond the comments on its earlier manifestation. A single quotation

(Ex. 13.9) sums up its approach although the extravagant curlicues in the epilogue are not structural. The basis is as it was in 1919 (given a

Ex. 13.9: *As ever I saw* – bars 40-43 & *The fairest may* – bars 40-45

few unimportant alterations); it serves as a warning to those who would describe Warlock's work from a standpoint influenced by his other interests. The research may have affected the composition but only in a superficial way. Those who profess otherwise are guilty of the biographical fallacy.

After two years (1930) finds Warlock on familiar pentatonic ground and his use of what will be termed the *And wilt thou*-motif[15] is chronologically inevitable. An abstracted sense of B flat minor creates a romantic (in two senses) atmosphere although there are a number of attempts to disorient the piece away from an indisputable centre, not least at the final cadence.

The vocal line is essentially based on two pentatones a 5th apart and the introduction incorporates a scalic figure that is an exposition of the fact; there is no G flat (Ex. 13.10). Its descending line creates another motif that serves as an inter-verse device and, inverted, as an

Ex. 13.10: *After two years* **– piano introduction with pentatonic derivations**

two pentatones combined to form a mode

instrumental decoration in the last verse. But the pitch-availability stated by the introduction appears to be immediately contradicted at the vocal entry for G flat is encountered three times in the space of two bars. However, these appearances account for all but one (the other is in bar 12) of the note's melodic soundings and, of these, only one is given rhythmical prominence by being located on a significant beat. In this B flat environment – substantiated by the occasional use of A natural (in bars 14, 27 and 29) – the absence of G flat creates, as elsewhere[16] a Dorian/Aeolian ambiguity. But the leading-note misfires at the end of the melody; instead of rising to the expected B flat, it shifts to a D flat, an anticipation of the harmonic deviation that will occur in the final bar. This association is the one that will be heard in *Carillon carilla*; it may refer to the relative but it is really another manifestation of Warlock's fascination with the mediant major, a relationship apparent since *My little sweet darling* and *Late summer*.

The song has verse-like sections but there is no literal repetition from one to another, rather a unity that emanates from a shared harmonic and motivic vocabulary. In this through-composed environment, chordal substitution associated with the verse-melody – a feature of Warlock's strophic songs – no longer applies. Instead, alternative harmonisations of the inter-verse material prepare for the final cadence on to D flat. Several times, the *Curlew*-chord takes on a pivotal rôle although it occurs in other situations too. This is not to imply a marked sense of functional harmony and the instrumental epilogue, the introductory figure once more, emphasises this in the way that the final chord is achieved: the A natural in the penultimate, minor 7th shape mirrors the close of the vocal line (Ex. 13.11).

Ex. 13.11: *After two years* – bars 30-32 (piano epilogue)

In these songs, the texts of which express relatively unsophisticated sentiments, Warlock underplays his techniques. He keeps his material simple and even conventional. Perhaps he realised how unsuitable his developed methods were to the sort of words he wanted to set but, while some of these pieces are among his best (*Milkmaids, Passing by* – despite its atypicality – and *The fairest may*) others are unworthy of him; they lack the assurance of the named examples, particularly their balance of melodic and chordal resources. Warlock had a genuine sympathy for popular and light music and, in these songs, seeks to emulate it. In attempting something he believed morally and aesthetically desirable, he misjudged the situation for the best of motives. His strengths lie elsewhere.

Notes
1   Most of these are listed in IC p.12.
2   PW omits four of the original nine verses. See MP p. 139.
3   See IC pp.195 & 214.
4   See IC pp. 198 & 214.
5   PW lived there from January 1925 until November 1928, a time of stable productivity approaching that of the Welsh period. His cottage became a centre for work and play of the most strenuous kind, not just for himself and E J Moeran who shared it with him but, from time to time, for some of the most prestigious figures in English music. Among the visitors were Arnold Bax and ". . . probably Patrick Hadley also . . ." (Foreman (1988) p. 224), Constant Lambert, Diana Poulton, Lord Berners, John Goss, Hubert Foss, Gr and BvD. See note 6, Chapter 14.
6   IC pp. 120-1.
7   See IC p. 289.
8   Curiously – and erroneously – Ernest Bradbury (New Grove vol. 20, p. 213) attributes the melody of this song to Hal Collins, its dedicatee. See note 13.
9   This song and the next six (1928) were entitled *Seven songs of summer* but never appeared as such. PW was anxious for cash so he was prepared to break up the set (IC p. 132). His time at Eynsford would soon end – he could not afford to live there (FT1 p. 44). The songs were published separately by different houses – see MP pp. 154-7. The proposed publication/performance order was: *The passionate shepherd, The contented lover, Youth, The sweet o' the year, Tom Tyler, Eloré lo, The droll lover*. The collective title suggests the season of their composition rather than anything else.
10   The *Seven Songs of summer* were all written in July (FT1) but MP p. 154 gives August – an error? The holographs (BL Add. Ms. 52907) are clearly dated.
11   *Bethlehem Down* is a case in point.
12   See pp.97-8.
13   The tune is based "almost entirely" (PW's expression) on an improvisation by his manservant, Hal Collins. See IC p. 137.
14   Not only does the metre oscillate between 6/8 and 3/4 but the verbal stress takes precedence – "without any regard for bar-line accentuation" according to the score.
15   See p. 306 et seq.
16   As in *The distracted maid*. See p. 195.

CHAPTER 14

Three pseudonyms (2)
Rumbustious and hedonistic

Twelve oxen (1924), a perfunctory amalgam of techniques and devices, lacks a consistent approach beyond its strophism. Although the melody stays intact through all four verses, the imposition of modally derived harmonies on to a strong tonal scheme is unsatisfactory and the assumption of pentatonicism during the refrain is but a distraction. The instrumental opening presents a number of familiar features, chordal parallelism, (tonic) pedal, Mixolydian tendency and chords built on 4ths; with a change in metrical stress it is recycled as inter-verse material through the piece. Variation in the piano part is minimal too; the first and third verses use identical shapes and second-verse material reappears, staccato, in the last. The principal difference between the two manifestations is textural, blending alterations of pitch and rhythm, but the harmonic bases are substantially the same.

The main difference lies in the abandon, verbal and tonal, of the respective refrains where the obbligato second voice emphasises the tonal movement and the social aspect of the words ("With hey! With how!"). Those to the odd-numbered verses favour a circle-of-5ths progression (chords on C sharp-F sharp-B-E-A-D) that, using the vocal C natural as an enharmonic B sharp, lurches to G sharp (which should have stood at the head of the circle – see Ex. 14.1a). The refrains to the even-numbered verses are more harmonically extreme to contextualise the nonsense words. They also start with circles-of-5ths that, some of the additional notes aside, move further to the flat-side (B-E-A-D-G-C-F) against the retained vocal material. They validate the sudden G sharp jump (four places to the sharp-side from E) in the other pair of verses; a decorated chord of F, five steps away from E on the flat-side, takes its place in verses 2 and 4 (bars 35/73 – see Ex. 14.1b). This latter version justifies its flat-side tendency by sounding the Mixolydian 7th, a reference to the introduction/interlude, before settling back on the tonic, a course of action that the earlier harmonisation had not found necessary. Both progressions reach the tonic via a pentatone- (or 4ths-) based chord although the shapes used are different: the one associated with the flat-side circle is a 5th lower than its predecessor and, because

Ex. 14.1: *Twelve oxen* **– bars 12-16 & 31-35**

of the tonal instability caused by the Mixolydian Ds, is reshaped to form a dominant.

Twelve oxen, then, sees Warlock in character, aware of chordal progress, even though the effect relates to tonal, rather than modal or chordal-family practices. The result is, in this case, unsatisfactory. *The toper's song* (1924) reveals a similar situation. The words and tune are of the 18th century[1] so the piece is simply an arrangement of existing strophic material. There is no recomposition, as in the *Folk-song preludes* or *An old song* – the work is a harmony exercise and, since there is no simultaneous composition of vocal and instrumental components, the interest lies in what fits the melody. Despite the tune's not being original to Warlock it accords well with his methods; it is largely Aeolian, on E, but generally avoids the seventh degree; when it does occur, both natural and sharp Ds are used, the latter directly after the former in a semitonal contrast that serves as a reminder of his earliest methods. These features apart, there is little to surprise; the pentatone chords are lost in the rush between the rests and, once more, the differences between verses are largely textural, a few chromatic bursts apart. *The toper's song* fits firmly in the "pot-boiler" category[2] and the false start in A minor is its most exciting feature.

The text of *Peter Warlock's fancy* (1924) resembles that of *Good ale* but the music replaces imprecatory vitality with unsubtle pleading. It is strophic, in five verses, the first of which is expositional. Thereafter there are two harmonic variants, one for verses 2 and 4, the other for 3 and 5. The Ionian mode melody is retained, intact, for all of them. The pentatonic harmonies that punctuate verse 1 give it some respectability but the Mixolydian 7th in bar 18 is a cliché rather than a delight. Some of the harmonic changes are equally unremarkable.

Yarmouth fair (1924) could have gone the same way but its Ionian melody – once more not by Warlock himself – is stronger and the piece, another arrangement, perhaps, rather than an original composition, is more successful. Perhaps it should not be called *Yarmouth fair* at all but *The magpie*.[3] Now that the original text is reunited with its musical partner,[4] it may be more correct to do so. Hal Collins's words must have necessitated minor rewriting for his juxtaposition of three- and five-line units is not as in the original.

Most treatments fit the original words better: accented dissonances towards the end suit "He rained such blows upon my clothes/I feel them to this day;/He kicked me too . ." (*The magpie*) far better than "The lads and lasses cheered us on,/My bonny maid and me,/We danced till stars were in the sky" (which replace them in *Yarmouth fair*) – in fact, while they have some harmonic character, they only work as word-painting in relation to the original version. The piano part, imaginative and entertaining in this respect, uses chromaticism and syncopation both as atmospheric and technical devices.

The lady's birthday and *One more river* (both 1925) are also arrangements, this time of antique, vernacular melodies and very much in Warlock's lighter style but they should not be dismissed for that. *The lady's birthday* is scored for baritone solo, male voice quartet and piano; in spite of the eclectic and inconsequential nature of both tune and text, the harmonic and textural treatments have much to recommend them, not least in the rollicking invention that characterises both elements (and, very often, harmony is texture). On this occasion, Warlock's chords make no concession to the simplicity – the banality, even – of the original melody yet contrives not to get in its way, a real achievement and another indication of the way in which his vocabulary can be manipulated according to circumstance.

The chords-on-4ths, part of the introductory, vocal figure, recall manifestations elsewhere. As in *Lillygay*, the ephemeral gratification of certain chords is no longer enough; there has to be some kind of constructional justification – the force behind recent chordal progress. Here, the chords-on-4ths do not exist for their own sake but relate to the melodic shape. One can only speculate whether the melody appealed because of its chordal associations (as could be claimed for the *Preludes* or *An old song*) or *vice versa*. That there is a link is undeniable. The ensuing pentatone-based chords also link with the earlier melodic stages which use only four notes from the five.

In this strophic song, the verses are identified by harmonic changes, slight in the earlier ones, more marked later. Vocal harmony very much depends on the introductory figure which, as in the solo songs, becomes an interlude between (most) verses; now it penetrates them too and has more of the quality of a ritornello than elsewhere so alterations to it are small and it is left to the piano to perpetrate chordal change, another feature from the solo songs. The only real exception to this state of affairs is the short, parallel passage in verse 4 (Ex. 14.2) and this decorative (rather than constructional, vis-à-vis the song as a whole) statement can be compared to others; the emphasis on 4ths and 5ths is evident and in keeping with chordal statements already made but its immediate function is to enhance "four and twenty singing men". Of

Ex. 14.2: *The lady's birthday* – bars 59-62

greater importance to the total shape are events such as the onomatopoeic chatter (verse 3, Ex. 14.3a), cries of anguish (verse 7, Ex. 14.3b) or aggregate confusion (verse 8, Ex. 14.3c) because there are established points of reference from earlier verses with which comparisons can be made. The last instance is particularly noteworthy

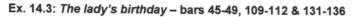

Ex. 14.3: *The lady's birthday* – bars 45-49, 109-112 & 131-136

for it presents a moment of rare, but undeniable, Warlockian bitonality.
The choice of G against the prevailing B flat derives from the G major
(rather than the more predictable minor) chord used to set the second

syllable of "birthday" in all verses but the seventh. Its climactic appearance is not out of character with associated material but its daring prominence within a particular verbal context draws attention to its uniqueness. Previous examples have approached the phenomenon but have fought shy of total commitment. Only in such an extreme verbal situation does Warlock feel completely able to go to such ends.

This song has no metaphysical statement to make, refers to no moment of angst or privation and the verbal emphasis, skilfully matched by the musical imagination, is placed on parody, irony and stereotype, qualities deemed to be aesthetically undesirable. The song is therefore subject to denigration, abuse or, worst of all, neglect.

One more river, another strophic piece arranged for similar resources, lacks the vitality and exoticism of *The lady's birthday* but compensates somewhat by the tongue-in-cheek provision of some semitonally regulated refrain harmonies. It is not just the symbolism of the River Jordan that excites these ironic and exquisitely deplorable chords but their utter inappropriateness to this staple of anthologies for "community singing" (Ex. 14.4). In the previous piece, the chord-choice possessed many moments of interest and even distinction, but did not upset the impetus; now the purpose is just the opposite and some of the

Ex. 14.4: *One more river* – bars 31-34

harmonies are consciously – gloriously – devoid of subtlety. (Those who would pick on such moments in Warlock's output as typical of an assumed decadence miss the point.)[5]

Maltworms (1926) was a collaborative venture with Jack Moeran who shared the Eynsford house with Warlock.[6] The tale of its speedy concoction and Warlock's melodic contribution is well documented.[7] Which harmonies are his and which are Moeran's must be open to conjecture but some are very much in the Warlock mould. The treatment of the choruses to the last two verses with their drone basses and family chords would appear to come from Warlock's pen rather than Moeran's (Ex. 14.5). Like *Captain Stratton's fancy* it has a strong, functional melody; it seems to have had some sustained currency as an alehouse song, too, a real mark of its worth![8]

Ex. 14.5: *Maltworms* **– bars 92-97**

The two verses of *Jillian of Berry* (1926) only last half a minute and its infrequent performance may stem from the effort necessary to make it work. The hedonism of the drinking-song words belies its melodic, harmonic and rhythmic invention (and the instrumental agility it demands) and its diversities imbue it with a quality that may have otherwise proved elusive. The introduction, a single figure in B flat repeated a tone lower (Ex. 14.6) and a clever variant on Warlock's favourite 6ths, demonstrates an evolution from harmonic parallelism to parallel motif: an initially chordal device becomes a linear one. But the figure is also consistent with a multi-modal B flat statement. The ambiguities continue, inevitable when shapes employ the same

Ex. 14.6: *Jillian of Berry* **– bars 1-3**

pitch-material with varying note-centre emphases. The first melodic phrase (the first line of verse) appears to be focused on F; the harmony, inspired by the A flats of the introduction, favours E flat at first. The suggestion of F in the melody is substantiated by the harmonic E natural (in bar 4, the end of the phrase) but only as a point on a circle-of-5ths, a tonal statement to counterbalance the modality that regulates the surrounding detail.

The melody, and the piece in general, reverts to B flat, but note-choice is shaped largely by F-based modes. Apart from a chromatic (*Curlew*) chord at the end of bar 16, accidentals suggest this centre in preference to others – A flat signifies the Dorian, E natural the Ionian/major and D flat the Aeolian. In this context, the overt references to F in the second and sixth bars of each verse are not so much modulations as more forceful manifestations of the modal focus. They explain the otherwise minimal alteration to the harmony of the second verse and the cluster-chords that close the song (Ex. 14.7). The latter create a carefree, almost careless mood to match the anticipation of "thither will we go now". Not only do they have their own distinctive character, the bass notes apart, they confuse the finality of B flat.

Ambiguities similar to those in *Jillian of Berry* mark the opening of *Away to Twiver* (1926),[9] "one of [Warlock's] most original achieve-ments"[10] and, at seven verses long, one of his most extended and triumphant strophic structures. The techniques intensify verse by verse as the narrative develops and its separate incidents aggregate. The piano's opening drone announces the B-centre that is to predominate although, because F sharp is below the B – in second inversion, as it were – the statement is enigmatic. Upper (right-hand) figures proclaim a

Ex. 14.7: *Jillian of Berry* **– bars 21-23:**

B-centred Aeolian mode but their starting point, an E-plus-B open 5th, is momentarily at odds with left-hand information. This is subsequently remedied but, upon the entry of the voice, the left hand assumes an open E chord that persists, albeit with a decaying dynamic to be sympathetically stimulated throughout the first verse. The right hand persists with the B Aeolian exposition (Ex. 14.8). The B/E dichotomy encapsulated in the first chord is also present, but over a longer timescale, in the verse-melody. The rising 5th, E-B, (after the anacrusic D) and the third phrase (bars 8-10) reflect the E-based drone; the G sharp in the latter, though a Dorian signifier in B, marks the Mixolydian in E.

Ex. 14.8: *Away to Twiver* **– bars 4-8**

The second verse is characterised by a pedal B but the associated chords do not resolve the question of note-centre beyond that. Most shapes form a pentatonic ostinato of five- and four-note chords while the only other chord used until well into the verse is that of G major (Ex. 14.9). The reappearance of G sharp (bar 20) and D/D sharp substitutions can be interpreted in terms of E or B modes. Bars 23-24, intermediate

Ex. 14.9: *Away to Twiver* **– bars 13-16**

between verses 2 and 3, offer a resolution of sorts in the 3rd-less B chord to which a D sharp is eventually added; the Aeolian progressions of the third verse, though diatonic (in the style of Vaughan Williams), cannot confirm or deny the superiority of one over the other. The disparity is symbolised by the piano's change of metre: 2/4 against the voice's 6/8 is barely multi-metrical but the difference is enough. C natural (bar 27), incompatible with B, implies an E Aeolian scenario. This is not exclusively maintained and references to G (bar 28) and F sharp (bar 30) cloud the issue. When a B major chord is achieved at the end of the verse it is mocked by the attendant flourish (Ex. 14.10) and launches the harmony back towards E for the start of the next.

Harmony in verse 4 is based on that of the previous one. While subject to amplification, it is not just thickened in the way noted elsewhere: for example, the open chord of bar 30 becomes a pentatone-chord in bar 38. Nevertheless, the similarity between the two verses means that the second of them, at the centre of the song, becomes an area of relative stability, recognised by the voice's assumption of the instrumental 2/4. Even if the B-centre achieved in bar 40 is hailed with an ironic gesture, it is the strongest recognition yet of its hegemony.

The instrumental echo of part of the verse's closing phrase, though, is transposed to E and sets off further, more extreme, deviations from this

Ex. 14.10: *Away to Twiver* **– bars 30-33**

And a - way to Twi- ver a - way,   a - way

centre as the post-nuptial revelry intensifies. Chords once again favour G before the bare dissonances that enhance the "fuddling-cap" carry the confusion into the harmony; the return to B at the end of the verse (without a 3rd in the chord) is surreptitiously effected. In verse 6, all caution is relinquished to evoke the debauch. This is achieved not so much by indeterminacy of centre as brutal dissonances, family chords to which wrong notes have been added (Ex. 14.11). Like the ambivalent attitude to the note-centre before it, this is a preparation for the last verse.

The first half of this appears to be based, harmonically, on G sharp, the first melodic accidental sounded back in bar 10; bass notes are the dominant, tonic and subdominant. To emphasise the discrepancy, Warlock incorporates the vocal melody within the piano part, a feature that would be less remarkable elsewhere for it would be seen as part of his chordal technique. Here it exaggerates the rift between the two note-centres, even if the return to B is, based on past practice (the end of *Sleep* is a ready precedent), not in doubt. Perhaps the *Curlew*-chord that facilitates it is equally inevitable, and the pentatone-chords that disguise it might be predicted, too. Less easy to anticipate is the *Frostbound wood*-chord at the very end that pushes the tongue further into the cheek after the octave Bs appear to have settled the issue (Ex. 14.12). This extraordinary song may well be another of "those songs about beer"[11] but should not be denigrated for that. By blurring the boundaries between individual modes it extends Warlock's attitude towards modality in general and sheds new light on the linear manifestation of his chordal vocabulary.

Ex. 14.11: *Away to Twiver* **– bars 49-54**

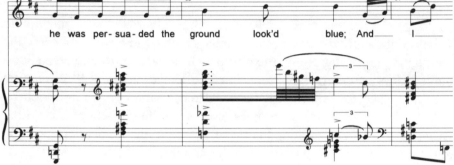

Ex. 14.12: *Away to Twiver* **– bars 64-68**

The jolly shepherd (1927), a "pot-boiler", is much less interesting; four substantial verses/refrains take a great deal of sustaining and, although Warlock's techniques are in evidence (alternative 3rds, Mixolydian 7th, circle-of-5ths) they are produced with so little originality that the song is difficult to take seriously.

Queen Anne (1928), though, is a piece of tongue-in-cheek, Baroque pastiche, mock-heroic to the point of irony to accord with its verbal material ("I am Queen Anne of whom 'tis said/I'm chiefly fam'd for being dead"). Its virtue is its simplicity, the vehicle for its humour, and Warlock's chordal homorhythms, witnessed in *As dew in Aprylle* are utilised again, albeit within a more dignified metre. Limited discussion here should not, in this case, be taken as a comment upon its quality.

Queen Anne was intended for unison voices although it can be considered – and performed – as a solo song. So can *What cheer? Good cheer* (1927). It has a pleasant enough, E flat Ionian melody with a homorhythmic accompaniment that includes the vocal line. Although there are a few non-triadic chords based, in the main on pentatones, there is a marked sense of functional harmony and, apart from an added dominant pedal in the refrain to the last verse, the same chordal outlay serves all verses. Even the Mixolydian 7th is only part of a subdominant modulation. Perhaps Uncle Evelyn was unlikely to be swayed by anything too outré.[12]

Fill the cup Philip (1928) is a plain, jolly and easily overlooked song. But, as with *Captain Stratton's fancy*, a delve beneath the surface reveals a bit more, in this case something about Warlock's attitude towards archaisms. The Mixolydian 7th (D flat) is forced harmonically on the two occasions (bars 2 and 5) where it is not dictated by melodic shape. On both of these occasions it flouts *ficta* conventions, especially when followed by a raised but falling seventh degree (Ex. 14.13); later manifestations, though, are more conformist, doubling or paralleling the vocal line. The suspension at the modulation in bar 12 has a similarly strained quality – it breaks with the dotted homorhythms that have become an established feature of the song. Such contrivedly disingenuous, attention-seeking appearances in a short (16 bars plus 2 bar epilogue) drinking song ("Come fill every tankard . . .") question the rôle of such devices as essential to Warlock's methodology and, thereby, substantiate observations made earlier about the place of Elizabethanisms. Here, their function is to mock, to create an air of respectability when the words are just about having a good time down at the pub. They are as ironic as the Baroque confections of *Queen Anne*.

Ex. 14.13: *Fill the cup Philip* – bars 1-6

Otherwise, the melody exhibits Warlockian characteristics, particularly the motif that will become associated with *And wilt thou leave me thus*. It first appears as a rising 4th variant at the beginning, a derivative, also, of an anacrusic figure, and the associated vocal/instrumental homophony establishes the textural practice of the song. It reappears melodically throughout. It is not used to the same extent as in *And wilt thou . . .* itself. It is, nonetheless, interesting to encounter its use in a song that many (including, perhaps, its composer) would dismiss as unimportant, a hastily concocted bagatelle.

Fill the cup Philip and its contemporary, *The cricketers of Hambledon* were intended for performance with brass band. Indeed, both sound splendid when this is the case, the dotted rhythms of the latter and dogged quavers of the former being particularly suited to the medium. *The cricketers . . .* is of lesser consequence than its companion; the pentatonic promise of the first vocal bar is unsustained and the tonal scheme hackneyed. But this does not indicate Warlock's weakness as a composer; firstly, the song is atypical and, secondly, it is a joke written for a particular circumstance that was, itself, a conscious incongruity (a cricket match to be played on New Year's day).[13] The over-prominent key shifts, chromatic harmonies, chordal density – even the Mixolydian 7ths – should, like all bombast, not be taken seriously.

Considered as a whole, the songs in this category are more successful than those in the previous one although, once again, verbal character demands that Warlock write in a style that is consciously less intense than will be evident in the next grouping. But now he is more prepared to be adventurous within the textual limitations he sets for himself (for, as in the previous grouping, there is a lack of verbal subtlety in most of these pieces too). Songs of this nature have elicited the "beer-swilling" kind of sobriquet favoured by sensationalist copywriters. A broader examination reveals a rhythmic invention not so freely exhibited elsewhere but which was revealed in earlier, exuberant songs: one need only examine the metrical divergences of *The shoemaker* and *Rutterkin*. Now it is a feature of *Jillian of Berry* (the opening and some bass-line syncopations), occurs in the counter-rhythms of *The lady's birthday* and the off-beat chords of *Maltworms*.

These manifestations, although hardly extreme, must be viewed in the whole Warlockian context. He adheres to the metrical and rhythmic demands of his texts most of the time; given that the majority of these are either antique verses with distinctive, regular metres and rhythms or poems by his own friends and contemporaries that use similar, traditional structures, the musical translation can be similarly conventional, even predictable. Of course, since the chords and related melodic shapes are the primary structural focus, the rhythmic element becomes more subdued anyway (as in the music of Erik Satie and, in particular ways, Olivier Messiaen). So when Warlock does respond this way, it is a reaction to a particular kind of stimulus. It is even possible to interpret such innocuous devices as the dotted crotchets in the introductions to *Fill the cup Philip* and *Maltworms* and the brisk quaver/semiquavers figure that begins *The lady's birthday* as part of this process.

Notes

1   IC p. 198. It appears in Chappell (1893) p. 179, citing *The banquet of Thalia* (York, 1790) as a source. FT1 (p. 29) ascribes it to ". . . a ballad sheet. Sung by Joseph Grimaldi towards the end of the century." There are similarities too with the dance-tune *Goddesses* in Playford (1651).

2   See note 35, Chapter 3. "Pot-boiler" could have been a term acquired from CT.

3   IC p. 113; the origin of the melody is explained here too.

4   In T(v).

5   "Heseltine was a martyr to the inter-war spirit of negative pseudo-romanticism." (Whittall (1966) p. 124).

6   Moeran, badly wounded during the First World War, appears to have spent many years thereafter reliant upon the social and financial generosity of friends. See Self (1986) passim.

7   Cockshott (March 1955) pp. 128-130.

8   ". . . to be heard in The Crown at Shoreham" – Cockshott op. cit.

9   Generally accepted pronunciation rhymes "Twiver" with "river".

10   Hold (1975).

11   See note 1, Chapter 9.

12   *What cheer . . .* and *Where riches is everlastingly*, "a couple of silly carols" (PW's words) were dedicated to the brother of PW's late father, a wealthy target who was, unfortunately, not forthcoming. See FT1 p. 44.

13   See FT (1981) pp. 11-18 and IC p. 208.

CHAPTER 15

Three pseudonyms (3)
Metaphysical and introspective

Two Herrick settings, both dating from 1923, are monostrophic songs that, consequently, have an air of through-composition although their melodies, like those in *Candlelight,* would have been strong enough to allow further use if required. Yet, because of their brevity, the chordal content is more powerful than otherwise might have been the case. The insistence on a dominant-tonic bass-line in the introductory bars of *I held love's head* creates momentary (four-note) pentatone chords. Such a harmonic cliché announces that the interest will lie not so much in the choice of chords (because, as has become more and more evident the chordal vocabulary is now so stable – so established – that it often needs little comment) as chordal progress. There are no real modal references in the melody and the modulatory nature of the piano part (closely followed by the voice) makes this piece more overtly tonal (the key is F minor) than most.

D naturals in the piano introduction can be thought of as Dorian signifiers; the voice omits them in bars 3-4, a classic use of the *And wilt thou*-motif. Their employment here, though frequent, has tonal rather than modal implications; they are basically chromatic although a structural function emanates from this chromaticism. The semitonal bass-line between bars 4-8 terminates once A flat is achieved but the D flat that follows – a dominant-tonic progression – shifts to the C that is, itself, the dominant of the original key. Warlock proffers the conventional result but in a personalised way. The chromatic climax occurs at the end, beyond the verbal and melodic component, in the piano coda (Ex. 15.1).

The ironic allegretto scherzando and the structure of its companion, *Thou gav'st me leave to kiss,* strengthen the association with *Candlelight* but the density of some of the chords precludes too much levity. The emphasis, again, is on juxtapositions of chords rather than their specific nature but there is much more of the dominant-tonic progression than had been the case in *I held love's head.* The G tonic is carefully established from the outset but with a curious side-step to E

Ex. 15.1: *I held love's head* – bars 18-21 (piano coda)

Ex. 15.2: *Thou gav'st me leave to kiss* – bars 1-2 (piano introduction)

flat which suggests that a related moment may follow later (Ex. 15.2). The notes refer fleetingly to another G-centred mode (an Aeolian) but the A flat (and its strong, dominant-7th quality) states otherwise. Using *Rantum tantum* as a precedent, though, and the relationship of procedures in that song to the 4ths and 5ths of the preceding items, it is possible to consider *Thou gav'st me leave to kiss* a similar, more self-contained number. The rising 4th, A-D (at the outset) and the construction of some of the introductory chords confirm this possibility. This relationship of 4ths is developed later, after the principal modulation (to the dominant – inevitable in the context); a secondary one, to the subdominant (a further confirmation of the 4th) engenders a shift to the subdominant minor (the promise of the E flat chord fulfilled) prior to a return to the tonic. The introduction reappears to serve – as elsewhere – as an epilogue. Its structural position is more than just a finishing device, however: it further confirms the intervallic statement made at the start and used to regulate other sections of the piece.

The unaccompanied choral song *All the flowers of the spring* (1923), a setting of John Webster, is one of Warlock's most intensely dramatic pieces. He makes of this metaphysical verse a slow processional that, in a manner at times rhythmically barren, describes the inevitable, if gradual, "progress from our birth". Individual lines are chromatic although most of the motion is stepwise. Not only does this make the piece easier to perform (it is within the capabilities of an experienced, amateur choir) but maintains a methodology apparent since *The lover mourns for the loss of love*. Its genius, if not its achievement, is Delian, for it depends on the juxtaposition of chords that are individually spectacular and so it reflects its composer's first inspirational impulses. It is through-composed but divides into a number of well-defined sections that, although of varying lengths, can stand as verse-substitutes.

The first of these introduces the whole song and establishes a tenuous G-centre; by its end in bar 4, the minor 3rd, emphasised to the point of dissonance in the opening bars (Ex. 15.3), has been relinquished and a chord with the semitonally modified mediant (B natural) established. This is, in fact, a first inversion chord of G major but the doubled 3rd and its positioning (stepwise part-motion from a second inversion E

Ex. 15.3: *All the flowers of the spring* – bars 1-4

major chord) make the chord's relationship to any prevailing or assumed note-centre more fragile than might otherwise be the case. The intervening chords are enhanced mainly by parallelism or appoggiaturas. One of the features of the developed, post-1917 piano songs is harmonic progress, the nature of chordal juxtaposition. Here it is largely linear but, elsewhere, it may draw on functional (or quasi-functional) relationships. Warlock will not – cannot – avoid triadic shapes but, especially in the ultra-chromatic and tonally unstable environment of *All the flowers of the spring*, he makes them less obvious by means of inversions or the nature of adjacent chords.

One other feature of this opening statement is particularly worth noting. The chord at the beginning of bar 4 is isolated by the quaver rest that follows and has a cadential quality as a result. It sounds like a major 7th chord and, as such, is a member of the chordal family; but it has one note semitonally displaced, giving it qualities associated with an augmented chord. It is actually a double suspension but the resolution does not occur until after the rest, a musical feature that emphasises, and is given credence by, the text's metaphysical inevitability.

After this opening homophony, counterpoint – strict imitation of a figure that combines falling semitones and minor 3rds within a texture regulated by unbroken crotchets – symbolises the ineluctable nature of existence. There is a brief array of family chords (*Curlew* and German 6th) before appoggiaturas and suspensions resolve on to the tonic (Ex. 15.4). A short, tonic pedal (bars 6-7) prophesies greater things to come. Warlock's employment of this device in the past has mostly provided constituents of family chords; in bars 13-27, the effect is that of a constant dissonance-point – many of the chords in the earlier part of this block derive from the family with the pedal as an irritant. From bar 23,

Ex. 15.4: *All the flowers of the spring* – bars 5-7

the pedal more frequently becomes a chordal constituent although, largely because of inversions and the pitch of the pedal note itself, the resulting shapes perpetuate the instability initiated by the foregoing dissonances. After bar 27 the pedal continues but the contrast is startling as ominous concords prevail, emphasising the finality of "And consequently this is done", so that the pentatonic resolution (bar 31) has to be semitonally distorted to complete the cadence (Ex. 15.5).

Ex. 15.5: *All the flowers of the spring* – bars 27-32

The melismatic nature of these distortions is very much a cadential device; it can be found, in a limited form, at the end of the opening section (bars 4-5) and at the end of the contrapuntal passage that follows it (bar 7). The device that closes the temporary homophony that immediately ensues is more extended (bar 10), and, although short, semitonal melismas appear more generally in the G-pedal section, the original purpose is restored, first in the figure that ends the pedal (bars 31-2) and then in the elongated, onomatopoeic treatment of the word "wind" that occupies the last 21 bars.

Otherwise, parallel motion is an important means of getting from one chord to the next. This can produce the moaning figures of the conclusion (where often there are only two moving parts at any moment) and the equally evocative, but more active, setting of "weave" – based on horizontal *Curlew*-chords (Ex. 15.6) – that precedes it, The process is begun by the easier, parallel 3rds in divided sopranos and tenors that set "To leave a living name behind" (36-40); all subsequent material employs 3rds as well, but the changes in the way pitches and rhythms are deployed create different dramatic effects.

In complete contrast, the solo song *Consider* (1923) is remarkable for its piano part. To enhance the unconfined joy of Ford's poem, an exuberant battery of arpeggios is unbroken except during a couple of

Ex. 15.6: *All the flowers of the spring* – **bars 36-44**

bars towards the end. The consequent power of the "accompaniment" swamps the simple, pentatonic vocal line, the most extreme statement of the fact that the piano parts of Warlock's songs are more compositionally important than the vocal content. As with *Dedication*, the linearisation of what are essentially vertical components gives Warlock the opportunity to introduce additional material into his chords although, for the most part, his choice is just as it has been all along; he merely changes the format in which that choice is presented.

The modified strophism depends very much on the perpetuum mobile of the piano to maintain the piece through the melodic changes, although the consistent pentatonicism of the vocal line is another stabilising factor; only two passing-notes in the entire part lie outside the shape. The reliance on the *And wilt thou*-motif (the pentatone-shape is composed of two of them) provides the basis of this latter integration, especially as the melody is open and expansive to proclaim the tone of the words.

These aspects apart, the song proceeds in a familiar manner: the chords of the instrumental introduction, interludes and (to a lesser extent) ending employ more passing-notes or other harmonic diversions than those used during the verses themselves. These additions can transmute one familiar chordal shape into another such as the pentatone and *Curlew* forms that characterise the first two of these sections and, true to past practice, the same material in different guises – see Ex. 15.7. In this particular piece, some descending, chromatic parallelism in the final stanza decorates the long note on "heath" and replaces the more static arpeggios – the norm in the preceding two verses – although they sound unnecessarily complicated in a song that is supposed to extol the simple pleasures of the natural world. Other chromaticisms are less obtrusive; sucked into the endless and rapid flow of notes they add a careful piquancy to the vigorous harmonic continuum.

Ex. 15.7: *Consider* – bars 1-4 (piano introduction)

The strophism of the equally Quilteresque *Sweet-and-twenty* (1924), the Clown's song from Act II scene iii of *Twelfth night*, is compact and presumes nothing. Not even the relationship between the introduction and the interlude/postlude is predictable for, although based on a common motif, the harmonies are subject to change, as those of the second verse are when compared with the first. Copley remarks[1] that, in this "light-hearted setting of the lyric", Warlock chose "to ignore its underlying sadness". This is not so; chordal choice is heavily dependent upon verbal meaning. In the strophic songs so far there has been a sense of development; the harmonic content of later verses is an extension or re-working of the first. This also explains those few occasions where material is largely unchanged in the second verse to emphasise the expositional function of initial statements before going on to make changes (as in *Tyrley tyrlow*). In *Sweet-and-twenty*, the second verse is substantially different from the first, the harmony in the first half is markedly, even radically, altered to reflect the change of mood in the text from wantonness to metaphysical introspection, although the melody stays the same. And where the harmony is the same as in the first stanza, the melody is different, another recognition of the change of mood. Only at the very end, where the clown uses uncertainty as an excuse to reassume the abandon of the first verse, are original melody and harmony re-instated together, a satisfactory conclusion both emotionally and constructionally.

The metamorphosis begins with the inter-verse, instrumental passage. As in many predecessors, it resembles the introduction but, on this occasion, not literally so; it retains motifs rather than a complete outline and extends the harmony rather than merely repeating it. This modification to the opening is, however, retained intact for the song's closing statement. Of the 33 chords that constitute the first half of the second verse (that is, where the melody is identical to that of the first) only eleven are unchanged in essence, and some of these may be subject to inversion or other manipulations. The new harmonies are chromatic and, although they never lose sight of the A flat tonic, they contrast strongly with the equivalent section of the first verse (Ex. 15.8) where accidentals were few, being restricted to a single Mixolydian 7th (G flat), a chromatic E natural (in a C chord prior to one of F minor, a brief reference to the relative) and a couple of modulatory D naturals (the leading note of the new key, the dominant E flat). The second verse makes the same modulation, retaining the richer harmonies of the first verse's second half for these both anticipate the new harmonies of the second verse and complete it.

Two settings (1925) of Arthur Symons are intended as a linked pair[2] despite the fact that nine years elapsed between their inspirations. The first, *A prayer to Saint Anthony of Padua* (the second written), is less texturally dense than its companion. It anticipates the C minor qualities of the second with a strong sense of E flat at the beginning although this breaks down as the song progresses, also a feature of the other. The voice, in fact, has a line shaped by a C Aeolian; the mode is strictly maintained until near the end where, for the final appeal, a prominent, chromatically derived G flat twists the melody towards an E flat centre as the piano becomes less secure in this respect (Ex. 15.9). *And wilt*

Ex. 15.8: *Sweet-and-twenty* – **bars 5-10 and 32-37**

Ex. 15.9: *A prayer to Saint Anthony of Padua* – **bars 13-17**

thou-motifs in bar 13 identify this song as not contemporary with its partner; the descending, vocal shape and the ascending, instrumental figure (with appropriate harmony) mark this song as a product of Warlock's maturity.

The second song, *The sick heart*, has already been referred to in terms of its earlier incarnation, *The cloths of Heaven*.[3] The swap of text is curious – Yeats's romantic fantasy for Symons's metaphysical irony – because the music retains most of the content of the original and most amendments relate to syllabic quantity and stress in the melody. In the process, though, one of the anomalies of the first version is remedied.

Both forms have an elusive sense of C about them and, while they avoid specific reference to it at their respective endings, *The cloths of Heaven* included the note in its final chord. But there is an equally elusive sense of G in the melodies. In a modal context this is more difficult to prove than in an exclusively tonal one and the rising, anacrusic 4th, G-C, that opened the vocal line of *The cloths of Heaven* states the one while concealing the other. But the syllabic deployment of *The sick heart* does not need this anacrusis and, in the new material that sets "I am sick of a malady" (bar 7), introduces an F sharp. In the earlier manifestation, this had only appeared during the ambiguous, whole-tone passage at the end. The new vocal line is built around the notes of a number of G-based modes with only a few chromatic amendments. Apart from this new material and the incorporation of some of the original melody into a short piano interlude (bar 5), the main difference between the two songs lies in their endings. *The sick heart* retains an instrumental echo but now delivers the whole of the last, short, vocal phrase a minor 6th higher than before and over a held chord; this can be thought of either as an A chord with an added 6th or an F sharp minor 7th, its derivation is clouded by inversion and context. Either way it semitonally contradicts both of the centres which have been observed operating during the course of the piece (Ex. 15.10).

Two more Webster settings, *Call for the robin redbreast and the wren* and *The shrouding of the Duchess of Malfi* (both 1925), are for women's and men's voices respectively; even *All the flowers of the spring* can not fully prepare for the extraordinary chords of the second of these. Meanwhile, *Call for the robin . . .* begins with a C-centred, 6th-less, modal statement, a linear device that contains a rising 6th/falling 3rd like a child's call. The eventual Aeolian 6th (bar 4) is replaced in the next bar by a Dorian (A natural) in combination with a Mixolydian 3rd (E natural – Ex. 15.11).

Ex. 15.10: *The sick heart* **– bars 9-12; cf. Ex. 3.3**

Ex. 15.11: *Call for the robin redbreast and the wren* **– bars 1-5**

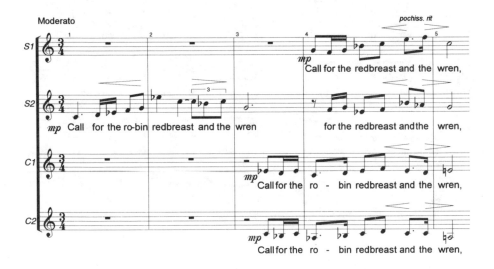

The F sharp at the start of bar 6 is the first wrench away from C-based material. Its brief sharp-side reference is more effective in the following bar if only momentarily although a chromatic flurry (Bars 7-11) safely restores C (Ex. 15.12). An echo of the opening, rising figure has an air of Warlockian strophism about it and the re-assumption of the succeeding shape confirms that impression. But the chords are now made to shift suddenly, first to suggest F sharp and E Dorians –

Ex. 15.12: *Call for the robin redbreast and the wren* **– bars 6-11**

sharp-side areas anticipated by those F sharps of earlier bars – thence to G minor/Aeolian, a flat-side balance also consistent with the F sharps. After these clear, if tiny and non-functional statements, the purpose of the following section is to cover them up, to lose them in a tirade of family chords that proclaim allegiance to no note-centre. By the end of this passage any sense of strophism has gone and the new emphasis is one of homophonic declamation.

The homophony continues into the next section (22-25) to combine with the parallelism that is increasingly a feature of Warlock's writing at this time. The two voices in parallel 3rds create false-relations that defy ascription to a particular centre although their concluding chord, consisting of D and F sharp, serves as a not very assertive dominant; it announces the G-centre that regulates the remaining eight bars (26-33). Thus, the entire song can be seen as an extended modulation, prepared by the early F sharps, where the process is incidental rather than crucial. It gives a framework, a simple logic, that contains the characteristic Warlockian shapes but is not itself so demanding that it overwhelms them, just like strophic form. The G pedal that pervades the closing section is but one of its veneers; the parallelism that precedes it is another and it generates a whole-tone situation (into which the G does not fit), then one that depends on parallel 4ths before the eventual, 3rd-less, G chord is attained at last, unconventionally, by means of an Italian 6th (Ex. 15.13).

Ex. 15.13: *Call for the robin redbreast and the wren* – bars 22-27 & 31-33

Parallelism is prominent too in *The shrouding of the Duchess of Malfi* but the initial cell is a chord. A tenuous C-focus, heavily concealed most of the time, pervades the piece. C occurs in the *Curlew*-chord that is the starting point, a Dorian mode encapsulated in a chord this time rather than as a linear figure. Stepwise part-motion, often semitonal, dictates the progress. The function of the semitone is epitomised by the parallel shift at the beginning of bar 2 (Ex. 15.14) and the consequent chords. With a few exceptions they are all family shapes and are summarised in

Ex. 15.14: *The shrouding of the Duchess of Malfi* **– bars 1-2**

Ex. 15.15: *The shrouding of the Duchess of Malfi* **– bars 1-5 (summary)**

Ex. 15.15. Many chords are semitonally distorted, a characteristic of *The lover mourns for the loss of love* and the *Preludes*. The latter work lacked the tight discipline of the former and there was much incompatibility between melodic and harmonic components; here, a thinner texture and softer, vocal timbres allow the technique to characterise the ominous qualities of the text.

There are two chordal types that complicate explanation. The second chord in bar 3 incorporates a passing-note D between E and C sharp and may just be that; it is a four-note pentatone chord, as previously described, in which one note has been semitonally modified, a fusion of two technical practices. The other chord, an open 5th that incorporates an added 2nd, appears once in bar 4 and twice in bar 6, the last time as a cadential constituent. It has affinities with pentatonic chords, especially the *Frostbound wood*-chord; its ambiguity makes it particularly suitable here for there is an attempted modulation to the dominant at bar 7 at the mention of the "shroud". There is no true perfect cadence and not even a new leading note: a D minor chord precedes the two cadence-chords. The first of these could be an amended dominant-of-the-dominant; certainly, the short, horizontal figure that follows (bars 8-9) confirms the sense of a G-centre but, by bar 12, C is re-established by means of Dorian, Mixolydian and minor references (Ex.15.16). The return of the original centre completes the first, extended section of a piece that, like *All the flowers of the spring* and other pieces (not just choral songs), is made up of a large number of sub-sections.

Ex. 15.16: *The shrouding of the Duchess of Malfi* **– bars 6-14**

Bars 16-29 contain some of Warlock's most severe and stark dissonances. They appear to start from a D-centre although a D flat may refer back to the semitonal shift in bar 2 from the preceding C-based material; in neither case is the prevailing focus upset. The upper tenor maintains the sense of a D-mode but the remaining parts sing parallel chords in a flexible F sharp major, the point most distant from the original, if only loosely stated, centre (Ex.15.17). The bitonality of *The lady's birthday* had been a joke, a moment of contrived confusion; here both effect and intent are very different: the strength of the parallel chords – the "wrong" key – is such that they push aside the established

Ex. 15.17: *The shrouding of the Duchess of Malfi* **– bars 21-25**

focus and make it sound at fault. The stimulus is verbal (the deviance of "sin their conception") but, significantly, Warlock responds chordally at first; the ensuing material, though homorhythmic, is more linearly devised. Part-motion depends on the semitone, a continuation of techniques heard at the beginning – and yet not just in that respect. The resulting harmony can also be explained as semitonally-amended family chords, often *Curlew* shapes, placed alongside unmodified forms of the same shape.

The sense of F sharp, while logical, is suddenly imposed, a procedure noted from time to time elsewhere. Equally important in this passage are the rising 3rds that contain the stepwise motion. When they reappear at bar 31, they are again employed as parallel elements within a texture that relates to earlier ideas through a triple-time metre and horizontal construction. There is a harmonic logic too; the first chord is a version of the three-note, pentatone-derived shape of bar 4 (Ex. 15.18). The

Ex. 15.18: *The shrouding of the Duchess of Malfi* **– bars 31-34**

semitone still distorts family chords; others in the passage are less easy to identify. Chords with semitone dissonances are now the essence, a position partially created by and reflected in the second basses whose promised pedal becomes a chromatic ascent until the ultimate resolution on to an array of family chords (Ex. 15.19).

The final section (bars 47-64) opens with a monophonic line that portends imitative polyphony. Actually, it turns into a 5ths-based exercise in parallelism that creates family chords (Ex. 15.20; they are unaltered here, a reference back to bars 43-6). The piece ends with another statement of chromatic lines bound by family chords and their distortions. It comes to rest, as in *Call for the robin* . . on an open chord. Warlock puts the 5th in the bass, a reminder of those second inversions he has used in the past to disguise triadic chords.

Ex. 15.19: *The shrouding of the Duchess of Malfi – bars 43-46*

cru - ci- fix let bless your | neck,____ a | cru - ci- fix let bless your | neck

Ex. 15.20: *The shrouding of the Duchess of Malfi – bars 49-53*

'Tis   now, 'tis   now full tide 'tween night and day___

'Tis   now   full tide 'tween night and day, 'tis   now full tide 'tween night and day___

In his book on Gesualdo Warlock wrote as follows:[4]

> . . . the so-called homophonic revolution which is supposed to have
> dethroned polyphony at the end of the sixteenth century is a mere figment
> of the historians' imagination. Gesualdo was always a polyphonist, yet
> there are harmonic passages in his work.

So, if there really is a piece in Warlock's oeuvre that displays the
influence of the late Renaissance, this is it, even if it is devoid of those
pretty Elizabethanisms, mistaken elsewhere as proclaiming the same
antecedent. And perhaps this piece, rather than *The full heart*, deserves
the dedication to the Prince of Venosa.

The opening of another choral song, *The spring of the year* (1925),
combines several stylistic features. The emergent tendency towards
parallelism as a means of chordal progress and the importance of 4ths
and 5ths in his harmonic make-up are linked — chordally of course – by
family shapes; the resultant association demonstrates the interrelationship of these techniques. Also, except for the multiple, chromatic

appoggiatura in bar 3, the first phrase uses no notes outside a G-centred Dorian mode ("Key F" boldly states the tonic sol-fa edition) before the cadential breakdown (Ex. 15.21). At this point, the Mixolydian 3rd (B natural) is closely followed by a chord that reinstates the Dorian version and introduces, chromatically, G flat and D flat – the F sharp and C sharp of the semiquaver chord in bar 3. Not only is this a relationship between pitches but the major 7th chord that results is also consistent with the preceding harmonic array.

Ex. 15.21: *The spring of the year – bars 1-4*

Tonal convention demands that, once the new centre is established, it is quitted. Warlock's response rejects the predictable by, at first, appearing to offer it and, then, diverting elsewhere. Chromaticism in bar 5 seems to settle on to what sounds like the dominant 7th of D at the end of bar 6; it resolves on to a D chord but (the bass leaps a 9th) in the second inversion. This is a delaying tactic; parallelism and an E flat major 7th, along with some rare verbal repetition ("primroses") steer towards E. This time, second inversion (bar 8i) gives way to first (9i), further disoriented by the insinuation of a major 7th (Ex. 15.22).

Ex. 15.22: *The spring of the year – bars 5-9*

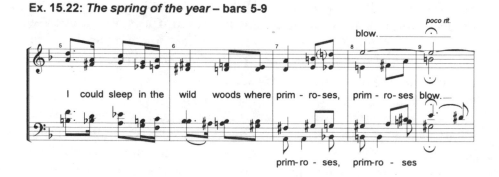

This chord is not only a favourite shape, it is part of the means for a return to G. The shift is executed by parallel motion in all but the soprano part; it fulfils all those occasions in earlier pieces where, as a result of semitonal alteration, the original tonic or note-centre was distorted. The situation here is very similar: the original G, converted to G sharp by the E major chord, then exploits that relationship in a return to the initial centre by the most direct linear route. The falling shape suggests an abstracted Delian procedure.

A truncated reference to the opening confirms the restoration of the G-centre despite the disguise of the *Curlew*-chord (there can be no unequivocal declaration). It also starts the second verse aided by a variant of the opening soprano figure. This is a more evasive affair than its predecessor, in keeping with the text's intimations of mortality, although an abstracted sense of G is provided by alternative major and minor 3rds, F sharps and, particularly, the descending, Aeolian bass-line between bars 11-14. Major and minor triadic chords at bar 16 are a surprise after the chromaticism that precedes them but also because of their association with a new centre, a Dorian C. Like the earlier shift to E, this is reached by steps of a semitone but parallel motion is tempered by contrary (Ex. 15.23). And dissonance combined with rhythmic distortion might be all very appropriate for "the finger of death" but

Ex. 15.23: *The spring of the year* – bars 10-18

concords, as in *All the flowers of the spring*, have the more sinister task, they set "closing them to sleep" – a verbal and musical euphemism.

Each of these two verses ends with a different centre from the one it started with; the last is no exception. The first two both began from G; this is less obvious in the last although a reference in bars 21-2 to bars 3-4 – hardly a strophic re-use, more of a quotation – remedies the situation somewhat. What is perplexing, like the earlier moves to E and C, is the climactic achievement (less a modulation than an insinuation) of what is really D minor; but, because the last chord is in the first inversion, it has affinities with a chord of F with an added 6th. There is no C in the chord (Ex. 15.24). Here is another example where the centre-associations of the last chord are disguised in some way, a procedure encountered in *Call for the robin . .* and *The shrouding of the Duchess of Malfi*. The music actually and finally gains the dominant (thereby realising the prospective achievement of "I'll meet them both in Heaven") but the mood is inevitability rather than triumph.

Ex. 15.24: *The spring of the year* **– bars 22-28**

In *The spring of the year* Warlock, with his increasing sense of chordal purpose and progression, incorporates his chords (included for their individual character) in a process that is not so much a key-scheme as a manipulation of conventional procedures. As suggested above, there are no real modulations, just a sense of one note-focus at one point and another somewhere else, a game played with lip-service to the rules. In retrospect, the description could apply to aspects of the 1911 songs too.

The birds (1926), a setting of Hilaire Belloc, contains several notable features not least of which is its own flexibility of note-centre: it begins and ends in E flat but, amongst a host of (very) sharp-side references are short, but stable, statements focused on D and A. There is a lack of the chordal and technical unification found in *The spring of the year* and verbal sectionalisation, often followed musically by Warlock, now results in very short statements of adjacent and diverse techniques as Ex. 15.25 testifies. The opening of predominantly family chords is first shaped by a falling-semitone run followed, in turn, by other figures that point toward E flat major/Cminor. There is the sense of an interrupted cadence at the end of them (bars 1-2, the first line of the poem). To set the second line, a short burst of parallel chords leads to another, semitone-dependent progression that anticipates the sharp-side tendencies of the second verse (the third inversion 9th on B, bar 4i, contains an enharmonic tonic). All this happens in just four bars; the third, and last, line of the verse – two bars of text-setting followed by one more from the piano – also starts with parallel chords (of the 9th) before more chords suggest C minor.

The melody binds these potentially conflicting ideas together and relates them to the verbal narrative as it also accumulates. The

Ex. 15.25: *The birds* – bars 1-6

frequency of G in the last one is musically satisfying for the stability it brings while the two F sharps substantiate "no man". Alone it declares E flat then, with C minor as a pivot, G minor, another mediant move.

Any doubts that may linger disappear at the beginning of verse 2 as a new clarity emerges. (The same thing occurs in the words: after the mystery of the miracle recounted in the opening, the story continues in a more matter-of-fact way). The C-centre is substantiated and proclaimed by parallel 6ths over a tonic pedal, a startling reversal of the song's equivocal opening and a striking example of Warlock's strophic process. As in the first verse, each line of text prompts a new form of expression and both the C-centre and established melody are abandoned to an extraordinary sequential passage in which the steps not only rise in whole tones but the rising bass 4ths are in canon with the melody (Ex. 15.26). This achievement is countered by a pentatonic melody and an ascending passage (to colour "flew away") that states D major with an added 6th. Reduction to three-note chords here is particularly effective.

Ex. 15.26: *The birds* **– bars 9-15**

Ex. 15.27: *The birds* – bars 16-18

The poem has an isolated Latin line in the middle (like Squire's parody in *Mr Belloc's fancy*) which is given an Aeolian setting on A; its contrary part-writing, exaggerated suspension and tierce de Picardie create a deliberately forced liturgical quality (Ex. 15.27). The irony of this statement strengthens the preceding material but the concluding verse offers nothing new. After a pivotal *Curlew*-chord, there is no material substantially different from that of the first and the ending is disappointing. Warlock shunned conventional religion and this paraphrase of a story from the Apocrypha is as close as he comes to setting a Biblical narrative.[5] It is difficult to assess whether his chordal choice suggests disdain or unease; it is also possible that the nature of the song's recipients[6] affected his selection.

The first, introductory bar of *Robin Goodfellow* (1926) is pentatonic. So, to begin with, is the strophic melody until the G sharp passing note in the fourth bar of each verse-melody. And, apart from the B flat in the seventh of each, the melody is consistent with A-centred modes. This gives considerable chromatic freedom. The pitch-demands of the piano are greater: bar 2 uses all 12 pitches in three consecutive (family) chords, a feat almost matched by the subsequent bar (Ex. 15.28). In the latter instance, the *Curlew*-chord is a pivot prior to the sudden A major dominant 7th that announces the start of the melody. The insistence on B flat in piano figures, stated then cancelled in bar 2 and reinstated in bar 3 (with whole-tone associations), anticipates later moves. The vocal entry moderates this sort of display – notes conform to A major apart from an E sharp, also anticipatory, in bar 6 – until the imperfect cadence in the dominant (bars 7-8), a signal for much insecurity of note-centre. The *Curlew*-chord at the end of bar 9 once more works as a pivot, this time between A and what could be F (an inconclusive pentatone chord

Ex. 15.28: *Robin Goodfellow* **– bars 1-4**

in bar 11 is replaced by a more conclusive major 7th in the next), the reference prophesied by the E sharp in bar 6 and, more strongly, the B flats of the opening bars which semitonally challenge the A-centre. The *Curlew*-shape constitutes four-fifths of a dominant 9th on C and so, in this functional context, conforms to the philosophy of omitting a note from a five-note chord and creates a family shape in the process.

After all of this foregoing material, the harmony restores the A-centre (there is a pentatonic pivot in bar 12 – Ex. 15.29). It is unstable and is overtaken by what promises to be a familiar, Mixolydian-instigated circle-of-5ths that diverts, through an F sharp minor 7th and a semitone shift, to make a fleeting reference to F again (bar 14). The pentatone chord at the start of bar 15 raises doubts about the real centre – it too has a pivotal function of a sort – and the situation is not remedied by the

Ex. 15.29: *Robin Goodfellow* **– bars 11-13**

fusillade of *Curlew*-chords in the subsequent bar. This Warlockian, strophic modification does not, this time, moderate the verse-content but, rather, the instrumental material of the introduction/interlude.

The relatively straightforward and tonally stable chords employed in the earlier stages of the first verse are not so much modified in the second as completely replaced. The emphasis is on chromaticism, especially the descending variety, as Ex. 15.30, a comparison of the relevant passages in both verses, indicates. The rest of the verse, effectively a refrain, is largely unaltered beyond chordal thickening and octave transposition, a policy that suggests stability of a kind (by what is, essentially, repetition) after the excesses of what preceded it. The next significant change is to the interlude material. To begin with, it is just as it was before the first verse; however, it is rhythmically and motivically extended ("capriciously", as the tempo instruction requires) and again draws attention to – emphasises – the whole-tone element observed at the start. The use of the whole-tone scale (as opposed to

Ex. 15.30: *Robin Goodfellow* – bars 3-7 & 16-20

other devices derived from whole tones) is rare in Warlock's music, although it can be occasionally prominent and *Rutterkin* provides the most obvious example of its use. While its manifestations have been principally linear, it can be harmonically justified – a necessity, given Warlock's methodology – by a chord-shape that appears from time to time. It is a fusion of *Curlew* and German 6th chords and occurrences in *Robin Goodfellow* can be found in bars 2 (twice) and 30, in fact at the same times as the whole-tone runs are evident. Displayed horizontally and vertically, it can be seen to contain all of these elements (Ex. 15.31). The first chord in bar 34 is yet another example.

Ex. 15.31: *Robin Goodfellow* – **chordal aggregations in bars 2 & 30**

Ex. 15.32: *Robin Goodfellow* – **bars 36-41**

Some of the harmonisations associated with the third verse extend those of the first; the original dominant 7th at the start of the melody now has an added minor 9th and major 13th, and the F sharp minor chord at the end of bar 5 is given a minor 7th. But the majority are different either from that disposition or the second. A substantial amount of the refrain repeats those of the preceding verses but there are some notable, even amusing, differences. The sequence in bars 36-8 that complements that in the vocal line is combined with the transposition down a minor 3rd of the figure that occupies the first half of bar 40; it gives a gentle but wry jolt in the midst of the security offered by what is otherwise repetition (Ex. 15.32). In all these respects *Robin Goodfellow* represents one of the most powerful examples of Warlock's strophic outlook, a case of continual chordal substitution and growth over three consecutive verses. The song lies halfway between the vigorously rumbustious and the philosophical and possesses features associated with both types. The intellectual, rhetorical manipulation of material exemplifies the latter but there is also a rhythmic vitality and invention that was so much a feature of songs such as *Rutterkin* and *Away to Twiver*.

Three more Belloc settings, allocated by Tomlinson to 1926,[7] overlap into 1927.[8] *Ha'nacker mill* begins with three arpeggiated, parallel, minor chords. The first, D minor, is immediately denied by those on B flat and G flat. If there is a unifying element it is B flat; the six notes the chords use are consistent with modes/scales based on that note. This analysis proves not to be very satisfactory over the work as a whole, though; the voice favours D and its multimodal tendencies in the first verse are gradually distilled during the second into the 6th-less ambiguity (Dorian/Aeolian) of the third. The opening chords disorient: their disparity denotes the despair at Sally's departure. The major 3rds that separate them contrast with the minors of the chords themselves (Ex. 15.33).

Ex. 15.33: *Ha'nacker mill* **– bars 1-2**

The same could be said of the string of *Curlew*-chords that ensues; the first three in bar 2 are the opening minor chords with added 6ths – the way that *Curlew*-chords appeared in the 1911 songs. The last chords of the opening two bars are the same *Curlew*-chord to which an extra note has been added, F natural in the first, F sharp in the second. That these are alternative 3rds in D-centred modes is difficult to discern in a progression that is very unstable in terms of a single note-centre but they are both succeeded by D-root chords with minor 3rds, implying a pivotal, even cadential, function. The *Curlew*-chords close the song in the manner of a short, abstract fantasia like that at the end of *Sleep*. Here, curiously, they also open it, a harmonic mutation encountered before, rather than after, the expositional statement.

The chordal language of *Ha'nacker mill* stretches back as far as the *Folk-song preludes*; the incidence of simple, major and minor chords is rare (despite the announcement in the opening bar); instead, the emphasis is on family chords, especially the *Curlew*-shape which was so much the measure by which the tonal instability of those earlier pieces was assessed. Warlock chooses to set this "threnody for the passing of a way of life"[9] in very personal terms; his wholesale resumption of techniques that, in this form, had recently become less prominent displays the same eclecticism as his use of Elizabethanisms. As the next two songs will immediately demonstrate, this is not the vocabulary of the whole set.

The night is altogether more straightforward and, in its contemporary context, familiar. Harmony is regulated by E-based modes, the Aeolian implied by the signature, the Dorian evoked by the interpolated C sharps and, ultimately, the Ionian, although not all accidentals can be fully explained this way. The centre is stated by a pedal, vocal this time, throughout the first verse. The irritant quality of such a device in, for example, *All the flowers of the spring* is here reversed so that the low Es stand for the dark security of the night. Repeated quavers emphasise its constancy while the piano sounds the melody and makes statements about modality (Ex. 15.34). The F major chord in bar 8 is not readily explicable; it could be a shift two places to the flat side, a balance for the move two places to the sharp-side that soon follows. On the other hand, it could represent a semitone shift from the original centre.

The achievement of A in bar 10 is more than just a modulation; it further explores the E modes. The C sharp of the A chord is the Dorian signifier from bar 4; the G sharp that prefaces it is the raised 3rd of an E mode that turns it into an Ionian or a Mixolydian – it will recur later in the song. Despite the apparent strength of E as a centre, an alternative view of this first verse is substantiated by later material: given that one of Warlock's practices involves transferring between different modes that are redistributions of the same declared pitches, the first verse can be viewed – if only theoretically – in terms of A-centred modes. This

Ex. 15.34: *The night* **– bars 1-10**

would explain the F natural (an Aeolian 6th) without contradicting any other accidental.

Chromaticism in the second verse grows from the Ionian and Mixolydian 7ths of bar 13; D sharp reappears as E flat in the next bar to trigger the subsequent B flat. A flat and G flat (bar 15) are already established enharmonically and the E major and A major chords at the end of the verse also have precedents. But both the first two verses end on the chord of A, a gesture that partly validates the hypothetical basis of the first verse. In the process, it maintains the modal relationship with the assumed E-centre and also avoids the E major to E minor chords that might otherwise have been sounded or implied. The transition between third and fourth verses is less cautious in this respect although the very full chord at the beginning of bar 29 actually combines E minor and A minor, an Aeolian composite. The third verse itself is transitional; it perpetuates the chromaticism of the second by transferring accidentals into a heavily modified melody made to differ substantially from the others.

The last verse re-establishes the melody which, it will be recalled, is itself regulated by the Aeolian mode. The composite chord referred to above recognises the fact. Indeed, the chords ascribed to the first half (bars 29-32) adhere to this mode and, with one exception, all later accidentals are multi-modal signifiers, C, D and G sharps. The exception is the enigmatic F natural, first encountered in bar 8 and now a constituent of a D minor chord. But its primary purpose has become very much the semitone irritant to the note-centre that was speculated upon earlier; this closing verse has an E pedal throughout and the note in question is particularly astringent during the setting of "cheat me with your false delight", a mannerist oxymoron if there ever was. The dispute between A and E as claimants for the real centre is not satisfactorily resolved. The last vocal note is supported first by a chord of A and then, more wistfully, by an open chord of E.

Warlock made no arrangement[10] of *My own country* for other instrumental resources but its linear nature makes it eminently suitable for such treatment (as in *Sleep*). It is constructed substantially, though not exclusively, of linear motifs derived from family chords. It begins with an instrumental pre-echo, heard four times, of the initial vocal motif, a four-note shape that can be viewed either as a dominant 7th outline or the inversion of the *Curlew*-chord/motif, a relationship noted during discussion of the eponymous work. Sounded with it are two different, pentatonically derived patterns (Ex. 15.35). The associated chordal logic

Ex. 15.35: *My own country* – bars 1-4

is less easy to define. Although there are references to the family here too, some shapes are puzzling for they have no origins that can be described in terms of the family or multi-modality, the two linked processes that order Warlock's style at this stage; they are, however, bound together by the F pedal that survives as far as bar 7. Nonetheless, the chromaticism of bar 2 seems to be there largely for its own sake; the

E flat (and consequent natural) are modal markers but the B natural and C sharp are, at this stage anyway, gratuitous.

Whatever their justification, these remain the only accidentals for half of the song. B natural appears – at the same pitch as in bar 2 – on three more occasions before bar 26 and C sharp just once. The bar referred to is the point at which the C sharp is justified, as the 3rd of a chord of A that becomes a temporary centre and spawns a new batch of accidentals appropriate to it. The shift is angular, logical and, although reinforced by tonic and then dominant pedals, unconvincing. The pentatonic pivot that enables the reversion to F is equally unsubtle. A reversion to expositional material (the B natural of bar 7 is converted to B flat) reaches a climax on a fragmented chord of G flat (F sharp) with an added 7th (Ex. 15.36), actually the dominant 7th of B, the other chromatic note of bar 2 that has remained unjustified until this point.

Ex. 15.36: *My own country* **– bars 41-44**

But there is no resolution, let alone any sustained use of it as a centre. Such a relationship, as with the C sharp and its place vis-à-vis an A-centre, may seem tortuous but is part of Warlock's search for environments in which his use of modes can function. In *My own country* and other, contemporary songs, he is in the process of rejecting the note-centre relationships of regular tonality although, in this instance, his choice of modulatory direction is dictated by other factors.

The semitonally motivated part-motion and dependency upon family chords in *Sorrow's lullaby* (1927) declares a lineage stretching back to *The lover mourns for the loss of love* and the earliest manifestations of

Warlock's mature style. There is also a link in the way that material is condensed, compressed even, to heighten the melancholy and the verbal irony. Now, though, the compression extends beyond chordal shapes to the structural logic that binds it together. In the process, *Sorrow's lullaby* becomes one of Warlock's most theatrical and uncompromising songs (and, alas, one of his least performed, too). It presents another view of the composer as a miniaturist, one who could manipulate the form of a short work to emphasise its emotional and atmospheric qualities, an alternative to the more familiar, strophic usage.

It was conceived as a piece for string quartet (the instruments are muted throughout) with soprano and baritone soli – it is not an arrangement of a piece for other media. The opening consists of four bars of predominantly *Curlew*, minor 7th and pentatone-based chords, a statement of established harmonic resources. This process continues in the string parts upon the first vocal entry, but both voices frequently sound notes that are at variance with the instrumental component (Ex. 15.37). Some of these sung pitches extend the coincident harmony by converting the instrumental chords into 9ths or 11ths; some are appoggiaturas; others are less easy to explain beyond deliberate disorientation. The aggregate complexity is exemplified by the vocal B flat in bar 5: it could deliberately clash with the B natural of the second violin, but both of these notes anticipate different C-centred modes by simultaneously announcing their respective seventh degrees.

The adjacent or simultaneous use of different modal signifiers is part of Warlock's method, of course. They are regular manifestations of the influence of the semitone on the relationship between horizontal and vertical elements in his music. But, in *Sorrow's lullaby*, he is more inclined to develop the resulting dissonances, abstracting them to a point where they exist for their own sake. With *The lover mourns . . .* once more a precedent, the ensuing structural uncertainty is appropriate to the poetic melancholy.

Modal associations are not the only source of disparities between vocal and instrumental material, a reminder of the anarchic melodies of *The water lily* or *Take o take those lips away* (in *Saudades*). Semitones may be a starting point for the piece both conceptually and physically (declared by the second violin) but they are soon stretched into major 2nds and both intervals dominate. The voice uses them to begin and end its opening statement; indeed, the linearity of the piece rests entirely on them, both in the construction of the vocal lines and in the way that instrumental harmony is modified. As if to emphasise the point, apart

Ex. 15.37: *Sorrow's lullaby* – bars 1-6 & A1-3

from a repetition of the quasi-refrain ("Let us sing his lullaby . . .") there is little common material, melodic or motivic, beyond the intervallic relationship. This is most apparent in the refrain itself where, despite the employment of both voices and the staggering of their entries, there is no attempt at standard, contrapuntal techniques such as imitation or inversion. A vague, descending figure of a 2nd (major or minor) followed by another interval of variable width (though often a perfect 4th) is used a few times; to all intents and purposes, though, the two lines are consciously different.

After a short interlude, the second quasi-stanza exhibits a similarly cavalier attitude to verse-melody – the next two couplets get a new vocal line; despite the novelty, the constructional criteria remain the same as before. The incentive to work this way may well have been prompted by Beddoes's verse.[11] Warlock's deployment of the vocal soli follows the poet's requirements absolutely (for a first voice, a second voice then both together). But changes in the positions of the syllabic stresses within the lines of text would have made melodic repetition, even in a modified form, clumsy and Beddoes does not divide his text into verses anyway. So there is a sense not so much of strophic repetition as regeneration; because of harmonic conflicts between vocal and instrumental forces and the vocal independence that results, there is a greater sense of autonomous melody than usual.

Warlock cannot leave such a deluge of constantly changing material to run its course unchecked and a repeated couplet referred to briefly above stands as a refrain; the eight bars from F1-G2ii are identical to A5-B6ii, an oasis of relative familiarity immediately preceding the short coda (G3-8).

Sorrow's lullaby possesses no stable note-centre; although there are references, they are fleeting and disguised. As a result, it falls into that part of Warlock's output that can be classed as paratonal. The introductory passage, bars 1-4, projects a loose sense of B, the unison sounded by the three instruments that begin it and from which the material unfolds. The first chords in bars 5-8 suggest a circle-of-5ths that rises rather than falls (G-D-A-E); but conflicting information in the second halves of those bars could suggest references to chords on A, E, B and A respectively. Precise identification is difficult because of the nature of these chords. To complicate matters even more, the first section (bars 1-12) appears to move towards a tenuous C-centre; this is substantiated by the soprano's line and anticipated by the coincident B flat/natural in bar 5 mentioned above. If the circle-of-5ths in bars 5-8 is genuine (and its existence is open to interpretation), then the B and C centres on either side of it are reversed (in that C should precede G and B should follow E). There are precedents, of course (as in *Twelve oxen*), but not on the scale presented here. Whatever the origins, the result – disorientation of centre in tonal terms – is the same.

Although the foregoing accords with Warlock's practice, there is an alternative reading: the chord at the beginning of bar 5, a minor 7th on G, interrupts the introduction and announces the vocal entry. The chord is hardly what might have been expected: the voice, the chromatic B flat apart, appears to insist upon an A-centre and, indeed, a chord rooted on A could have followed what is, effectively, a dominant 9th at the end of bar 4. (There are other possibilities for the orientation of this melody, D minor or F major are candidates; bar 5 is, also, a vocal exposition of the whole- and half-tones discussed above.) The sudden G could suggest a shift occasioned by a modal seventh, a reorientation that, via the ensuing, inverted circle-of-5ths, reverts to the dominant at the start of bar 8.

The vocal melody, meanwhile, employs a variant of a procedure already encountered numerous times, a move from tonic to mediant. Here, the implication of a modulation to the relative once more suggests a basis in accepted, tonal practice even though the harmony ultimately suggests a mode with a minor, rather than a major, third degree, a feature of the chromatically complex part-writing that frequently denies any centres alluded to by the voices. In just this way, the C-centre achieved by the soprano is maintained by the baritone at letter A even though the strings are reluctant to confirm it. The baritone's line is so strongly centred on C that it regulates the instrumental harmony, even that which contradicts it, a situation that its timbre emphasises.

Note-centres in the remainder of the song are more abstruse although the vocal lines of the quasi-refrain gravitate towards an A mode with a minor third. The chord at the beginning of bar B3 is the least ambiguous statement but only two bars later, the situation is reduced to a pedal. It is often contradicted by other material, especially when it attempts to work its way into the following section.

For it is in the ensuing material that the already fragile sense of centres begins to disintegrate totally. Note-foci in the second quasi-stanza ("What sound is that . . .") are even less readily defined than those that preceded it. The family chords that characterised the harmony in the introduction and the first verse are now subject to distortion either by amendment or addition, irritations created by semi- or whole-tone contradictions of established constructions. The emphasis is heavily upon stepwise part-motion; the vocal lines also continue to be shaped by the major and minor 2nds presented at the outset. Even an appearance of the "gloom" figure at bar C3 eschews the drones usually associated with it; they are replaced by trills that further obfuscate any

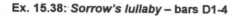

Ex. 15.38: *Sorrow's lullaby* – bars D1-4

sense of centre that they might otherwise suggest (although the first violin/cello figure substantiates the soprano's first notes by recycling them in a transposed form). But from this tonal chaos emerge the clearest note-centre references of the entire piece: indisputable B minor chords at D4i and D5i, although negated by adjacent shapes, recall the opening. A coincident leading-note-tonic progression by the baritone is so obvious after the way that material has been disguised elsewhere as to verge on caricature (Ex.15.38) but it effectively colours "suddenly awakening", a nice use of tonality as symbolism, although in a different way from that which was the case in *Rantum tantum*.

But no sooner is B re-established than it is dispersed in a flurry of string activity, a preface to the return of the refrain. Again, material is ambiguous and self-contradictory in terms of centres. Nevertheless, the short epilogue that follows the repeated passage finally asserts A as the focus. The chord of D in bar G5 suggests a plagal cadence although the last chord is a fusion of *Curlew* and German 6th configurations that maintain the element of concealment there has been throughout. But it also contains five notes of a Dorian mode on A; only the second and seventh degrees are absent. Pure modal references are rare in this piece and such a presentation at the end, substantiating as it does other aspects of Warlock's technique, takes on much the same sort of rôle as the last chords of *Sleep*. There they restored the diatonicism that had been continually under threat; here, the modal element, largely swamped in the course of the piece, reasserts itself.

Sorrow's lullaby is one of several experimental pieces that Warlock chose not to take (or was prevented from taking) further. (A list would also include *Consider*, *Dedication* and the *Folk-song preludes*.) While the intervals that shape it – 2nds and 3rds – are constituents of the family chords which form the harmonic basis, there is no significant, developed motif of the kind used in *The curlew* or that will regulate *And wilt thou leave me thus* and its contemporaries. Consequently, melodic material is diverse; it lacks the unity that comes from either the use of readily definable modes or the strophism that has become such a regular feature of Warlock's music even, as *Capriol* will readily demonstrate, his non-vocal output. Note-centres, heavily disguised to the point of being scarcely recognisable, are bound together by a logic that is based on intervallic rather than functional relationships, however loose.

These are not negative comments; the piece has a distinctive character that aptly mirrors the fatalism and impending doom that Beddoes declares in this and many another text. It possesses an intricate structural logic that begins with the first notes of the instrumental opening: the unison Bs (that represent the initial centre) move to C (second violin) and A (cello), the other two distinguishable centres, by means of minor and major 2nd motion respectively, the two intervals that shape the vocal lines. This begs a comparison with *Lillygay*. There, the semitone regulated linear and chordal growth and determined the relative centres of the constituent songs; here, the situation is contracted so that centres within a single movement are shaped by melodically strong intervals. This piece demonstrates once and for all Warlock's ability to manipulate material that is interrelated and in keeping with his technique. Its attitude towards dissonance and diatonicism, though, is more extreme than in most other pieces that have been examined.

The lover's maze (piano and voice, 1927), while redolent with archaisms, has more notable features and to describe it as "pseudo-Elizabethan"[12] again misses the point. In this song, though, rather than providing a decorative veneer, the devices heighten the neurotic underlay of "unquiet thoughts" that must "be still". Unlikely as it may at first appear, there is a similarity between this song and the more trivial *Fill the cup Philip* where archaisms also acted as a foil to the mood of the song.

A chord of F (major, despite the four-flat signature, but see below), to

Ex. 15.39: *The lover's maze* **– bars 1-3**

which a flattened 7th is added after the manner of many Mixolydian precedents, launches the song with a broken circle-of-5ths. Upon reaching A flat, the cycle is interrupted to recommence from a G chord that reinstitutes a modified form of the sequence to land back in the tonic, F, again (Ex.15.39). These capricious shifts of allegiance anticipate the modulations that are an important feature of the song; all three verses of this strophic piece make the same moves, to the relative (A flat, the break-off point in the opening circle-of-5ths) in the fourth bar, to the dominant in the eighth and to the subdominant in the twelfth. Each stanza reverts to F four bars later at the verse-end. Yet, in this excessive, even parodic, tonal scenario, there is room for more than just modal references.

The F-centre is ambivalent, oscillating between uses of major and minor 3rds. The issue remains unresolved at the end of the song as both are declined. The epilogue, a modified re-run of the introduction, uses both at different points but is so unstable (because of the circles-of-5ths) that an A flat immediately before the final cadence fails to provide a totally convincing answer. These alternative 3rds are the most obvious among many semitonal variants for which modal shapes offer a rationale. Ds and Es, consequently, may be flat or natural and, after the move to A flat, G is also subject to flattening as a Mixolydian gesture. Warlock's use of modality, of course, has already been traced back to his chordal family and the semitonal differences between the chords, so it comes as no surprise to find the phenomenon occurring here. The song is remarkable, however, for the intensity of its use; although adjacent positionings of alternatives are fairly frequent, moments of simultaneous use, such as those in bars 11 and 35, are more rare (Ex. 15.40).

Ex. 15.40: *The lover's maze* – bars 11 & 35-36

(De-) light not your- selves   I should be___ re -   jec - (ted)

Ex. 15.41: *Sigh no more ladies* – bars 1-6

Fast and in strict time (Allegretto con moto)

Sigh   no   more,   la - dies,

sigh   no   more;   men   were   de - cei - vers   ev - er.

Key-shifts in *Sigh no more ladies* (1927) are more audacious and are prepared by the heavy disguise of the E flat tonic (for this song must be discussed in tonal terms) at the beginning. Chromaticism and dissonance arise not just in terms of stepwise motion but chordal distortion (see Ex. 15.41). There is, also, a strong dependence on motif, in this case a

Ex. 15.42: *Sigh no more ladies* – bars 10-17 & 28-35

three-note figure that rises by step. It occurs first in the piano introduction but as a retrograde (or inversion) of what will be its usual form. Nevertheless, the principal basis is still chordal choice, particularly in the second half of each verse. The respective first halves have much in common. This results both from their common intent – modulation from tonic to dominant, a tonal convention that does not fully prepare for what is to ensue – and from the material employed: there is substantial repetition in the second verse beyond the use of the introductory bars as a new accompanimental figure.

As in *Rantum tantum*, the modulatory principle, when established, triggers more of the same. So, after a short series of temporary dominant-tonic relationships, melody and, to a lesser extent, harmony achieve A, the most distant point from E flat. Starting and finishing points are the same as in *Suky you shall be my wife* but the route between them is less predictable here than the circle-of-5ths in the earlier song. Reversion to E flat is achieved via an extended dominant and modally generated chromaticism in the melody, abstracted in the upper piano-part (bars 15-16); it is superseded by the motivically regulated sequence, dependent upon pentatone-chords, that incorporates and eventually states the tonic. Ex. 15.42 compares the six bars in each verse that effect the move from B flat up to the restatement of E flat; the significant difference between the two lies in the semitonal alterations made to the second, most apparent in the bass and particularly in the two bars prior to "Hey nonny . . ." – the E flat reversion. There is still a sense of the dominant (at the end of bar 34) but this is achieved by a parallel, semitone shift rather than a conventional pivot. Self finds the modulations "tortuous" and they "make his melody sound contrived".[13] But, despite the change of centre, they are not modulations in the conventional sense, being primarily chordal progressions with an incidental sense of focus; likewise, the melody is (as usual) a compositional convenience, subservient to the piano-harmony.

Sigh no more ladies charts Warlock's continuing search for a way to progress from one vertical statement to the next but is less modally dictated than most of its contemporaries. In its use of semitones to manipulate the content (and its motivic counterpoint) it is closer in spirit to a song like *Take o take those lips away* (*Saudades*). This suggests no regression on Warlock's part; the piece is strong with a greater sense of purpose than its predecessor, largely as a result of the paratonal excesses that exemplify the "fraud of men".

Cradle song (1927), possesses the perfect Warlockian song-structure; melodically multimodal and literally strophic, it has exciting chordal changes from verse to verse. Centred on G, the introduction presents the modal diversity. The restless infant may well be comforted: Es flat and natural suggest, as major 7th attempts to resolve on to *Curlew*, Aeolian and Dorian modes respectively (Ex. 15.43). The F in the chord under the

Ex. 15.43: *Cradle song* – bars 1-5

first vocal note prepares for later developments: the unraised 7th is deliberately used when it could have legitimately been otherwise. The point is made more strongly by the voice as it leaps a 7th (bar 5 etc.) to F; it resolves on to and, hence, draws attention to the Dorian 6th immediately afterwards. Although little used (five appearances in each verse), it persists, unaltered, throughout the melody.

The Dorian is the principal melodic mode (implied by the signature), but there are other references: F sharp (bars 8, 10, 14, etc.) suggests the minor/ficta or, in conjunction with B natural (another alternative), the major/Ionian. The piano is largely independent of these melodic accidentals; it uses them but incorporates others, especially E flat from the introduction. While instrumentally prominent, it has no melodic significance. The first vocal F sharp coincides with a piano modulation to D (as does the third), but the melody can be consistently thought of in terms of the G modes above. The modulations recur in all three verses.

The introduction appears, ritornello-like, between the end of the verse proper and the refrain. It is at this point (bars 10-12) that the process of amendment begins: an F sharp – effectively a minor 3rd in addition to the major – is added to the original, anacrusic major 7th to create a more complex, more dissonant shape. The *Curlew*-chord is unaltered. When the figure reappears as an interlude a few bars later it reverts to its initial form and the opening of the second verse is, some octave doubling apart, just like the first. Alteration, when it comes, is prompted by verbal repetition; the phrase "lullaby baby" recurs in both verse and refrain and its return at bar 20 results in a more chromatic (descending, stepwise) treatment that grows out of the texturally variant octaves. The formal (not the emotional) climax of this passage is the superimposition of alternative 7ths at the end of bar 21, a device that prepares for the pandiatonicism of bars 23-5 where chords are suggested by the alternative Fs and Es. There is no tonally satisfactory resolution to these bars; the expected G chord (with either major or minor 3rd) never materialises (bar 25); a pentatone is substituted but with a G in the bass (Ex. 15.44). G is only achieved fully at the beginning of the refrain (bar 29); the material that precedes it, especially the extended A chord, makes its arrival the more remarkable.

The modified, pre-refrain ritornello of the first verse appears in the second with a superimposed dominant drone to complement the interpolated F sharps of the earlier manifestation. On its last inter-verse presentation, though, the chords are expanded into pentatone-related shapes that spill into the verse (Ex. 15.45). Chordal progress in this

Ex. 15.44: *Cradle song* – bars 21-28

Ex. 15.45: *Cradle song* – bars 31-33

verse is largely dictated by circle-of-5ths statements and, again, they begin at the "lullaby baby" textprompt. But it is the chordal choice associated with the verse ends that is arresting. The final line of each stanza is treated with varying degrees of pandiatonicism; that of the second verse was commented upon above. Now there is a bitonal element also but of a particular kind. There is no sustained centre in either the left- or right-hand writing but, in bar 39, a D7 shape (left-hand) is juxtaposed with E major and C minor triads (in the right) as detailed in Ex. 15.46. The pentatone-chord at the start of the passage is the pivotal point after the functionality of the preceding modulation.

Ex. 15.46: *Cradle song* **– bars 38-40**

Ex. 15.47: *Cradle song* **– chordal aggregations in bars 27 & 48**

Such simultaneous polarisations were suggested by an arpeggiated chord in bar 27, a dominant 7th shape with an added minor 9th and, another interpolated dissonance, a flattened 12th; it can also be viewed as a chord of A on to which has been grafted one of E flat (Ex. 15.47a), its most distant relative on the circle-of-5ths. The chord at 39i could be an extended chord of E (one of Dr Day's chords)[14] but the cadential chord at 48ii (Ex. 15.47b) is a 7th chord on F sharp with a superimposed one of E flat, a variant of the example in bar 27. Its F sharp component means that it becomes a dominant substitute before the G (major) chord that is to close the song. This avoidance of specific, functional, tonal references has been observed elsewhere; it is a part of the dilemma that Warlock set himself for, having developed a modal methodology, he cannot evade diatonic chords. He can, however, develop stratagems to maintain a sense of centre without necessarily making them tonally conventional. In this respect, the ending of *Sleep* must be seen as an early example of the process at work; the dissonant, instrumental passage that succeeds the vocal component does not need to approach the final G-chord by means of regular methods. Indeed, Warlock makes a strong, even exaggerated, statement to the contrary.

The lack of a key-signature that heralds *Mockery* (1927) could be taken, along with the plethora of accidentals that are to be encountered, to imply no fixed centre.[15] There are tracts of this song where note-foci are as impermanent as the marital relationships that are the verse's subject-matter. The published form employs a G Mixolydian environment despite all the information that contradicts it. Vocally, F natural is preferred to F sharp until the refrain although the latter note has put in an appearance as G flat (bars 8-9). The descending, cuckoo-3rds of the introduction, like the figures that begin *Sigh no more ladies* or *The lover's maze*, create an element of confusion; no clear centre emerges and they avoid references to Fs either natural or sharp. The first note, B flat[16] launches the eight different pitches that constitute the introduction (Ex. 15.48). The falling, interlocked triads create a cynically distorted "Day"-chord that suggests other structures: they imply two dominant-tonic relationships, E flat-A flat minor and E-A minor, a semitonally related gesture. Similarly, the opening B flat is semitonally altered an octave below to C flat; G is transmuted to G sharp, E flat to E natural, C flat to C natural and G sharp to A. These

Ex. 15.48: *Mockery* – bars 1-20; verse-melody and some chordal detail

origins prepare nicely for the rest of the song where, although there is a sense of G, pandiatonicism like that of *Cradle song* is also present but now in a more concentrated form in a faster tempo. The welter of triadic chords, sometimes decorated with additional notes, have little or no functional relationship with one another; they are abstractions of circles-of-5ths and other unstable tonal procedures observed elsewhere. So complex is the material in *Mockery* that new chord-choice in the second of the two verses is precluded; the musical content is identical.

A strong, linear basis is epitomised by the melody, one of the most active that Warlock wrote in terms of its derivations; Ex. 15.48 shows this melody and such harmonic detail as will be described. As stated, it is essentially focused on G and, although the first note is written as A sharp (a chromatic appoggiatura on to the B) it can also be thought of as B flat, an alternative 3rd. Bar 4 presents alternative 6ths, E natural (Dorian) and E flat (Aeolian); the resulting B flat-E flat 4th at the end of the bar has flat-side implications ripe for extension and abstraction, hence the D flat (bar 6) and A flat (bar 7). In bar 8, a falling 4th, C flat-G flat, completes the flat-side adventure often effected elsewhere by circles-of-5ths – the 4ths here can be seen as a version of it. The four notes of bar 9 are a retrograde of those of bar 5, semitonally transposed; they make a horizontal minor 7th, a pentatone-chord. Another pentatonic reference occurs in bar 7 but such use is not extensive.

Warlock fits a melodic snatch of Mendelssohn's *Wedding march* to the words "Mocks married men for thus sings he". Of course, the intent is ironic but motivic reasons validate his choice and not just because the first chord of the original would have been a *Curlew*-shape. The chromatic C sharp chimes with his own practice, as does the pentatonic shape described by the fourth to eighth notes of the quotation. In fact, the last of these is distorted to avoid a specific reference to G, initiating a few sharp-side gestures.

The introductory, falling 3rds have more implications. Notes 1-4 – in fact, apart from notes 3-6 (a major 7th) any four consecutive notes – produce a semitonally-altered minor 7th. These chords appear from time to time in the piano-part, particularly in the pseudo-dominant associated with the anacrusic A sharp. With other, less easily quantifiable shapes, they generate "wrong-note" harmony. Some of the most startling chords colour the Mendelssohn quotation. Here, each hand at the piano plays an individual, parallel statement: the chords in the left hand are augmented triads, those in the right are augmented 5ths with a minor 3rd on top, a distortion – a caricature perhaps – of a major 7th. Despite their individual parallelism, the two chordal lines work in contrary motion; the G-centre of the melody is consequently – and conveniently – swamped by the instrumental component.

Musical information is repeated in the second verse so the inter-verse figure now recalls not only its earlier manifestation as the introduction but, also, the shape used (but without the 3rd) in the upper piano at the Mendelssohn quotation. It also appears in the coda and, along with the remaining four notes, is used vertically to approach the final G. The centre is only stated by the very last, isolated note; there is no perfect (or any regular) cadence (Ex. 15.49). Warlock therefore confirms – in a song with a marked linear intent – the relationship in his music between horizontal and vertical components; the linearity derives from chords or has chordal associations.

Ex. 15.49: _Mockery_ – bars 40-44

It is worthwhile drawing a brief comparison between the experimental nature of some of these Eynsford songs and the earlier pieces published by Rogers. In the latter he was establishing a new, linear vocabulary based on his chordal background and inclination; the result was a diversity of approaches. In these later pieces a similarly wide range of results occurs as he continues to refine his methods for progressing from one event to another. The similarity is one of spirit rather than detail but nonetheless valid for that.

Sometime in, perhaps, 1927,[17] Warlock met the poet Bruce Blunt. Their friendship and association was one of the most positive features of Warlock's last years and Blunt provided the texts for five songs (_The first mercy, The cricketers of Hambledon, The fox, The frostbound wood_ and _Bethlehem Down_) which must rate among the composer's most successful ventures. The poems that Blunt wrote have artistic limits but, also, a directness and, occasionally, a strength of image that inspired Warlock. _The first mercy_ (1927) is an ingenious fusion of modal and tonal elements that favour the former by emulating the latter. Material at the start of the song is familiar enough: a G Dorian intro-duction anticipates a melody with the same basis but the semitonally adjusted B natural in bar 6 converts it into a Mixolydian; E flats in the piano-part suggest Aeolian. Chromaticism in bar 7 (Ex. 15.50), however, is modally unsatisfactory in terms of G; while the F sharp can be tolerated as a ficta – or even an Ionian – signifier, the C sharp is less easy to justify except as a chromatic passing-note, echoed by an overlapping inversion (or retrograde). It could suggest a move to D that fails to materialise just here. The chord that includes it is ambiguous; it

Ex. 15.50: *The first mercy* **– bars 1-8**

contains only three notes that could be a segment of a dominant 7th shape. The D flat at the end of the bar is a *Curlew*-chord constituent.

The second-verse melody, in fact, is amended to take in C sharp/D flat, first presented within a linear diminished triad, another *Curlew*-chord element. It prompts a flat-side harmonic shift that anticipates the A flat of the next bar (Ex. 15.51). The modal

Ex. 15.51: *The first mercy* **– bars 13-16**

implications of the move to a B flat-centre, hinted at in bar 10, are Dorian (with D and A flats) or Mixolydian (reverting to D natural) in the harmonic underlay. The G flat of bar 15 suggests Aeolian. Had Warlock left it at that the song would have been remarkable for its adherence to a modal methodology while paying lip-service to the tonal practice of changing the centre, even if the moves do take place without tonally conventional cadences. The C sharp/D flat of bar 7 can be retrospectively viewed as an expectation of later developments. The melodic C sharp of bar 18 also creates the air of a dominant modulation from the initial G-centre, but it is saved from being too convincing by the underlying *Curlew*-chord and ensuing part-motion.

To redress the balance after such upheavals, the third verse reverts to earlier material, reassuming the melodic outline of the first over pure, Dorian harmony as implied by the signature; this turns out to be a glorious statement of pentatonic usage, mostly in four-note chords, but within a G-framework (see Ex. 15.52). Verse 4 adopts the melodic line of verse 2 and much of its harmony, too. Differences, the parallel opening apart, depend upon semitonal amendment (such as the word-painting of "frighten" in bar 39). Similarly, the last verse recycles the first, including the C sharp/D flat of bar 7. Whether this is a successful reminder of its use in the even-numbered verses is questionable.

Where riches is everlastingly (1927) has a four-part version of the refrain (ad lib.) to close the third verse although the vocal harmony just duplicates what has been heard instrumentally. The D Aeolian adds a little more potential interest than the Ionian of its companion (*What cheer* . . .) but, harmonically, Dorian becomes minor and B natural, the Dorian signifier, is but the vehicle for a modulation to C, the dominant of the relative.

Ex. 15.52: *The first mercy* **– bars 23-32; vocal melody & chordal summary**

I saw a fair maiden (1927) is for unaccompanied four-part chorus; like its choral contemporaries, it incorporates a certain amount of harmonic repetition: verses 1 and 2 use the same material; verses 3 and 4 share a variant which verse 5 only slightly alters – the refrain is effectively the same for all five. The texture is homophonic, the chordal language substantially that of the family and the whole has the freshness, even the innocence, of earlier examples of the genre such as *Benedicamus Domino*. Some of the spacing creates surprising (and delicious) dissonances but their effect is softened by the vocal timbre and the low dynamic level. There is no modulation from the F-centre; the number of accidentals is smaller than in just about any other piece and, with one exception, these are only the raised or lowered 7ths, E or E flat. That other instance is a B natural in bar 13; it could indicate a vestigial modulation but its use, in two adjacent triadic chords is

Ex. 15.53: *I saw a fair maiden* **– bars 11-14**

consciously non-functional (Ex. 15.53). It is also noteworthy that parallelism, an important device in pieces where Warlock was endeavouring to establish credible, alternative techniques of chordal progression, is reduced to a merely decorative level in bar 36; in other respects the principle of stepwise part-motion, the method of the earlier choral songs, is maintained.

The motion of individual parts within the texture is an important structural feature of *Bethlehem Down* (1927) too. The result is a piece dependent almost exclusively on family chords although, despite the slow tempo, a quasi-polyphonic fluidity arises from the way the crotchets move. (The piece has a 6/2 time-signature, an unusual, ominous, but textually appropriate reversal of Warlock's sprightly compound metres elsewhere). Most of the harmony remains constant for all four verses; the only variants are in the first two bars of verses 3 and 4 (which, like verses 1 and 2, use common material). All of the 1927 choral songs show a marked reluctance to vary chordal choice between verses; this may have resulted from the speed at which they had to be written (to raise cash),[18] but the quality of the part-writing and the credibility of the harmonic language suggest that this is not the only conclusion. Given Warlock's search for an improved technique of harmonic progression, it must be recognised that, in *Bethlehem Down*, there is so little alteration because change without compromise would be difficult. The chordal progression, as it stands, demands no major alteration.

The piece depends on the progress of the chord-choices – any melodic implication of the soprano part is of secondary interest, merely a device to assist the harmonic passage. As in earlier examples, even the passing notes conform to the harmonic logic as Ex. 15.54 demonstrates. But there is also a note-centre plan; the main one is D and the harmony at

Ex. 15.54: *Bethlehem Down* (choral version) – bars 4-6

the start suggests both Dorian and Aeolian tendencies. By the end of bar 4 the centre has moved to F, a predictable event had this been a strictly tonal situation. In fact, the result is an F mode rather than the key of F as the bass line of bar 5 attests. The F chord in bar 4 has no 3rd and quickly transmutes into one of B flat, hardly convincing as a key-change. A similar situation arises at each verse-end; the reversion to a D-centre should not be thought of in terms of D minor. The octave Ds and the Dorian figure in the tenor part state otherwise (Ex. 15.55).

Ex. 15.55: *Bethlehem Down* **– bars 7-8**

Warlock's choral-song technique was established early, in the first examples, in fact and alters little over the course of his career. As other aspects of his composition were undergoing changes, this suggests that, despite his customary self-denigration, he was satisfied with his achievements; if the description of how this one was rattled off is accurate,[19] it is his natural medium. Certainly, in *Bethlehem Down* he adheres exclusively to his preference for four-note chords.

Warlock's employment of melody as a prime force in his music has been shown to be a severely restricted practice. The horizontal constructions of *Saudades* aside, the motivic dependency of sections of *The curlew* may be recalled as well as the energetic lines of *Captain Stratton's fancy*, *Maltworms* or other, convivial songs. It has been suggested earlier that Warlock's vocal-lines lack the self-generating and autonomous properties that are normally assumed to be a part of the melodic process, the drinking songs being, in this respect, the better examples of the art. *And wilt thou leave me thus* (1928) breaks with this situation for it employs a recurring motif that relentlessly shapes the line. It is the chordally derived shape of a whole-tone and a minor 3rd first encountered at any length in *The curlew* and identified sporadically afterwards. Sometimes it has appeared in a modified form but not to the same extent as here.

Warlock's technique now recalls the chordal usage of early works where the semitone was also used as a modifying instrument. Of course, the interval has always been used melodically, principally as the device that converts one set of modal characteristics into another. But here it is brought to bear on the three notes of the identified motif more intensively than it has previously been possible to record. The whole-tone component is often reduced to a semitone and the minor 3rd extended to the major so that, after the first, every note of the first-verse melody – with the possible exception of the A flat in bar 8, a component of a modified *Curlew*-chord (or an extra minor 3rd) – can be justified in terms of different forms of this motif (see Ex. 15.56). The intent is announced in the introduction, a two-bar, contrapuntal statement that anticipates both the impending linearity and the opening vocal phrase. It confirms the relationships that exist within the chordal family and, thereby, their modal relatives as well. Whole-tone and minor 3rd is a component of minor 7th, *Curlew* and pentatonic shapes; semitone and major 3rd signify major 7th; whole-tone and major 3rd derive from the German 6th shape.

Ex. 15.56: *And wilt thou leave me thus* – bars 2-9 (vocal line only)

As well as the predominant motif, this figure contains a rising semitone (A natural-B flat) to contrast with the preceding – falling – whole-tones and interrupts the falling minor 3rd (D flat-B flat) (Ex. 15.57). The A natural itself should come as no surprise for it is only the leading note of B flat minor, the principal key – in this case the welter of chromaticisms precludes modal references. Nevertheless, the A

Ex. 15.57: *And wilt thou leave me thus* **– bars 1-2 (piano introduction)**

possesses more of the character of the chromatic than of a genuine leading note, a fact substantiated by the E natural that mirrors it in bar 3. But B flat as a centre is hardly over-stated; there are no unequivocal tonic chords after the one that concludes the introduction and the motif prevents a further leading-note reference at the end of the verse. Nor is there a modulation to heighten the importance of the tonic.

Except for a B natural in bar 15 (another semitonal amendment), the melody of verse 2 is intervallically identical to that of the first. Its rhythmic changes result from verbal demands rather than any developmental process. Melodic material in verse 3 is new in that it does not reuse the line of its predecessors literally. But its dependence upon the motif – indeed, its reworking of it – mark it as developmental. Change results from reordering, a technique also noticed in *The curlew*, and is catalogued in Ex. 15.58; the process continues into the fourth, final verse that also contains some recapitulation from the first two. This emphasis upon more logical motivic procedures is a particular aspect of Warlock's style at this time and he will present another approach in *The frostbound wood*. Yet, however much the compositional basis gravitates towards a linear methodology, it must always be borne in mind that the origin of the motif presented here is chordal. It may be convenient to relate the process to the van Dieren encounter but the result, the semitonal modification of a vertically inspired technique, is wholly Warlockian.

In the third and fourth verses, the motif is again re-ordered and to a greater extent than in *The curlew*. In the first (and second) verse Warlock had employed it in prime, inversion, retrograde and retrograde-inversion forms; in the later verses it becomes a pair of intervals rather than a single, distinct shape and, in this manner, surrenders its chordal origins and transforms into a more consciously horizontal entity.

Ex. 15.58: *And wilt thou leave me thus* – bars 18-33 (vocal line only)

Another feature from past practice reveals itself in the harmonic change of the second verse. The differences arc not so much a development as a complete rewrite. Family chords again provide the material but the *Curlew*-chord predominatcs and appoggiaturas feature strongly. The technique continues into the third and fourth verses (where, as described above, the melody amends the original motif) although the prevalence of the *Curlew*-chord is reduced. It does, though, conclude the song in a widely spaced arpeggio on to which a major 7th (an inverted semitone) is grafted, a more direct, less compromising statement than the chromatic reminder of the interval at the end of *Rantum tantum* and one that echoes the last notes of the vocal part (Ex. 15.59).

And wilt thou leave me thus is among Warlock's best and most significant songs. It was the last song to be composed at Eynsford and it makes thereby a fitting envoi to what was a highly productive time in his compositional life, even though its results did not quite match the sustained quality of those of the Welsh period.

The choral songs of 1928 were mostly arrangements of existing solo songs;[20] *The rich cavalcade* was the only new part-song of the year but

Ex. 15.59: *And wilt thou leave me thus* – bars 32-34

it would not be published until 1973.[21] Its through-composition is
refreshing after the strophic repetitions of recent examples of the genre;
nor is it without moments of declamatory beauty. It maintains the
Warlockian homophony already shown to be an important characteristic
of his work for this medium and – another peculiar feature – is written
throughout in four parts.

Like many of its contemporaries, this piece makes use of a motif but
not, in this case, the *And wilt thou*-shape prevalent elsewhere. It has
some affinities with it in that it is scalic, as are some manifestations in
the song with which it is particularly identified. But Warlock's music
has always used adjacent-note material and, in this respect, *The rich
cavalcade* is not extraordinary. Rather, it could be said that the *And wilt
thou*-motif is a crystalisation of scalic figures, shaped by those chordal
associations that have already been discussed.

The motif is presented chordally on a number of occasions but this is
not unique; other pieces have done the same from time to time. It is not a
frequently used shape but its affinity with other family chords – which,
once more, dictate chordal choice here – is plain. It is a curious work
that does not appear particularly strong on the page, but a sympathetic
performance reveals some pleasing and typically Warlockian sounds.[22]

Warlock's melodic and harmonic attitudes to the pentatone have been
revealed in a number of ways. Sometimes pentatone chords employ all
five notes although, often, only four are used. Melodically, the pentatone
can also be used as it stands but it is usually a transitory device, readily
altered, by addition, into another modal shape. On occasion, it is fused
with another pentatone a 5th away and, particularly as demonstrated in
The curlew (at "I know of the sleepy country"), the resultant hexatone

can have modal implications of its own. In *The frostbound wood*, (1929) the melodic tetratone D-E-G-A is derived from the common notes of two such pentatones (Ex. 15.60). Some of the four-note chords that appear from time to time in Warlock's music are transpositions of the same tetratone and have been referred to, consequently, as "*Frostbound wood*-chords". There is no doubt here that the vocal material is so dramatically reduced to portray the shattered landscape of Blunt's verse. Yet it is both an extension and a refinement of material that stimulated the opulent excesses of the *Folk-song preludes*.

Ex. 15.60: *The frostbound wood* – **pentatonic derivations**

Because of the limited information presented by the notes, a centre is difficult to discern. All four notes could be contenders although the piano seems to favour the A (minor/Aeolian to begin with). The short, introductory figure has more than a suggestion of (modal) E about it and the A minor chord that coincides with the vocal entry comes as something of a surprise. E predominates in the voice – it is the most frequently used pitch – to the extent that it assumes the rôle of a frequently interrupted pedal-point. Yet A is always quitted to E so there is an occasional sense of A in the vocal melody as well; the consequent ambiguity has some affinity with the polymodality experienced from time to time elsewhere.

But this song is remarkable not just for the concise encapsulation of its composer's attitude towards pentatonicism. The four notes describe the three-note, *And wilt thou*-motif, in both prime (the shape heard in the introduction which, therefore, has an expositional rather than just a tempo or pitching function) and retrograde inversion forms. It is these two presentations in particular that regulate the melody. The retrograde is used on a couple of occasions but the inversion itself never appears (Ex. 15.60 again). This is curious; given the piano's A-focus, G natural in a descending shape would have been acceptable within both modal and minor usage. But, perhaps because it is too obvious, Warlock declines its use this way, reserving it for ascending figures only. This heightens the vocal ambiguity of centre. The voice's limited note-choice provokes a comparison with Cage's better known *Wonderful widow of eighteen springs*; yet the manner in which the notes are used has a greater affinity with the note-row of Stravinsky's *In memoriam Dylan Thomas* (for its restricted pitch-use within what should be a wider note-choice situation) or even that of Webern's *Concerto* (for its internal relationships).

The continual retention of the tetratonic outline (which is largely pentaphonic, E-D-E-G-A) and the equality of time-span (four bars) allocated to each stanza of the poem, maintains a strong strophic quality. But chordal change from verse to verse is more extreme and, generally, more logical than before. In earlier, strophic forms, Warlock generally exercised chordal variation in much the same way that he made his chord-choices in the first pieces – for their intrinsic, self-contained interest; indeed, his attitude to strophism allowed him, short bursts of functional harmony notwithstanding, to perpetuate his love of chords-for-their-own-pleasure while the form superimposed a logic. Here, his choice of new chords is, to begin with anyway, the result of modal decoration and interrelationships. The chordal family, as a set of identifiable, vertical devices, is extended beyond recognition but in its place is a different, chromatic chordal language, a more logical version of that found in, for example, *Burd Ellen and young Tamlane*. The considerable rhythmic variation in the melody is motivated, some short melismas aside, by natural speech patterns and this, too, contributes to Warlock's most imaginative – and compact – strophic use.

Apart from a chord of G created by the D passing-note at the end of the second, the first three bars are dominated by minor triads. The run is broken by the minor 7th on D (bar 4), a preface to the chromatic, dissonant chord at 4iii (Ex. 15.61). The G sharp in the latter fits with an A centre and it will, in the Warlockian tradition, become a constituent of an alternative note-pair. The A sharp is less easily explained beyond the fact that, firstly, the chord of which it is part, a spread, whole-tone cluster, resolves on to another spread cluster, this time shaped by A minor/Dorian/Aeolian material; secondly, the two notes constitute a double, chromatic appoggiatura. G sharp reappears at the beginning of bar 5 (to be contradicted a crotchet later); A sharp is held in memory for future use.

So, until A sharp reappears (as B flat) in bar 12, all intervening accidentals relate to different manifestations of A-centred subject-matter. F sharp, a Dorian signifier, is used in the bass at the end of the seventh bar (but denied in the subsequent one) and C sharp,

Ex. 15.61: *The frostbound wood* **– bars 1-5**

denoting major or Mixolydian, appears in bar 9 only to be immediately cancelled. G sharp, meanwhile, is preferred to G natural sporadically, but not exclusively, throughout. Chordal choice in the second verse initially matches the first, albeit up the octave; a *Curlew*-chord, often an instrument of change in the past, prefaces new material here too. The E chord at the beginning of bar 8 is more than just a dominant, though; it has, if momentarily, the sensation of a new centre and, despite the raised 3rd, confirms vocal references. The dissonant chord that colours "Pitiful" (bar 9ii) is less easily explained. Its effect is to deny or cloud any sense of a note-focus, yet it embodies A-centre signifiers – the alternative sevenths (G and G sharp), the raised third (C sharp) and the Aeolian sixth (F natural). Although A itself is missing from the chord, E is present. It substantiates the voice; that Warlock sees fit to double it emphasises the fragility of A as the principal centre (Ex. 15.62).

The third verse settles on C (bar 11iv), a brief resolution rather like the E chord three bars earlier. The chord that ensues is interesting, too. It

Ex. 15.62: *The frostbound wood* **– bars 6-9**

contains a *Curlew*-chord component, again with a pivotal function, but it can also be viewed as an extension of the D minor 7th at the corresponding point in the first verse. The G sharp in the bass is an adjunct to the *Curlew*-configuration but the total chord, like that at 10ii, is an aggregation of A-mode signifiers, a description that fits the next shape too (12iii), a minor 7th (on C sharp) with an extraneous note (F natural). The dual derivations (either family chord with an added note or verticalised mode) of these chords prompts others in the ensuing bars, as Ex. 15.63 attests, but it may be taking the matter too far, even in the light of Delian chromaticism, to draw attention to the fact that the foreign notes in some successive chords are chromatically adjacent (F natural-F sharp at 12iii-13ii, C sharp-D-Dsharp at 15iii-16i-16iii).

Rhythmic enhancements of the strophism are heralded by the introductory figure that has become an inter-verse device. Because the verses are brief and the time-span between recurrences consequently short, Warlock modifies it by truncation (bar 6) and diminution (bar 10). In bar 14, reduced by three crotchets, it becomes a rhythmically bland

Ex. 15.63: *The frostbound wood* **– bars 11-15 & 23**

figure that only uses D from the original note distribution; in bar 20 it becomes a single note, an A which the original figure aspired to but did not achieve.

And, in the end, the whole song refuses to recognise it; the preceding allusions and references aside, the final cadence is inconclusive in terms of a specific note-centre. It goes a step further than the *Curlew*-chord with a 7th (a widely spaced 7th at that) which concluded *And wilt thou*; that did contain an element of the B flat minor stated at its outset. Here the voice proclaims E, as it has done all along, and the piano appears to be about to confirm A (as it has done, more or less, all along). But, at the last moment, it gives way to a semitone-modified *Curlew*-chord that, through the C and G sharps, only refers to an A-centre in the most tenuous way. As if to emphasise the fact the upper notes are all a semitone away from an A minor triad. The piano, meanwhile, has the *And wilt thou* shape with a chromatic interpolation (F sharp), indicating a motivic (rather than a tonal or modal) raison d'être.

The limited melodic note-distribution and harmonic dissonance of *The frostbound wood* reflects Blunt's penitential text, a Marian carol transposed from Epiphany to Holy Saturday. *The five lesser joys of Mary* (1929), which expresses more optimistic sentiments, is less satisfactory. Conceived as a part-song,[23] it eventually materialised for unison voices and organ. The melody uses the *And wilt thou*-motif but in a half-hearted manner; given the precedent of *The frostbound wood* – a demanding paradigm, it is true – it is disappointing. It relates to the pentatonicism of bars 8-12, another feature that fails to develop. The song is strophic in form, the same chords being retained for the first four verses, changing only in the last. Speculation that Warlock retained his harmonies because alteration was not desirable – because it could neither improve nor significantly change a chordal statement (as in *Bethlehem Down*) – does not apply here. The chromaticisms of the opening bars may offset the dullness of the parallel, first inversion triads but they are no more successful, and the close on to a chord of F major in bar 8 (from a D flat base) is inexcusable. The vocal line is doubled in the instrumental part giving the impression of a chordal improvisation; it aggravates the melodic weakness. Unfortunately, the status of this non-tune is increased in the last verse where it becomes the basis for some fanciful harmonic procedures. *The five lesser joys . . .* does not represent Warlock at his best; that said, it is no worse than many another Christmastide offering.

Although Warlock continued to edit, arrange and transcribe other people's music, the last two years of his life were compositionally lean. 1929 had witnessed only two works although *The frostbound wood* must be considered one of his own most distinguished pieces and one of the most startlingly original songs by any contemporary, British composer. He appears to have become disillusioned with writing songs although for commercial rather than artistic considerations.[24] But, if his continued association with the poet Bruce Blunt is a reliable measure, an appropriate text could still inspire him.

Warlock wrote four solo songs and a partsong in 1930; however, this statement is not entirely accurate for the last of the solo songs was a rewrite of an earlier, choral composition, another one is a new version of a piano-song and the partsong also exists in a version for unison voices. While arranging his solo songs for differing combinations of voices was a continual aspect of Warlock's output, the new version of *Bethlehem Down* is the only example of the situation in reverse and, as such, it raises aesthetic questions, particularly about its composer's attitude towards melodic and harmonic constructions and the relationship between them.

Carillon carilla would be Warlock's last carol. The choral setting is the one to be discussed here as it contains all the material of the unison version. It is a strophic song that might pass with little comment if it did not contain some unusual harmonies, especially those that open the fourth verse. The prevailing melodic mode is an E-centred Dorian in which C sharp can become C natural (to create an Aeolian mode) and G natural to G sharp (to suggest the Mixolydian). What makes *Carillon carilla* different is the frequency of interchange between these discrepant notes and the impression of interpolated chromaticism that results. D sharp, the raised 7th, is an early *Curlew*-chord component (as E flat) but the chief irritant is B flat, also introduced harmonically as part of a *Curlew*-chord in the second bar of the introduction and an augmented 4th away from the implied centre. The consequent instability is only resolved at the very end and, even then, on to G (major) rather than the initially stated and continually implied E (minor).

But another way to examine the piece, as with the recent solo songs, is to consider the melodic construction. In this way, the soprano line is seen to be made up of basic and modified *And wilt thou*-motifs (Ex. 15.64); occasional parallelism allows them to appear in other parts as well. The resulting vertical and horizontal fusion is not as successful as in *And wilt thou leave me thus* itself for, the accidentals notwithstanding, there is an increased sense of note-centre here that makes them sound the stranger. However, the resultant disorientation creates an appropriate atmosphere for the tale of the Holy Family's search for accommodation; the final verse, more joyously contemplative, abandons

Ex. 15.64: *Carillon carilla* – bars 2-16 (vocal line only)

Ex. 15.65: *Carillon carilla* – bars 54-58

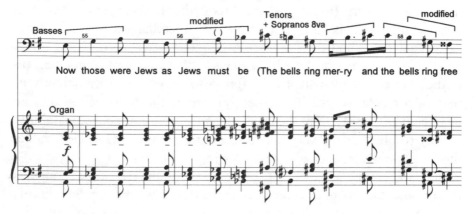

the extraneous B flat altogether and, although there are still chromatic additions, they lack the disquiet that prevails elsewhere in the song.

And so to the curious chordal juxtapositions of the fourth verse. Their extravagant incongruity could mock Belloc's anti-semitic text but may, actually, give it some substance it by drawing attention to it.[25] The B flat minor chord in bar 56 is the most distant point possible from the initial E centre and justifies (or is justified by) the B flats that precede it (Ex.

15.65). This is but one extraordinary chord among many. The C minor chord that follows the pivotal *Curlew*-shape at the start of the passage is also surprising although it incorporates the leading note of the E-centre (D sharp written as E flat, as at the beginning); the forced modulation to the dominant in bar 57 mocks tonal procedures. Warlock makes a statement of some kind about Belloc's words but his intention is not plain. It shows up what is, in fact, a weakness in Warlock's technique for he never really makes clear where he stands on the tonal issue. Perhaps his own modal usage never allows him to fully divorce himself from its constituents, something that an increased dependence on motif would, in fact, allow and which will seem to be developing in *The fox* (yet to be discussed). He very often appears to deny tonality; the avoidance of specific references, at the end of *The frostbound wood*, for example, suggests that he is not dependent on it. But the fact that there are doubts about his intent is a significant criticism. His handling of linear material marks him as a modernist although, in his attitude towards centres and chord-shapes he is still a romantic. To describe him as a transitional figure between the two may be both convenient and correct – *Carillon carilla* epitomises his position.

Furthermore, Warlock had his own doubts about the effectiveness of all the chords in *Carillon carilla*; his manner of expressing it was both unusual and characteristic. In a letter to Arnold Dowbiggin he wrote a parody[26] on Belloc's text, a description of the music of the carol, in which the harmony is ". . . a mixture of Bax and Vaughan [Williams]". By so doing he appears to put himself into the romantics' camp. If what he meant is that his harmony is still, in general, looking backward (though Bax and Vaughan Williams were contemporaries) rather than to the future then this ties in with the foregoing comments. Nonetheless, *And wilt thou leave me thus*, *The frostbound wood* and *The fox* demonstrate something of a change in his compositional approach, one that suggests a different way of thinking chordally. It would not have the chance of being taken further, alas.

Apart from a small number of 5ths, the melody of *The fox* depends upon 2nds and 3rds, minor and major. But the note-choice is much more free here than has been the case; the *And wilt thou*-motif, even in its modified forms, is overtaken by its constituent intervals or semitonal modifications of them (Ex. 15.66). Sometimes shapes recur, creating a kind of vestigial strophism but through-composition is the real basis. Blunt's stanzas are so short (each is only a couplet long) that a purely strophic treatment would not work.

Again – virtually at the end of Warlock's career – chords are chosen for their intrinsic interest rather than their functional relationship, a situation in place for nearly 20 years. Their spontaneity does not deny an

Ex. 15.66: *The fox* – bars 1-6

underlying note-centre or interval-related logic, though. So, the introductory, 5th-plus-3rd (triadic) hunting-horn device would assert F (twice) but gets little support from material associated with it. The E flats could have Mixolydian 7th connotations and the F sharps – a semitonal aberration – could seek to assert D major, an attempt to influence the interpretation of the D-plus-A open 5th that will conclude the song. After a reiteration of the F-triad figure, the falling, parallel 3rds of the second bar suggest a double appoggiatura on to a first inversion A minor chord, the dominant of the D minor chord that initiates the pandiatonic parallelism of the subsequent bar and another contender for the completion of the last bar. These falling semitones still recall the Delian influence, of course, but the irony is that the device that inspired the young Heseltine with its thrilling beauty, isolated and elongated here in a slowly moving texture, now symbolises decay and death.

Chordal progress in bar 3 depends on the semitone: D minor conforms to the key-signature and a D centre has already been suggested; F minor semitonally contradicts the F major that began the piece; E minor is a semitone away from F and the parallelism emphasises the fact rather than seeks to disguise it; A flat minor picks up on the semitonally-altered note of the second chord as well as the E flat of the introduction, itself a distortion of a tonal leading-note; the whole chord semitonally denies the A minor chord that closed bar 2 and announced D minor. In this transition through a tritone Warlock attains in four chords – and with more justification – what he needed a circle-of-5ths for in *Suky you shall be my wife*. The highest note of each chord doubles the melody but, in the light of the harmonic logic, it makes more sense to consider the voice in parallel with the chords; the structurally important 3rds linearly shape the vertical component to create motif-driven harmony, an important advance and the most developed manifestation of the melody of chords.

Warlock's chords generally retain their familiar, four-note structure. There are deviations from the practice but, usually, only when the voice rests. What is of particular interest is that the intervallically driven juxtapositions of bar 3 continue; the top notes of each chord constitute a counter-melody, working in 2nds and 3rds, only coinciding with the vocal line towards the end of the song. Ex. 15.67 demonstrates a longer process that really commences in bar 3 and culminates in a scalically chromatic descent in bars 19-20. This essentially linear basis generates the associated chords such that there is now, in the context of two simultaneous melodic events, a much stronger element of

Ex. 15.67: *The fox* **– bars 3-20 (chordal summary)**

vertical/horizontal interrelationship – and one within a paratonal framework – than has previously been the case. In this context, it is significant that *The fox* follows so quickly on the heels of *Carillon carilla*. Questions raised in discussing the latter are eloquently answered here.

If *The fox* provides some solutions to Warlock's approach, his new version of *Bethlehem Down* asks more questions. His last composition[27] is disappointing in several ways; in others, though, it exemplifies his attitude towards the relationship between horizontal and vertical components in his music within a context of increasing linear awareness – just the sort of environment that *The fox* was concerned with and in which it began to suggest a way forward.

This version is superficially the same as the choral piece written in 1927. All four verses there had used, essentially, the same progression of chords and it was proposed that this arose from a satisfaction with the deployment. It was also suggested that the soprano line was less a tune than just the adjacent, highest notes of the chords. Yet that very line is here granted the status of a melody.

In fact, by virtue of its 2nds- and 3rds-based construction, it does have some credibility in the context of contemporary melodic shapes although much of this stems from a quasi-pentatonic quality; there is none of the semitonal manipulation found in *And wilt thou leave me thus* or *The fox*. Its rhythmic structure is simple and metrical, just the opposite of the freer, speech-dictated shapes that characterise *Sleep* or *And wilt thou leave me thus* where Warlock regards the bar-lines as convenient rather than regulatory.

Some of the harmonic content of the 1927 setting is retained but, for most of the piece, Warlock introduces new material. Passing-notes, utilised in all parts in the choral version and most obviously by the sopranos in the third line of each verse, created a strong sense of forward motion and they assume an even greater importance in this one. The continual quavers (note-values are halved) become obsessional, in fact, not unlike those of *The distracted maid*. As in that song, they do more than simply ease the passage between chords, even though these remain the logical basis of the piece. In *Bethlehem Down*, passing notes are transmuted into stepwise motion, a motivic device though one lacking the character of the *And wilt thou*-shape. Semitonal modification, where it happens, is regulated by considerations of note-centre in the manner of one of the earlier songs, prompted, as Ex. 15.68 shows, by the interpretation of the E flat, Mixolydian 7th as a flat-side gesture, a situation from which contemporary songs appear to be moving away.

So, while it has a degree of the linear about it, the song's homophonic origin militates against its success and no amount of parallel-quaver motion can alter the fact. It is a statement about the relationship between Warlock's chords and melody: their evolution needs to be simultaneous and, as *The five lesser joys of Mary* demonstrates even more forcefully than *Bethlehem Down*, when the harmonic raison d'être is removed, the melodic remnant cannot survive. If (the conditional qualification is important) Warlock was influenced at all in this song by the Renaissance practice of producing solo and choral ayres from the same material, he is unusually ignorant of the importance of the homorhythmic quality inherent in both instrumental and vocal components. His reversion to a strongly chordal – though not exclusively homorhythmic – treatment for passages in verse 3 and for most of verse 4 suggests what really lies at the heart of his work. In just that one way this otherwise not very important piece provides an appropriate ending to Warlock's compositional career.

It is in these more contemplative songs, then, that Warlock finds his true voice. This is not by any means because of the elevating or philosophical nature of the texts but simply because his musical vocabulary is tight, interrelated and subject to regulation by the semitone which can create ambiguities and doubts. These factors generate an ambience more suited to verbal introspection or rationale. It is a great pity that much of the output discussed in this chapter has but a

Ex. 15.68: *Bethlehem Down* **(solo version) – bars 9-15; cf. Ex. 15.54**

limited currency in the solo-song or choral repertoire, though. For whatever reason, Warlock's best music has been largely ignored; why this is so when it can be shown to constantly demonstrate ingenuity and sensitivity remains a mystery. One piece by Warlock has not suffered the same neglect, however; although it is to be discussed out of chronological order, it will be the subject of most of the final chapter of this survey.

Notes

1 IC p. 111.
2 ". . . however, they can stand separately, and indeed they do not really both suit the same voice." MP p. 145.
3 See pp. 24-27.
4 p. 120. See note 5, Chapter 8.
5 The story appears in the apocryphal Gospel of Thomas. See James (1924).
6 It was written for Port Regis Prep. School, Broadstairs (IC p. 203).
7 FT1 p. 36 follows Kenneth Avery's chronology.
8 IC p. 122 states that the autograph – of all three songs – is dated January 1927, a fact recognised by Tomlinson (FT1 p. 9). It is conceivable that they originated the previous year.
9 IC p. 122.
10 Somebody else did! See FT1 p. 17. FT himself suggests that, while some of them may have been in PW's hand, they could have been made by BvD (conversation with BC, 29/09/90). The Ms. has disappeared.
11 *Song by two voices* by Thomas Lovell Beddoes (1803-1849) from *The bride's tragedy*, 1822.
12 MP p. 151.
13 op. cit. p. 85.
14 See p. 49.
15 PW's manuscript (now in the library of the RCM) is a semitone lower than the printed version (O), also sans key-signature.
16 It is misprinted without an accidental (O 1928); in T(vii) the error is corrected although the whole is given a tone lower.
17 FT (1981) cannot establish a precise date.
18 see note 19.
19 Blunt relates that he and PW produced the piece at speed to raise money for beer at Christmas! See IC pp. 204-5.
20 PW produced versions of *The bayly berith the bell away*, *The first mercy*, *Lullaby* and *Mourn no moe*, presumably to raise cash.
21 By T. See note 8, Chapter 6.
22 It ". . . is not a very characteristic Warlock composition . . ." (IC pp. 209-10). The Finzi Singers' recordings (see note 2, Chapter 8) present an opportunity to re-assess the work. It is strong enough to withstand numerous, repeated hearings.
23 See IC p. 210.
24 IC pp. 139-40 reproduces part of a letter from PW to Arnold

Dowbiggin, the dedicatee of *And wilt thou . . .* and *The frostbound wood*, in which he refers to ". . . the enormous decline in the music publishing trade".

25 See IC p. 211.

26 IC p.212 quotes PW's doggerel in its entirety. PW refers to the whole carol as "balls" because "The tune is trite and the style's outworn . . .". The latter fact, Warlock's general penchant for self-deprecation aside, substantiates the comment in the text about "looking backward".

27 The holograph is dated 1.XII.30. PW died on the 17th.

CHAPTER 16

Capriol and some conclusions

The suite *Capriol* typifies the general misunderstanding that has dogged Warlock's music for it is usually misnamed. A quick glance at the score will reveal that a "suite for string orchestra" (in small letters) is called "Capriol" (isolated and in larger type). The title "Capriol suite" is, therefore, a fabrication. But, whatever it gets called, it has come to represent its composer. It is heard on the radio with some frequency, figures on several recordings, often compilations of British or English music and is the single named work with which he is likely to be identified, even in musical company. Unfortunately its popularity has generated misunderstandings about the nature of his oeuvre for he wrote no other work like it; it is partly responsible for the Elizabethanist label that has been hung round his neck. But it is undoubtedly true that, had Warlock not already demonstrated a sympathy for and a knowledge of the music of the Renaissance, he would not have been approached by Cyril Beaumont to write the preface to the latter's 1925 edition of Thoinot Arbeau's *Orchésographie*.[1] Without this experience, Warlock could not have written *Capriol* the following year.

In two respects the suite does not typify its composer. It should be apparent from the argument this far that references to antique material in Warlock's music are not essential – they do appear from time to time but in momentary, eclectic gestures rather than as constructional necessities. There is no need to temper this opinion because of the very quantity of old tunes in *Capriol*. And, because it is an instrumental piece, it fits rather uncomfortably into the last phase of Warlock's career which, although he worked the while on transcriptions of old viol music and the like, otherwise consists only of compositions with vocal and verbal components.

But, if one can lift and set aside the obvious, decorative veneer of Arbeau's melodies, it will be possible to discern an altogether more familiar, Warlockian substance throughout the work. Despite the fact that it dates from some four years before the end of his life, it sums up some of his compositional achievements. It is not his best work – so much must be made clear; *The fox* and *The frostbound wood* are better by virtue both of their inventiveness and sensitivity; from their position nearer to his death they make a more fitting epitaph. The relative familiarity of the *Capriol* music, though, demands a separate treatment as well as a reappraisal.

Capriol recalls the *Folk-song preludes* and *An old song* written a decade earlier: much melodic material is not original to Warlock (although the modal outlines chime with his own) and harmonies result from his own chordal philosophy rather than one automatically implied by the tunes or their cultural ambience. In this context, *Capriol* further questions Warlock's method, as did those earlier works. In this case the problem is that of reconciling his attitude towards modality and tonality. The easy way out would be to cite his enthusiasm for the chordal progressions, often modally derived, that characterise Renaissance structures and mark their presence here accordingly. This will not work; the harmonies of *Pieds-en-l'air* may be excused (because the melody is mostly invented) as may the pandiatonicism and dissonance of *Matta-chins* (where the material also diverges from Arbeau). But this does not explain, for example, the deliberate false relations in the *Basse-danse* and the *Pavane* which have associations, and therefore origins, beyond musica ficta or other discrepancies that can only be consistently described in terms of Warlock's accumulating style. *Capriol* is a work as much affected by eclecticism as *My gostly fader* and its harmonic basis must be seen to lie elsewhere – in Warlock's own developed method, in fact. It must not be assumed that the idiom of the melodies will exclusively find its way into the harmonies; if this were the case, the suite is a reconstruction rather than the composition that it surely is (and which the following discussion will confirm) and it could, like the dance, song and other transcriptions, be left out of this survey. Comments apply to all versions of *Capriol* although examples are taken from that for string orchestra.[2]

The Renaissance practice of decorating sections on their repetition (akin to the Baroque double) matches Warlock's strophic methodology, except that his ornamentation is chordal rather than linear – he leaves the tunes alone. Thus, the first strain (in Morley's[3] terminology) of the *Basse-danse* is harmonised in terms of a D-centred Aeolian mode; its immediate reappearance is marked by the insertion of a G minor chord (bar 9) but, more significantly, by the A chord with an added 9th (a pentatone-derived chord) at the beginning of bar 12. This chord both denies the preceding C natural and anticipates the *ficta* dichotomy of bar 20 (Ex. 16.1) and, because the figure is strong, its literal repetition eight bars later. Warlock's melodic C sharp is editorial – the version in

Ex. 16.1: *Basse-danse (Capriol)* **– bars 9-12 & 19-20**

Ex. 16.2: *Basse-danse* **– bars 49-52 & 59-60**

Beaumont's edition, with which, after all, he was intimately familiar,[4] employs no accidentals. While precedents exist in early music, the simultaneous use of both 3rds is further evidence of Warlock the composer rather than the transcriber or arranger and has already been witnessed in *Sorrow's lullaby* and elsewhere.

The third strain converts to the Dorian, still D-centred, although it moves to A (minor) after four bars, restores D and then moves to A major. It is, therefore, reminiscent of the major/minor discrepancies of the earlier Rogers songs and, at the same time, relates to the dichotomous ficta passage of several bars previously; repetition extends this detail by sharpening the F of the D Dorian, converting it to a Mixolydian. The movement concludes with a truncated repeat of the entire dance: harmonies are different, individual strains are not repeated and the third one is omitted altogether in favour of a concluding figure. The rate of harmonic change is increased to begin with (bar 49 et seq.) and eventually uses both Aeolian and Dorian 6ths. Once more, a device is carried over into the next phrase, this time into the bass ficta motif (bar 60 – cf. bar 20 – Ex. 16.2). After some pentatone-chords this same motif closes the work using simultaneous ascending and descending forms (Ex. 16.3) for which the inspiration and derivation could be just as much Bartók as Arbeau.

The *Pavane* has a G Dorian melody which employs variant 7ths, once again according to the practices of musica ficta. The initial harmony uses the Aeolian 6th as well as the Dorian but it must be pointed out that it too emanates from *Orchésographie*. Most of the differences between the two presentations of this binary dance are achieved texturally; there is no harmonic change in the second. The melody returns at the same pitch but in the lower half of the deployed note-range instead of at the top. The real harmonic variants are reserved for the epilogue, a further reprise of the second half of the melody. They are effective without being extravagant and hinge on the D chord with a B flat in the bass (bars 65-6, a pseudo-pedal that appears out of nowhere) and the false relation between the alternative modal 7ths in bar 67 – see Ex. 16.4. The other, G-plus-D drone is introductory or intermediate and does not impinge upon the dance-melody. It has an atmospheric rather than a structural function (a reversal of such manifestations elsewhere) and must be viewed as another eclecticism.

The *Tordion* melody fragments in the course of the movement, a further abstraction of the reduced form supplied by Arbeau himself,[5] and is eventually distilled into a progression of two-chord statements. The

Ex. 16.3: *Basse-danse* **– bars 65-68**

Ex. 16.4: *Pavane (Capriol)* **– bars 62-69**

Ex. 16.5: *Tordion (Capriol)* – bars 1-4

(Basses rest)

first harmonic treatment of the tune prefers the Dorian 6th (just like the melody) so that, when the raised 3rd is employed (as at the end of bar 2) an impression of the Mixolydian is created. As well as these alternative 3rds, the 7th is subject to alteration; F sharp substitutes for F natural in other than ficta contexts. The raised 7th (violas bar 3, Ex. 16.5) is present to make much of the clash with the G from the first violins.

And the last discrepancy is that between Dorian and Aeolian 6ths; E flat and E natural also become interchangeable. Once these working practices are established they permeate the whole movement, even to the point of an E flat major chord in bar 13, immediately followed by one of C major (Ex. 16.6); the procedure is repeated in bars 25 and 29.

The *Bransles* is the most structurally complex of the six movements and Copley gives a full breakdown of the themes employed and their derivations from *Orchésographie*.[6] The repeated-note melody is less individualistic than its companions but this has advantages: the homo-rhythmic – and, consequently, chordal – element is heightened in this relatively unadorned texture so that it can express the transmutation of melodically generated progress into chordal statement, just what the *Tordion* was beginning to propose towards its end. As before, these are regulated by modal implications so that, although the overt linearity of the melody is reduced, the implicit linearity of the mode is retained, indeed, becomes the raison d'être. The following modal breakdown of

Ex. 16.6: *Tordion* – bars 13-16

the first 42 bars (up to the change of signature) can be superimposed on Copley's thematic sectionalisation. It does not include textural modifications such as octave-transposition that are used to generate variety. G is the centre throughout.

Bars 1-3   Aeolian

    4-6   Aeolian with raised 7ths in the melody; 3rd avoided in the final chord

    7-9   As bars 1-3

    10-12   As bars 4-6 but a Dorian 6th replaces the Aeolian and a Mixolydian (major) 3rd introduced into the final chord

    13-15   As bars 1-3 but with a counter-melody, a variant of the figure heard in 9-10

    16-18   As bars 10-12

    19-22   Dorian and Aeolian 6ths, minor and major 3rds, Mixolydian and raised 7ths – a fusion of all of the above

    23-26   As bars 19-22 without the cadential major 3rd but with the counter-melody

    27-30   A scalic melody reasserts G but harmony uses variant 6ths and 7ths

    31-34   As bars 27-30

    35-38   Similar to bars 27-30 but now with a chromatic counter-melody that uses notes beyond the alternative 6ths and 7ths

    39-42   As bars 35-38.

This kind of modal exposition is familiar enough from the songs. There is no modulation but the middle section of the movement (bars 43-82), while G-based, has its modal emphasis shifted towards the Ionian. Chromaticism (in bars 55 and 75, for example) is similar to what has already been experienced elsewhere in the suite but is not generated within this part of the piece – its validity depends on what has already occurred. In fact, the Ionian offers little scope for discrepancies and it is abandoned in favour of earlier techniques and material. These conclude the movement with what proves to be the most substantial of the three sections (bars 83-148). Although there is a small amount of new thematic content, harmonic processes are as at the start.

Pieds-en-l'air contrasts in tempo and texture with the movements on either side of it. The melody, only a small portion of which is quoted by Arbeau,[7] is G-centred with alternative 7ths, Mixolydian in the upper octave and Ionian in the lower. These discrepant notes mark the limits of the tune which is, as implied, mostly a Warlockian concoction. It is used after the manner of a two-verse, strophic song; the first appearance is expositional, the second an opportunity for harmonic development. But, because the melody itself incorporates an element of repetition that is open to modification, there is a sense of continuous growth within the "verses" and, hence, throughout the movement rather than in distinct, even predictable, locations.

However, the modality of the melody is the only compositional concession to the Renaissance. Chordal choice is family-dependent once more and has no modal associations beyond a greater than usual (for this sort of vocabulary) sense of functional progression; even the German 6th shape in the penultimate bar turns out to be a real one (Ex. 16.7). So the contrast with the *Bransles* is not just one of tempo but language and personality; it reasserts the chordal basis of the modal deployment at the moment when the linear manifestation seemed to be taking precedence.

The spectacular chords, the most memorable feature of *Mattachins*, serve as onomatopoeic sword-impacts but, also, test the F-focus of this last movement and, perhaps, even the note-centre allegiances of the whole suite. There is a logic to the relationship between these centres, a sense of progression from one to the next, that is modally rather than tonally derived. Apart from one, all the movements have a single-flat signature; this is consistent with their respective centres, D (*Basse-danse*) G (*Pavane, Tordion* and *Bransles*) and F (*Mattachins*). *Pieds-en-l'air*, with its single-sharp signature, extends the G-centre of the preceding movement but adds Mixolydian elements to the Dorian,

Ex. 16.7: *Pieds-en-l'air (Capriol)* **– bars 24-26**

Aeolian and Ionian characteristics already explored. This attitude is similar to, if less arresting than, the use of modal relationships in *Jillian of Berry* and *Away to Twiver*.

Otherwise, the apparently simple, Ionian melody of the *Mattachins* has a harmony to match, give or take a Mixolydian 7th and an Aeolian 6th. The rhythmic, bass drone that opens it is based on the drum-rhythm that would have accompanied the original monophonic dance-tune, an innocuous device from which the sword-chords will derive. It regulates nearly all the expositional material, giving way to a perfect cadence at bar 28 (although the C and F of the drone encapsulate dominant and tonic anyway). But melodic re-use reveals its own deceit; it has no 7th, could be Mixolydian rather than Ionian and the harmony exploits this.

And so begins the curious cycle of chords that serves as a coda to the individual movement and the whole work. The drone rhythm on which it is based is generated from within the *Mattachins* itself but is also related to the notes that begin the *Basse-danse* melody, the insistent drum-rhythm of the *Pavane* and motifs used in the *Tordion, Bransles* and, rather more tenuously, *Pieds-en-l'air* (Ex. 16.8). To begin with,

Ex. 16.8: *Capriol:* **rhythmic relationships between movements**

dissonant chords with a whole-tone component alternate with major chords. Among the former is the composite chord from *Robin Goodfellow*; the latter group comprises those on A, G flat, C, A flat and F. There is no consistent relationship one with another but some would deny the F-centre while others are there to substantiate it. After their repetition (bars 54-62) dissonances become more uncompromising: the chord in bar 63, a 13th, has seven different notes in it, that in bar 65, less readily defined, has six. This passage (Ex. 16.9) is the closest Warlock gets to "the stimulating harshness and dissonance of Bartók"[8] and it is acceptable to view its origins in those terms.

So, while aspects of *Capriol* summarise Warlock's procedures, there are also features to lead astray the unwary. In no other composition does he use echt-Renaissance melodies thereby so provocatively inviting the biographical fallacy ("he was a Renaissance scholar ergo his music is influenced by the Renaissance"). At the risk of crushing the kernel of truth with the sledgehammer of repetition, Warlock was no neo-Classicist (or neo-Renaissancist in his case) even though his music was contemporary with what are construed as observations of the past – *Pulcinella*, *Apollon Musagète* and other pieces by Stravinsky, as well as examples by Hindemith, Poulenc, Bartók etc.

Indeed, part of the problem of evaluating Warlock the composer is that he fits badly against the usual criteria used for assessment. Although he produced a big enough corpus of songs of one sort or another, there is very little else: a suite of piano preludes possesses limited artistic value (although it is an important indicator of his stylistic development) and a couple of orchestral pieces emulate his friend and guide to a greater or lesser extent. Again, while they are valuable in a survey such as this and are, of themselves, competent enough, they do not demonstrate the peculiar Warlockian character. In this sense, therefore, *Capriol* stands in a fascinating position, unique not only in the mature music but in the whole canon. It is relatively easy to analyse but difficult to evaluate or contextualise; in this respect it is just like its composer and further serves as a summary of his career.

Warlock established no school[9] and any group to which he belongs as a song composer is loose not to say disparate.[10] There were, of course, many British songwriters with whom he is contemporary or of whom he is a successor or predecessor of sorts. But it would be fatuous to materially relate Warlock to, say, Stanford or Britten. And although he knew and admired, among others, C W Orr, Roger Quilter, Arnold Bax and Alec Rowley, one should not look for (or expect to find) similarities

Ex. 16.9: *Mattachins (Capriol)* – bars 63-71

of approach. The situation is one of tradition – British composers write songs – rather than of a school with a shared philosophy.

The grouping with which he can actually be associated lies outside the European mainstream. The origins of Delius's music are, as Christopher Palmer has so ably shown,[11] multifarious and served the hedonism to which Warlock also aspired. Along with Balfour Gardiner, Jack Moeran, John Ireland, Alec Rowley again – hardly household names any of them – he sought out what we would now describe as the Delian backwater. Yet he was destined never to achieve the heights that his friend Arnold Bax did in his second symphony where harmonic and melodic shapes similar to those used by Delius himself are put in a grand frame imbued with a nobility, a majesty even, that the older man rarely achieved. The result is that Delius is, effectively, out-Deliused!

All of this draws attention to an assumed hierarchy of musical genres, a situation akin to that seen in nineteenth-century painting where not only were large canvasses depicting historical or legendary events considered to have greater aesthetic worth than, for example, landscapes or portraits but the worked-up, stylistically detailed, technically demonstrative oil painting had more credibility than the spontaneously executed water-colour sketch, however vital. For "history-painting" read "symphony" or "opera". Songwriters are not taken as seriously as symphonists unless they happen to be both. However, these observations are not intended as a list of excuses and a proper evaluation of the composer must only be based on factual data.

To begin with, Warlock rarely wrote for resources that did not feature a voice and voices require texts to sing. That he was verbally as well as musically aware is evident in his own written style and the volume of his output, his early championship of writers yet to be publicly recognised (such as Yeats and Roy Campbell), not to mention the breadth of his own reading. He would appear to have had a fascination with the very sound of language, hence his settings not just of Cornish, Latin and French (which together only make up four songs) but of Elizabethan and Jacobean English too. He may well have encountered the words as a result of his musicological investigations although throughout this survey it has been made clear that the real substance of his settings of such texts owe little, if anything, to their contemporary musical style. But the main reason for his becoming a song composer must lie in the nature of his compositional style – the resources of voice and piano are one means whereby melodic material can facilitate chordal motion. In other words, it can be perceived that Warlock in his songs does not so much employ an ongoing chordal logic which enhances a vocal melody, rather, he writes songs so that his chordal procedures can be melodically validated. Forms other than songs are possible, of course, but the textural division implied by his methodology coupled with his verbal sympathies make song his natural medium.

This being said, how does Warlock's technique complement his texts? To begin with, one feature that rarely needs mentioning is word-painting: there are very few significant examples of this process in his output and, while it is a factor of only minor importance, anyone who accepts the biographical preconception would have expected a greater frequency of the phenomenon from one who is, by reputation, influenced by the English High Renaissance. The misunderstanding apart, it is a fact that Warlock sets a wide variety of textual sentiments from the abandon of *Rutterkin* to the metaphysics, the nihilism even, of the Webster dirges.

What Warlock can achieve is the creation of musical imagery through his method. Some instances are more spectacular than others. In the most extreme example, *Sleep*, the dissonances and distortions that close the song are a fusion of abstracted Delian chromaticism an van Dierenesque polyphony. They have as their starting point the concordant G-shape, a temporary point of rest that, on the one hand, encapsulates Warlock's continuing diatonic reliance; on the other, it reflects the "sweet deceiving" of the text. *Sleep* is not about peace at all but the disturbances of dreams and fancies, a factor forcibly substantiated by Ivor Gurney's own setting, of course. Warlock's epilogue, a statement of troubled reality that counteracts any fantasy, is not pacified by the G chords that close it. Formally they represent a tonic dutifully appended; but the concords are too sweet in their context and only represent false hopes – "sleep", anyway, is a euphemism for "death" ("let my joys have some abiding") and the hidden metaphysical (and mannerist) agenda is never far from this interpretation. Fletcher's words have echoes in other, contemporary writings such as Shakespeare's Sonnet XLIII ("When most I wink then do mine eyes best see") and their universality and depth of meaning evoked a remarkably sympathetic response from Warlock. Musical imagery in *Autumn twilight*, *The full heart*, *The shrouding of the Duchess of Malfi* and elsewhere achieves comparable results. As a general observation, the semitonally regulated relationships that bind together Warlock's chordal family and its linear offshoots find a constant and sympathetic resonance in the fatalism, fragility or insecurity proclaimed by the texts of such songs.

Such a statement, though, raises doubts about the validity and efficacy of the lighter songs – *Mr Belloc's fancy*, *Captain Stratton's fancy* and the like. Most of the objections that have been raised about them in the past have arisen from what is perceived as their banality, an assumption that verbal inconsequence generates, ipso facto, music of little worth. In a number of specific cases this may be justified: *The jolly shepherd*, *Peter Warlock's fancy* and *The bachelor* have many deficiencies, it is true, and no claim is made here for their unquestioned acceptability; but it is necessary to examine Warlock's intentions. (They do not alter the quality of the outcome but may start to explain why Warlock bothered to write such songs at all.)

There are historical precedents and one need look no further than Purcell – whose music Warlock admired and, through his transcriptions, helped to popularise – to find a "serious" composer who could and did turn his hand to catches and other frivolous material. Antiquity is a great healer, though, and what is perceived as the charm of the ancient music now excuses the scatological or proletarian subject-matter. In Warlock's case, perhaps because of his suspicion of established or acclaimed figures (Stravinsky, Holst, Vaughan Williams), he perversely declared his support for alternatives, individual (Delius, Gesualdo, van Dieren, Bartók, Berlin) or stylistic (early music, brass bands, folksong). Nevertheless, he had a genuine enthusiasm for lighter pieces and attempted some himself. The results were varied but some worked well, especially where his musical vocabulary could suggest ironic humour, confusion or riotous jollity. *Away to Twiver* is the supreme example but, given their context – craftsmanlike songs with clearly defined and direct texts, musical and verbal – *Jillian of Berry*, *Rutterkin*, *Maltworms*, *Good ale*, *Milkmaids*, even *Fill the cup Philip* and *The cricketers of Hambledon* – are successful in what they set out to achieve.

Occasionally, Warlock tried too hard and his intentions misfired. The complimentary rectitude of *Piggesnie* is irredeemable. If the blatancy of the modulation is meant to suggest otherwise, as it does in *Rantum tantum*, then it fails for it lacks the preparation of the latter song within its cycle. And perhaps the lighter songs as a whole do not represent Warlock at his best, despite any short-term attractiveness they may generate. They constitute the more straightforward side of his oeuvre and have been taken up by singers as programme-fillers (*Captain Stratton . . .* is a particular and overworked example) that are deemed to balance weightier items by other, more respectable composers. This is one of the reasons why Warlock's output has been misunderstood. For in these songs Warlock was aspiring to something that he felt was both necessary and artistically valid and he did not recognise his own strengths and weaknesses in the matter. The chordal vocabulary that he developed right through his career was really much better suited to texts with altogether different sentiments.

Allied to the appropriateness of musical to verbal material is Warlock's rhythmic outlook. He displays great sympathy for the natural stresses of the words in his selected texts and, consequently, is often bound by the metrical demands of the verse he sets. As a result, his harmonies may sound pretentious (as in *Fair and true*) or he feels obliged to compromise to the point where tonality – in the form of more conventional shapes and procedures – dilutes his methods (*The jolly shepherd*, *The five lesser joys of Mary*). It must also be made clear, though, that this metrical fidelity can be positive as well. The verse of the *Candlelight* songs could have resulted in equally predictable settings. In fact, their simple brevity inspired concise refinement.

So, while Warlock creates an emotional ambience in his music that is appropriate to the mood of the words and can, at times, circumvent the obvious one and put a new slant on things, his principal technical reaction to his texts is bound by their metrical deployment. Conversely, it can also be said that he is at his best when the metre of the verse is unusual or less rigid. Yeats's poetry in *The curlew* is a case in point: it has a rhythm of its own and Warlock is happy to follow it, but its irregularity suits his musical vocabulary better than, for example, the unrelenting dactylic tetrameters of *The jolly shepherd* (again). Likewise, the mixed metre of *The shrouding of the Duchess of Malfi* (iambic and trochaic tetrameters) proves a positive stimulus. There are a few occasions on which Warlock is prepared to modify or override the verbal rhythms in some way. At its simplest this can simply be a matter of choosing the right tempo: the dactyls of *Bethlehem Down* could have become as tiresome as those of *The jolly shepherd* but, when performed "Very slow" such a problem disappears. Similar tempi in *The full heart* and *All the flowers of the spring* are equally effective but, in these two, Warlock has a greater than usual tendency to ignore the natural syllabic stress in order to produce a more dramatic result than would otherwise have been the case. Less typically, in *Call for the robin redbreast and the wren* and *My lady is a pretty one*, the metre is disguised by the use of melisma.

Finally, although this survey has been directed towards musical results rather than the details of a life, it is difficult to leave the subject of Peter Warlock without considering, if only briefly, the infamous theory established by Cecil Gray in his biography of 1934. The matter of a "split personality" is one that neither Gray nor the present writer was or is qualified to discuss; but it is a fact that, because of the place of the former's book in Warlockian studies, his opinion has achieved the status of a dogma rarely questioned openly outside the cognoscenti. Warlock the man did display some characteristics associated with cyclothymic or manic depressive personalities but, rather than pursue tiresome proposals of this nature, it makes sense to leave such a final detail to another song. *Sweet-and-twenty* demonstrates not so much two unreconciled sides of a single, complex character but a flexibility, an ability to identify and address the varying demands of circumstance.

The dichotomy is present in Shakespeare's words: the anticipated pleasure of the "lovers' meeting" prompts doubts about the future ("what's to come is still unsure"). It has already been stated that Warlock's vocabulary and technique are up to dealing with different emotional demands in separate songs; here they are called upon to deal with diversity within the same one. Not only is this further evidence of Warlock's compositional validity, it stands as an allegory of his personality. There is no doubt that he did seek out the selfish pleasure of the immediate present; but he also had a strong sense of insecurity about the future, a lack of confidence in his own abilities that appears time and time again in his letters to Delius, Taylor and others. Some of the latter, no doubt, arises from the tight financial constraint in which, rightly or wrongly, he felt he was placed by his mother; however, these are not unique circumstances and question, given the wealth of music he wrote, the value of such an exercise.

Notes

1   For details of Warlock's encounter with Arbeau's *Orchésographie* and its translator, Cyril Beaumont, see IC pp. 235-6.

2   *Capriol* appeared in versions for piano duet, string and full orchestras, but that for strings was the first in print. Other arrangements – of which there are many – are by other persons.

3   Morley uses the term to denote a self-contained section in *A plaine and easie introduction to practicall musicke* (1597).

4   The notated examples were prepared by PW for Beaumont.

5   p. 83 in Beaumont's edition.

6   IC p. 239.

7   Only the opening two bars are given by Arbeau "because the rest of it . . . [has] the same movements." Beaumont op. cit. p. 126.

8   See note 6, Chapter 11.

9   That the Warlockian style is elusive and difficult to emulate is discussed in Hutchings (4th July 1963).

10   "We are all individualists and no such school exists" (Arnold Bax on English composers) quoted in Pirie (Summer 1965) p. 23.

11   in CP.

Bibliography

A complete bibliography of all known books and articles written by or about Peter Warlock before 1976 can be found in Fred Tomlinson's *A Peter Warlock handbook* vol. 2 pp. 91-106 (see below). Material listed here inevitably duplicates this in part but also includes details of more recent publications as well as those on other composers or subjects that refer to Warlock or have a bearing on Warlock research. A comprehensive list of manuscript material held in the British Library is also included to aid further enquiry.

ApIvor, Denis (May 1985), "Philip Heseltine (Peter Warlock): a psychological study", *The Music Review*, pp. 118-132.

— (Nov 1986/7), "Bernard van Dieren: search and rescue one hundred years on", *The Music Review*, vol. 47 no. 4, pp. 253-66.

— (Autumn 1994), "A signpost at a fork o' the road", PWSNL no. 55, pp. 3-5. See also PWSNL no. 56.

Arbeau, Thoinot trans. Beaumont, Cyril W. (1925), *Orchesography*, Beaumont, 1925.

Baker, Frank (November 1936), "The artist's private life: notes upon Philip Heseltine", *The Chesterian*, vol. 18 no. 130, pp. 46-8.

Banfield, Stephen (1985), *Sensibility and English song*, Cambridge University Press, Cambridge.

Bartók, Béla trans. Brian Lunn (July 1921), "The relation of folk-song to the development of the art music of our time", *The Sackbut*, vol. 2 no. 1, pp. 5-11.

Bennett, Rodney (September 1923), "Peter Warlock: the man and his songs", *The Bookman*, vol 64 no. 384, pp. 300-2.

Blom, Eric (1 April 1931), "Warlock Memorial Concert" [review], *The Musical Times*, vol 72 no. 1058, pp. 360-1.

Carley, Lionel & Threlfall, Robert (1983), *Delius: a life in pictures*, T [reprint of O, 1977].

Chambers, E. K. & Sidgwick, F. (eds – 1907), *Early English lyrics*, A. H. Bullen, London.

Chappell, William (1893), *Old English popular music*, Chappell & Co. and Macmillan & Co. [revised edition by H. Ellis Wooldridge of original, ?1855 version].

Chisholm, Alastair (1984), *Bernard van Dieren: an introduction*, T.

Cockshott, Gerald (July 1940), "Some notes on the songs of Peter Warlock", *Music & Letters*, vol 21 no. 3, pp. 246-58.

— (November 1940), "A Note on Warlock's 'Capriol Suite'", *The Monthly Musical Record*, vol. 70 no. 821, , pp. 203-5.

— (March 1955), "E J Moeran's recollections of Peter Warlock", *The Musical Times*, vol. 94 no. 1345, pp. 128-30.

Collins, Brian (August 1986/7), "Rantum tantum: linear techniques in Warlock's *Lillygay*", *The Music Review*, vol. 47 no. 3, pp. 184-93.

— (July 1987), "Warlock and the *Lillygay* texts", PWSNL no. 39, pp.10-11.

— (October 1989), "The case of *The distracted maid*", PWSNL no. 43, pp. 9-10.

— (April 1990), "Besides *The distracted maid*", PWSNL no. 44, p. 7.

— (1992), "Peter Warlock: a pre-centenary re-appraisal" *Aspects of British Song*, (British Music Society Song Composer Year Book) , pp. 82-9.

Collinson, Francis (1966), *The traditional and national music of Scotland*, Routledge and Kegan Paul, London.

Copley, Ian (June 1963), "Warlock's Cod-Pieces", *The Musical Times*, vol. 104 no. 1444, pp. 410-11.

— (October 1964), "Warlock in novels", *The Musical Times*, vol. 105 no. 1460, pp. 739-40.

— (July 1968), "Warlock and Delius – a catalogue", *Music & Letters*, vol. 49 no. 3, pp. 213-18.

— (1979), *The music of Peter Warlock: a critical survey*, Dobson, London.

— (1983), *A turbulent friendship - a study of the relationship between D H Lawrence and Philip Heseltine ("Peter Warlock")*, T.

Cox, David (10 December 1964), "Warlock: the mask and the meaning", *The Listener*, vol. 72 no. 1863, p. 953.

— (With Bishop, John – eds) (1994), *Peter Warlock: a centenary celebration*, T.

Davies, Hywel *Philip Heseltine as seen through his letters to Colin Taylor*. Undergraduate dissertation.

— (December 1987), "Bernard van Dieren (1887-1936)", *The Musical Times*, vol. 127 no. 1738, , pp. 675-78.

— (January 1988), "Bernard van Dieren, Philip Heseltine and Cecil Gray: a significant affiliation", *Music & Letters*, vol. 69 no. 1, pp. 30-48.

van Dieren, Bernard (1 February 1931), "Philip Heseltine" [obituary], *The Musical Times*, vol. 72 no. 1056, pp. 117-19.

— (1935), "Down among the dead men" and other essays, O, London.

Dille, Denijs (September 1965), "Vier unbekannte Briefe von Béla Bartók", *Die Osterreichische Musikzeitschrift*, vol. 20, pp. 449-60.

East, Leslie (1975), "Busoni and van Dieren", *Soundings*, vol. 5, pp. 44-54.

Fenby, Eric (1936), *Delius as I knew him*, Bell and Sons, London.

Foreman, Lewis (1988), *Bax: a composer and his times*, 2nd Edition, Scolar Press, Aldershot.

Foss, Hubert (1 January 1931), "Philip Heseltine 1894-1930", *The Monthly Musical Record*, vol. 61 no. 721, pp. 1-2.

Gillies, Malcolm (1982), "Bartók in Britain 1922", *Music & Letters*, vol. 63, pp. 213-25.

— (Aug/Nov 1982), "Bartók, Heseltine and Gray: a documentary study", *The Music Review*, vol. 43 nos 3/4, pp. 177-91.

— (1989), *Bartók in Britain*, O, Oxford.

Gray, Cecil (November 1920), "Bela Bartok" [sic], *The Sackbut*, vol. 1 no. 7, pp. 303-12 (includes examples reproduced from PW's MS).

— (1934), *Peter Warlock: A memoir of Philip Heseltine*, Cape, London.

— (1948), *Musical chairs*, Home and van Thal, London.

Gray, Pauline (1989), *Cecil Gray - his life and notebooks*, T.

Hamnett, Nina (1955), *Is she a lady?*, Allan Wingate, London.

Harker, Dave (1985), *Fakesong; the manufacture of British "folksong" 1700 to the present day*, Open University Press, Milton Keynes.

Heseltine, Nigel (1992), *Capriol for mother*, T.

Heseltine, Philip (21 September 1912), "Arnold Schönberg", *The Musical Standard*, vol. 38 no. 977, pp. 176-8.

— (March 1917) untitled – relating to Bernard van Dieren, *The Palatine Review*, no. 5, pp. 25-9.

— (10 May 1917), "Predicaments concerning music", *The New Age*, vol. 21 no. 2, , p.46.

— (14 June 1917), "The condition of music in England", *The New Age*, vol. 21 no. 7, pp. 154-6.

— (1918-19), "The modern spirit in music", *Proceedings of the Musical Association*, vol. 45, pp. 113-30.

— (July 1920), "The scope of opera", *Music & Letters*, vol. 1 no. 3, pp. 230-3.

— (1 February 1922), "A note on the mind's ear", *The Musical Times*, vol. 63 no. 948, pp. 88-90.

— (1 March 1922), "Modern Hungarian composers", *The Musical Times*, vol. 63 no. 949, pp. 164-7.

— (September 1922 "Early chromaticism in the light of modern music", *The Chesterian*, vol. 4 no. 25, pp. 5-10.

— (1923), *Frederick Delius*, John Lane the Bodley Head, London. Reset (ed. Hubert Foss) 1952; repr. *facsimile* Greenwood Press, Westport, 1974.

— (4 August 1923), untitled review of Schoenberg's *Pierrot lunaire*, *The Weekly Westminster Gazette*, vol. 2 no. 77, p. 14.

(as Warlock, Peter)

— (November 1916), "Notes on Goossens' Chamber Music", *The Music Student*, pp. 23-4.

— (1925), Preface to Arbeau: *Orchesography* (see above).

— (September 1925), "Street music", *The Music Bulletin*, vol. 7 no. 9, pp. 270-1.

— (1926), *The English ayre*, O, London.

— (February/March 1926), "The editing of old English songs", *The Sackbut*, vol. 6 no. 7, pp. 183-6 and vol. 6 no. 8, pp. 215-20.

(with Gray, Cecil)

— (1926), *Carlo Gesualdo, Prince of Venosa: musician and murderer*, Kegan Paul, Trench, Trubner & Co., repr. *facsimile* Greenwood Press, Westport, 1971.

Hill, Lionel (1985), *Lonely Waters: the diary of a friendship with E J Moeran*, T.

Hold, Trevor (1975), "The art of the songwriter", *The Music Review*, vol. 36 no. 4, November , pp. 284-99.

— (1978), *The walled-in garden: a study of the songs of Roger Quilter*, Triad, Rickmansworth.

— (1980), "Two aspects of *Sleep*: a study in English Songwriting", *The Music Review* vol. 41, pp. 26-35.

Hutchings, Arthur (4 July 1963), "The Heseltine-Warlock nonsense", *The Listener*, vol. 70 no. 1788, p. 34.

James, Montague Rhodes (1924), *The apocryphal New Testament*, O, London.

Kelley, Philip (1985), *The influence of nature on the solo songs of Peter Warlock*. DMus constituent, Florida State University, (unpublished thesis).

Kennedy, Michael (1968), *Portrait of Elgar*, O, London.

Kennett, Christian (1986), *The development of Warlock's skill as a songwriter as seen in* Saudades, The curlew *and the last three songs*. Undergraduate dissertation (unpublished), University of Southampton.

Kington, Beryl (1993), *Rowley rediscovered*, T.

Lambert, Constant (1934), *Music ho! A study of music in decline*, Faber and Faber, 2nd ed. 1937; 3rd ed. 1966.

— (27 Dec. 1936), "The finest modern carol", *The Sunday Referee*, p. 17.

Lindsay, Jack (1962), *Fanfrolico and after*, The Bodley Head, London.

Lloyd, Stephen (1985), *H. Balfour Gardiner*, Cambridge University Press .

MacDonald, Keith Norman (1895), *The Gesto collection of highland music*, Oscar Brandstetter, Leipzig.

Mellers, Wilfrid (March 1937), "Delius and Peter Warlock: a comparative note" *Scrutiny*, vol. 5 no. 4, pp. 384-97.

— (1 December 1949), "The music of Bernard van Dieren", *The Listener*, vol. 42 no. 1088, p. 972.

van der Merwe, Peter (1989), *Origins of the popular style*, O, Oxford; (corrected edition with minor alterations, 1992).

Motion, Andrew (1986), *The Lamberts: George, Constant and Kit*, Chatto & Windus, London.

Nance, R Morton (ed.) (1955), *A Cornish-English Dictionary*, The Federation of Old Cornwall Societies.

Opie, Iona & Peter (1985), *The singing game*, O, Oxford.

Osborne, Charles (1974), *The concert song companion: a guide to the classical repertoire*, Victor Gollancz, London.

Palmer, Christopher (1976), *Delius: portrait of a cosmopolitan*, Duckworth, London.

Parrott, Ian (October 1964), "Warlock in Wales", *The Musical Times*, vol. 105 no. 1460, pp. 740-2.

— (May 1966), "Warlock and the fourth", *The Music Review*, vol. 27 no. 2, pp. 130-2.

— (1994), *The crying curlew - Peter Warlock: family and influences*, Gomer Press, Llandysul.

Pilkington, Michael (1989), *Gurney, Ireland, Quilter and Warlock*, Duckworth, London.

Pirie, Peter J (Summer 1965), "The 'Georgian' composers", *Music in Britain*, no. 69, pp. 23-7.

Playford, John (1651), *The English dancing master*, London, (ed. Mellor and Bridgewater, Dance Books, 1984).

Poulton, Diana (1972), *John Dowland*, Faber & Faber, London: rev.

1982.

Quiller-Couch, Sir A. T. (ed.) (1908), *The Oxford book of English verse 1250-1900*, O, Oxford.

Redwood, Christopher (ed.) (1976), *A Delius companion*, John Calder, London.

Ritson, Joseph (ed.) (1829) *Ancient songs and ballads from the reign of King Henry II to the Revolution*, 3rd edition (1877) rev. W. C. Hazlitt, Reeves and Turner, London.

Self, Geoffrey (1986), *The music of E J Moeran*, Toccata Press, London.

Shead, Richard (1973), *Constant Lambert*, T, (rev. n.d.)

— (1976), *Music in the 1920s*, Duckworth, London.

Shaw, Margaret Fay (1955), *Folksongs and folklore of South Uist*, Routledge and Kegan Paul, London.

Smith, Albert Eric Barry (1991), *Peter Warlock: a study of the composer through the letters to Colin Taylor between 1911 and 1929*. PhD, Rhodes University, Grahamstown, (unpublished thesis).

Smith, [A. E.] Barry (1994), *Peter Warlock: the life of Philip Heseltine*, O, Oxford.

Sorabji, Kaikhosru (15 January 1931), [obituary], *The New Age*, vol. 48 no. 11, pp. 128-9.

Stradling, Robert & Hughes, Meirion (1993), *The English musical renaissance 1860-1940: construction and deconstruction*, Routledge, London.

Taylor, Colin (Autumn 1964), "Warlock at Eton", *Composer*, no. 14, pp. 9-10.

Tomlinson, Fred (1974), *A Peter Warlock handbook* vol. 1, Triad Press, London.

— (1976), *Warlock and Delius*, T.

— (1977), *A Peter Warlock handbook* vol. 2, Triad Press, Rickmansworth.

— (1978), *Warlock and van Dieren*, T.

— (1981), *Warlock and Blunt*, T.

Trend, Michael (1985), *The music makers: heirs and rebels of the English musical renaissance, Edward Elgar to Benjamin Britten*, Weidenfeld and Nicholson, London.

Walker, Ernest (1952), *A history of music in England*, O, 3rd ed.

Watkins, Glenn (1973), *Gesualdo: the man and his music*, O, London; 2nd ed., 1991.

Whittall, Arnold (May 1966), "The isolationists", *The Music Review*, vol. 27 no. 2, pp. 122-9.

Wilson, Jane (1989), *C W Orr – the unknown song-composer*, T.

Yenne, Vernon Lee (1969), *Three Twentieth-Century English song composers: Peter Warlock, E J Moeran and John Ireland*. DMus Arts constituent, University of Illinois, (unpublished thesis).

Correspondence/other manuscript material in BL Add. Ms. Collection

48303   *Codpieces.*

49995   (van Dieren) Interlude from *Choral Symphony* ("Chinese") copied by PW.

50186   6 letters to Paul Ladmirault, 1925-30: 3 holograph, one typescript and 2 manuscript copies.

50505   *Rutterkin.*

52256   6 letters to Edward Clark, 1924-29.

52523   Transcriptions of *Abradad* (Farrant) *When May is in his prime* (Edwardes) *A doleful deadly pang* (Strogers) made by PW.

52547-9 Letters from Delius to PH.

52904   *Chinese Ballet.*

52905   *Kanow Kernow* I & II.

52906   *Saudades.*

52907   Seven songs [of summer] (*The passionate shepherd/The contented lover/Youth/The sweet o' the year/Tom Tyler/Eloré Lo/The droll lover*).

52908   *Corpus Christi* – version for string quartet.

52909   Six Songs (*The fairest May/My Lady is a pretty one/Sleep/Take o take../Chopcherry/My gostly fader*) – versions for voice & string quartet.

52910   Two songs (*A sad song/Pretty ring time*) – versions for soprano & small orchestra.

52911   *Maltworms* – arrangement for voices and small orchestra.

52912   *The old codger* [corresponds to version in Add. Ms. 48303 but without the first 16 bars]/*The cloths of heaven/The curlew* no. 3 (*The withering of the boughs* – short score)/*Jenny Gray/Queen Anne*. A short score arrangement of *Row well ye mariners* (anon. XVII C.) is on the reverse of *Queen Anne*.

54197   Letters to Colin Taylor.

54390   MSS of material published by A: *Folk-song preludes*; *To the memory of a great singer*; *Late summer*; *The singer*; *Captain*

Stratton's fancy; *Mr Belloc's fancy*; *Good ale*; *Hey troly loly lo*; *The bachelor*; *Piggesnie*; *Candlelight* [the individual pieces are without titles]; *Eloré lo*; *The contented lover*; *The droll lover*; *The cricketers of Hambledon*. Also:

    Transcriptions of a Concerto in E minor (Avison)

    Six Pieces for string trio (Hilton); Suite in C (Locke)

    Five short pieces (Wood).

54391   Arrangements of music by Delius made by PH (all published by A): Violin concerto (violin and piano); Double concerto (violin, cello and piano); *North country sketches* (piano duet); *A song before sunrise* (piano duet); *Dance rhapsody* no. 2 (piano duet). These all bear the name "Philip Heseltine" rather than "Peter Warlock".

57486A Letter to George —? concerning the publication of *Giles Earle his book*.

58079S Letters from PH to William C. Smith.

58127   Letters from PH to Olivia ("Viva") Smith.

59846W Letters from PW to CT and G. A. Thewlis

    Transcription of *When I taste my goblet deep* (Henry Lawes).

60748   Letters to E. Arnold Dowbiggin.

60749   *Mourn no moe* – version for voice and string quartet.

65187   Correspondence between PH and BvD; also includes some pertaining to other writers/recipients (Gray, Goss and Holbrooke).

71168-9 Letters from PH to Jelka and Frederick Delius.

71169   Letters to BvD from Delius, Blunt and Ladmirault, mostly following PH's death.

The [Cecil] Gray papers (selection only – items relating to PW)

57776   Gray: *Deirdre*. Score reduced for 2 pianos by PW (1928).

57794   Letters written by Heseltine to Gray and others ?1915-30.

57795   Correspondence etc. between PH and Robert Nichols.

57796   Drafts/typescripts of scatological verse etc. by PH; notes on *Dildos and Fadings*: offprint of Cockshott (JUly 1940). Notes by Robert Nichols on his letters from PH 1930. Offprint – Stanley M. Coleman (April, 1949), *The dual personality of Philip Heseltine*, Journal of Mental Science, pp. 456-466.

57797   Verse by Robert Nichols including *The water lily* and an untitled poem dedicated to PH ("You, Phil have heard full many a poem/Burst from my throat . . ."); Also contains a (printed) score of *The full heart*.

57798   Criticism by ?PH of two poems. (The hand is similar to that of PH but there are some inconsistencies.)

57803   9 photographs of PH with friends.

The Heseltine Papers (presented by Nigel Heseltine, PH's son)

57958   Letters from PH to his mother (1907).

57959   ditto (1908-10)

57960   ditto (1911-13)

57961   ditto (1914-20)

57962   Letters to PH from Jelka and Frederick Delius (1922)/ Gray (1921-3)/Joseph Heseltine [Uncle Joe] (1909-22).

57963   Letters to PH from Sorabji.

57964   Letters to PH from miscellaneous persons.
         Letters to PH's mother from miscellaneous persons.

57965   Kodaly: 2 songs for bar./orch op. 5. (but not in PW's hand, although some annotations may be).

57966   Song *Love ecstasy* (CT) copied by PW; *Good Ale*: printed version with annotations in PW's hand; arrangement of *Brigg fair* (Delius) by PW for 2 pianos (4 hands); sketch for arrangement of *In a summer garden* (Delius); analysis (principal material) of Kodaly's op.7/8. This on the reverse of some extracts in PW's hand from pieces by BvD: ("Chinese" symphony/*Levana*/*Diaphony*/second string quartet; – examples for ?article about BvD); Bartók: unidentified song (1916 – printed *facsimile*) dedicated to PH; Sorabji MS of music to *The rider by night* with annotations by PH ?prior to publication. Some pages missing.

57967   Miscellaneous papers including one dozen *Cursory rhymes* c.1919

57968-9 Working notebooks.

57970   Offprints of articles by/about PH.

Index

References to music by Peter Warlock are given under "Warlock"; principal verbal references are in bold type, those to notated examples are in italics and relate to page rather than example numbers. An asterisk denotes the title of a work in several movements where further mention may be found under the names of those individual movements. Works by other composers will be found under the composer's name. Main references only are given to features of Warlock's style; it would be impractical to list all occurrences of (for example) *Curlew*-chord".

Aberystwyth: University Choir 138; University College 193
Alkan, Charles-Valentin 63
Arbeau, Thoinot 327, 330, 343; *Orchésographie* 327, 330, 332, 343
Augener Ltd 118, 174
Avery, Kenneth 5, 325

Bach Choir (London) 192
Bach, Johann Sebastian 4, 11
Bailey & Ferguson 52
Baines, William 8
Ballet Russe 7
Ballett, William 85, 118
Banfield, Stephen 51, 118
Banquet of Thalia, The 252
Barnby, Joseph 53
Bartók, Béla 3, 7, 9, 12, 23, 34, 37, 169, 193, 197, 198, 205, 330, 336, 340; *Mikrokosmos* 65, 81
Bax, Sir Arnold 5, 55, 235, 319, 336, 338, 343
BBC 80
Beaumont, Cyril 327, 343
Beddoes, Thomas Lovell 286; *Song for two voices* 325
Beecham, Sir Thomas 2
"de Beldamandis Jr, Prosdocimus" 5
Beggar's opera, The 159

Belloc, Hilaire 272, 279, 319
Bennett, Sterndale 8
Berg, Alban 31
Berlin, Irving 159, 174, 340; *Alexander's ragtime band* 174; *Everybody's doing it now* 174
Berlioz, Hector 11
Berners, Lord 235
Blake, William 84
Blunt, Bruce 301, 316, 317, 325
Boosey and Co. 138
Bradbury, Ernest 235
Bridge, Frank: *String quartet no. 3* 54
British Library 11, 51, 52, 53, 80, 118, 131, 138, 175, 235, 344
British Museum 4, 118
Britten, Benjamin (Lord) 104, 336
Busoni, Ferruccio 4, 63
Butterworth, George 5, 8, 104, 193
Byrd, William 4, 99

Café Royal 105
Cage, John: *The wonderful widow of eighteen springs* 312
Campbell, Roy 338
Carnegie Foundation 56
Cefn-Bryntalch (Montgomeryshire) 54, 176, 193
Chambers & Sidgewick 138

Channing, Minnie Lucy "Bobbie" ("Puma") 55, 80, 118
Chappell, William 252
Chelsea 105
Chester, J. & W. Ltd 27
Cholla mo rùin 52
Chopin, Fréderic 11
Clare, John 176
Clarke, Rebecca 193
Cockshott, Gerald 11, 81, 174, 252
Collins, Hal 235, 238
Copley, Ian 1, 3, 4, 5, 11, 21, 36, 37, 51, 52, 53, 64, 65, 80, 81, 118, 119, 138, 149, 156, 157, 162, 169, 174, 175, 178, 192, 223, 235, 252, 325, 326, 332, 343
Covent Garden 11
Cox, Harry 193, 205
Crocker, Phyl 80, 118
de Croustchoff, Boris 80, 118

Davies, Hywel 130
Day, Dr Alfred 49, 53, 297, 298
Debussy, Claude 6, 7, 22, 65; *Sirènes* 81
Delius, Frederick 3, 6, 7, 8, 9, 11, 13, 16, 29, 42, 43, 44, 46, 52, 55, 59, 61, 63-4, 67, 84, 86, 128, 136, 147, 148, 153, 156, 176, 255, 337, 338, 339, 340, 342; *Brigg fair* 44; *On Craig Ddu* 67, 146-7, *147*, 148, 178; *On hearing the first cuckoo in spring* 43; *Sea drift* 54; *Song before sunrise, A* 149, 150, *150*; *Twilight fancies* 24, *25*, 51; *Two pieces for small orchestra* 44
Dent, Edward 11
van Dieren, Bernard Jr viii
van Dieren, Bernard Sr viii, 3, 4, 7, 8, 9, 11, 20, 23, 28, 33, 34, 46, 53, 55, 59, 61, 67, 77, 78, 86, 105, 136, 148, 149, 188, 235, 325, 339, 340; *Ich wanderte unter den Bäumen* 8; *Levana* 8; *The long barrow* 138; *Netherlands melodies* 8

Donne, John 175
Dowbiggin, Arnold 319, 326

Elgar, Sir Edward 5, 8, 11
Epstein, Jacob 105
Eton College 7, 13
Eynsford (Kent) 118, 221, 235, 301, 309

Farnaby, Giles 4
Fenby, Eric 1, 11
Finzi, Gerald 5, 8, 193
Finzi Singers 156, 325
First nowell, The 46, 127, 130
Fletcher, John 339
Foreman, Lewis 235
Foss, Hubert 80, 235

Gardiner, Balfour 338
Gesualdo, Carlo 3, 148, 156, 269, 340; *Dolcissima mia vita* 148; *Moro lasso al mio duolo* 148
Gibbons, Orlando 4
Gillies, Malcolm 12
Goddesses 252
Goossens, Eugene 1
Goss, John 235
Grainger, Percy 53
Gray, Cecil 1, 2, 4, 11, 46, 52, 53, 64, 80, 105, 118, 156, 205, 218, 235, 341
Grieg, Edvard 11, 29
Grimaldi, Joseph 252
Gurney, Ivor 8, 193, 339

Hadley, Patrick 235
Here we go round the mulberry bush 170
Herrick, Robert 253
Heseltine, Edith 54, 342
Heseltine, Evelyn 249
Heseltine, Nigel 80, 206
Heseltine, Philip: see Warlock, Peter
Hindemith, Paul 336
Hold, Trevor 174, 252

Holst, Gustav 3, 60, 340; *Sávitri* 60
Hood, Thomas 16
Hungary 7
Hutchings, Arthur 343

Ingle, Anthony 21
Ireland, John 338

James, Montague Rhodes 325
Jazz 7
John, Augustus 205
Jones, Walter Buckley 54

Karpeles, Maud 34
Kindler, Frida 4

Lambert, Constant 7, 235
Leicester University Singers 138
Liszt, Franz 63
London 81, 105

Messiaen, Olivier 189, 213
Mendelssohn, Felix 8, 301; *Wedding march* 300
Moeran, Ernest John ("Jack") 34, 235, 252, 338
Moffat, Alfred 52
Morley, Thomas 328; *First book of consort lessons* 231; *A plaine and easie introduction to practicall musicke* 343
Musical Standard, The 7, 81

Nashe, Thomas 175
Neuberg, Victor 193, 205
New Grove 235
Nichols, Robert 6, 11, 52

Opie, Iona and Peter 175
Original Dixieland Jazz Band 7
Ornstein, Leo 3
Orr, Charles Wilfred 336
Osborne, Charles, 1, 11
Oxford Book of Carols 180, 189
Oxford Companion to Music 53

Oxford University Press 156, 174, 175, 192, 325
"Palimpsest, Huanebango Z." 5, 11, 15
Palmer, Christopher 51, 52, 149, 337
Parrott, Ian 80, 138, 205
Pearson, Louis vii
Pilkington, Michael 174, 207, 217, 235, 325
Pimm's no. 1 Cup 175
Pirie, Peter 343
Pither, Anthony 138
Playford, John 252
Port Regis Prep. School 325
Poulenc, Francis 336
Poulton, Diana 235
"Puma" – see Channing, "Bobbie"
Purcell, Henry 159, 231, 340

Quilter, Roger 8, 259, 336; *Love's philosophy* 118

Ravel, Maurice 159
Richter, Hans 11
Ritson, Joseph 119
Rogers, Winthrop 26, 27, 46, 56, 60, 78, 82 et seq., 119, 120, 126, 139, 145, 148, 227, 301, 330
Rowley, Alec 336, 337
Royal College of Music 325
Russia 7

Sackbut, The 1
Savoy Orpheans 8
Schoenberg, Arnold 4, 6, 7, 11, 21, 37, 77, 81; *Harmonielehre* 11; *Pierrot lunaire* 4, 78; *String quartet no. 2* (op. 10) 21, 68, 81
Scott, Cyril 38, 53
Self, Geoffrey 252, 293
Shakespeare, William 8, 29, 342; *Measure for measure* 86; Sonnet XLIII 339; *Twelfth night* 259
Shanks, Edward 177, 178
Sharp, Cecil James 34

Shaw, Margaret Fay 52
Shoreham (Kent) 252
Skryabin, Alexander 8
Smith, Barry 1, 11
Spicer, Paul 156
Squire, Sir John 159, 275
Stalham (Norfolk) 205
Stanford, Sir Charles Villiers 8, 336
Strauss, Richard 7, 8
Stravinsky, Igor 7, 8, 156, 159, 340;
 Apollon Musagète 336; *In memoriam Dylan Thomas* 312; *Pulcinella* 231, 226
Symons, Arthur 24, 260

Taylor, Colin 3, 7, 11, 51, 52, 53, 80,
 118, 119, 138, 156, 174, 205, 252,
 342
Thames Publishing, 21, 27, 51, 53,
 118, 119, 138, 145, 157, 174, 175,
 192, 205, 252, 325
Tippett, Sir Michael 104
Tomlinson, Fred vii, 2, 5, 11, 21, 30,
 51, 52, 53, 80, 81, 118, 119, 120,
 125, 138, 145, 156, 174, 175, 184,
 192, 235, 252, 279, 325, 344
Trinity College (Dublin) 4, 85
Tristan-chord 22

Walker, Ernest 1, 11
Wagner, Richard 7, 11, 22, 156
Warlock, Peter, Life and musical style:
 And wilt thou-motif 62, 75, 187,
 233, 253, 258, 261, *307*, *309*, 310,
 311, 316, 317, 319 et seq., 323
 bitonality 65, 81, 97, 102, 108, 169,
 182, 183, 198, 241, 267, 297
 brass bands 250, 340
 British music, place in 5, 8, 9, 54,
 56, 63, 79, 104, 317, 336, 337,
 Celticism 34, 35, 42, 55, 85, 118,
 124
 chordal composition 4, 5, 6, 7, 9,
 10, 18, 20, 98 and passim
 chordal family 26, 27, 33, 35, 38,

 41, **47-50**, 51, *48*, 92, 116, *117*,
 153, 183
 chordal inversion 16, 22, 23, 35, 43,
 47, **49**, **57**, 63
 chordal vocabulary 18
 chromatic bases 15, 20, 35
 circles-of-5ths 15, 17, 91, 95, 97,
 115, 212 and passim
 clusters 138, 154, 155, 169, 201,
 213, 244
 Curlew-chord 22, 23, 30-1, 32-3,
 44, 48, 51, 61, 65, 67, 68, 77, 84
 Delius, influence of 3, 24, 29, 43,
 46, 54, 99, 102
 Delius, relationship with 3, 11, 45,
 153
 van Dieren, influence of 3, 23, 24,
 28, 33, 34
 van Dieren as his heir 64
 European music, place in 7, 9, 31,
 337
 expressionism 54, 81
 folksong 34, 35, 37, 38, 52, 53, 104,
 112, 191, 193, 194, 202, 203, 205,
 218, 223, 340
 Frostbound wood-chord/shape 49,
 65, 191, 247, 266, 311
 "gloom" motif 64, 66, 69, 75, 136,
 198, 287
 Great War, attitude towards 55, 118
 harmony 3, 9, 13, 15, 23, 24, 25-6,
 27, 38, 49
 harmonic/melodic relationships 89,
 94, 105, 161
 influences in general 8
 Ireland 55, 118
 lifestyle, 4
 key-centres 5, 6, 21, 52, 91
 linguistic choice 338
 melisma 13, 128, 129, 131, 142,
 257, 312, 341
 melodic attitude 15, 20, 86, 105,
 116-7, 306, 310
 "melody of chords", definition and
 usage 6, 11, 182, 216, 321

modality 4, 6, 9-10, 17, 25, 26, *35*, 36, 49, 60, 72, 73, 75, 91, *95*, 99, 100, *100*, 105, 116-17, 190, 193

motivic usage 4, 14, 15, 18, 29, 47, 61, 68, 72, 73, 187, 225-6, *225*, 229

multiple derivations in technique 14, 103-4

musica ficta 17, 102, 108, 111, 139, 185

musical work beyond composition 2

musical knowledge, breadth of 7

orchestral writing 45

parallelism 16, 73, 75, 130, 166, 181, 182, 226, 229, 236, 243, 256, 257, 264, 265, 279, 300

pedals 25, 41, 42, 129, 133, 139, 198, 236, 256 et seq., 280, 330

pentatonicism 17, 23, 25, 27, 28, 35, 39, 40, 48, 50, 61, 62, 67, 70, 71, 75, 77, *78*, *190*, 203, 310-11, *311*

piano, composing at 46, 160, 184

pitches of songs 21, 174

"pot-boilers" 53, 159, 238, 252

pseudonyms 1, 86, 218

Renaissance, influence of or otherwise 3, 10, 85, 93, 116, 142, 166, 169, 184, 231, 269, 323, 328, 339

Renaissance scholarship 85, 118, 327

rhythm 4, 18, 22, 33, 37, 42, 61, 75, 82, 95, 120, 160, 214, 243, 251, 255, 312, 341

semitonal usage 3, 9, 13, 14, 15, 18, 22, 23, 24, 26, 27, 28, 31, 42, 44, 48, 49, 56, 57, 65, 96, 102, 104, 203-4

song-cycles 27, 61, 69, 204, 206, 207

songs as a principal medium 338

sprechgesang 78

strophic form 15, 29, 37, 46, 61, 82, 85, 94, 97, 106, 111, 112, 127, 151, 159, 161, 177, 178, 180, 201, 215, 244, 274

stylistic origins 8

through-composition 46, 61, 82, 106, 112, 114, 177, 187, 229, 234, 255, 310, 319

tonal attitude 5-6, 9

Wales 54, 176, 235, 309

Works:

Adam lay ybounden **180-2**, *181*, 189

After two years **233-4**, *233, 23*

All the flowers of the spring **255-7**, *255, 256, 257, 258*, 262, 266, 272, 280, 341

Along the stream (Saudades) **33**

And wilt thou leave me thus 62, 220, 250, 289, **306-9**, *307, 308, 309, 310*, 316, 317, 319, 322, 326

Arthur o' Bower (Candlelight) **21**

As dew in Aprylle **120-22**, *121*, 128, 124, 125, 249

As ever I saw 53, **87-9**, *88*, 108, 111, 142, 231, *232*

Autumn twilight **187-9**, *187, 188*, 339

Away to Twiver **244-8**, *245, 246, 247, 248*, 279, 335, 340

Bachelor, The **166**, *167*, 169, 171, 340

Balulalow **139-40**, *140*, 141, 189, 219

Basse-danse (Capriol) **328-30**, *329, 331*, 334, 335

Bayly berith the bell away, The 9, 53, **91-3**, *92*, 94, **110-11**, 111, 325

Benedicamus Domino 120, **122-4**, *122*, 125, 304

Benneth Nadelik ha'n Bledhan Noweth – see *Kan Kernow*

Bethlehem Down (choral version) 235, 301, **305-6**, *305, 306*, 316, 341; (solo version) 317, **322-3**, *324*

Birds, The 219, **272-5**, *273, 274, 275*

Bransles (Capriol) **332-4**, 335
Bright is the ring of words **84-5**, *85*, **106-8**, *107*, 110, 112, 141
Burd Ellen and young Tamlane (Lillygay) **197**, **199**, *199*, **200-201**, *201*, 202, *202*, 204, 312
Call for the robin redbreast and the wren **262-5**, *263*, *264*, *265*, 268, 272, 341
Candlelight* 27, 119, **206-15**, 216, 253, 341
Capriol* 2, 230, 289, **327-36**, *335*, 343
Captain Stratton's fancy 141, **158-60**, *158*, 166, 171, 174, 218, 243, 249, 306, 339, 340
Carillon carilla 219, 234, **317-19**, *318*
Chanson du Jour de Nöel **221-2**, *222*
Child's song, A 220
Chinese ballet, A 5
Chopcherry (Peterisms set I) **166-8**, 169, 174
Christmas hommage to Bernard van Dieren, A **46-7**, *47*, 130
Cloths of Heaven, The **24-7**, *26*, 31, 33, 40, 41, 51, 80, 86, 94, 104, **115-16**, 164, 220, 262
Codpieces 5, 8, 34, 51
Consider 95, 149, **257-9**, *259*, 289
Contented lover, The **229**, 235
Cornish Christmas carol, A – see Kan Nadelik
Corpus Christi 120, **133-7**, *134*, *137*, 139, 141, 142
Countryman, The **223**
Cradle song 100, 225, **294-8**, *294*, *296*, *297*, 300
Cricketers of Hambledon, The 141, 218, **250-51**, 301, 340
Curlew, The* 9, 13, 15, 22, 24, 27, 30, 33, **54-81**, 146, 158, 176, 178, 187, 191, 193, 194, 196, 197, 204, 216, 218, 227, 289, 306, 308, 341

Dedication **95-98**, 96, 97, 98, 110, **112**, 118, 149, 228, 289
Distracted Maid, The (Lillygay) **194-5**, *195*, 197, 198, 199, 202, 203, 204, 218, 235, 323
Droll lover, The **229-30**, *230*, 235
Eloré lo **228**, 235
Everlasting voices, The 5, 13
Fair and true 151, **223**, 341
Fairest may, The **231-3**, *232*, 234
Fill the cup Philip **249-50**, *250*, 251, 289, 340
First mercy, The **301-3**, *302*, *303*, *304*, 325
Folk- song preludes* 8, **34-42**, 45, 46, 47, 56, 64, 67, 78, 84, 86, 105, 106, 112, 128, 159, 191, 237, 239, 266, 280, 289, 311, 328
Prelude I **35-7**, *35*, *36*
Prelude II **37-8**, *38*, *39*, 39
Prelude III **39-40**, *40*, *41*
Prelude IV **40-42**, *41*, *42*
Prelude V **42**
Five lesser joys of Mary, The **316**, 323, 341
Fox, The 218, 301, **319-22**, *320*, *322*, 327
Frostbound wood, The 49, 174, 231, 301, 308, **311-16**, *313*, *314*, *315*, 319, 326, 327
Full heart, The 120, **146-8**, *147*, 156, 269, 339, 341
Good ale 159, **162-4**, 174, 340
Ha'nacker mill 220, **279-80**, *279*
He hears the cry of the sedge (The curlew) 60-61, **70-73**, *70*, *72*, 216
Heraclitus (Saudades) **29-33**, *31*, *32*, 51, 84, 94
He reproves the curlew (The curlew) **60-63**, *62*, **64-9**, *66*, *67*, *68*, *69*, 71
Hey troly loly lo **164-6**, *165*, 220
How many miles to Babylon (Candlelight) **207**, *207*
I askèd a thief to steal me a peach

46, 53, **82-4**, *83*, *84*, **105-6**, 110

I had a little pony (Candlelight) **210-11**, *211*, 212

I have a garden **220-21**

I held love's head (Two short songs) **253**, *254*

In an arbour green **171-3**, *172*, 230

I saw a fair maiden **304-5**, *304*

I won't be my father's Jack (Candlelight) **207**, *208*

Jenny Gray **215-16**, *216*

Jillian of Berry 160, **243-4**, *244*, 251, 335, 340

*Johnnie wi' the tye (Lillygay)*194, 195, **196**, **198**, 199, 204

Jolly shepherd, The **249**, 340

Kan Nadelik 124, 125, **126-32**, *126, 127, 128, 129, 130, 132*, 133, 136, 138

Kan Kernow 124, **125**, *125*, 138

Lady's birthday, The **238-42**, *239, 240-41*, 251, 267

Lake and a fairy boat, A 9, **13-16**, *14, 15*, 29, 38, 40, 63, 71, 130, 148

Late summer **177-8**, 183, 187, 229, 234

Liadain and Curithir 120

Lillygay* 24, 27, 35, 40, 64, 104, 176, **193-205**, 216, 231, 289

Little Jack Jingle (Candlelight) **211**

Little Tommy Tucker (Candlelight) **209**, *210*, 210, 212

Little trotty wagtail **176-7**, *176*

Love for love **98-9**, 221

Lover mourns for the loss of love, The (The curlew) 9, 22, 25, 29, 44, 48, **56-60**, *57, 58-9*, 63, 64, 69, 73, 137, 177, 255, 266, 283

Lover's maze, The **289-90**, *290, 291*, 298

Lullaby 53, **94-5**, *94*, **111-12**, 325

Lusty Juventus (Peterisms set II) **171**, 174, 230

Magpie, The **238**

Maltworms **243**, *243*, 251, 306, 340

Mattachins (Capriol) 328, **334-6**, *337*

Milkmaids **218-19**, *219*, 234, 340

Mockery 225, **298-301**, *298-9, 301*

Mourn no moe **101-2**, *103*, **113-14**, 325

Mr Belloc's fancy **159-62**, *161*, 174, 275, 339

Music when soft voices die **16-18**, *16, 17, 18, 19*, 29, 39, 87, 99, 102, 220

My gostly fader 9, 53, **89-91**, *90*, 92, 94, 95, 99, **108-10**, *109*, 328

My lady is a pretty one 62, **142-4**, *143, 144*, 341

My little sweet darling **99-101**, *100, 101*, 102, **112-13**, *113*, 117, 178, 234

My own country **282-3**, *282, 283*

Night, The **280-2**, *281*

Old song, An 3, 34, **42-5**, *43, 44*, 238, 239, 328

O my kitten (Candlelight) **208-9**

One more river 238, **242-3**, *242*

Passing by 118, 170, **224-7**, *225, 226*, 234

Passionate shepherd, The **227-8**, *227*, 235

Pavane (Capriol) 328, **330**, *331*, 334, 335

Peter Warlock's fancy **238**, 340

Peterisms* 27, **164-73**, 174, 189

Pieds-en-l'air (Capriol) 3, 328, **334**, *335*, 335

Piggesnie **166**, *167*, 340

Play-acting **153-5**, *154*, 160, 162

Prayer to St Anthony of Padua, A **260-2**, *261*

Pretty ring time **222-3**, *224*

Queen Anne **249**

Rantum tantum (Lillygay) 188, 193, 194, 195, **201-4**, *204*, 211, 216, 254, 288, 293, 309, 340

Rest sweet nymphs 95, 169, 173, **182-4**, *182*, 187

Rich cavalcade, The 138, 309-10

Robin and Richard (Candlelight) **207-8**, *209*, 219

Robin Goodfellow 18, **275-9**, *276*, *277*, *278*, 336

Roister Doister (Peterisms set II) 168, **170-71**, 174

Romance **141**

Rutterkin (Peterisms set I) **169-70**, *170*, 171, 174, 251, 278, 279, 334, 340

Sad song, A (Peterisms set I) **168-9**, 174

Saudades* 8, 9, 22, **26-34**, 45, 46, 55, 64, 67, 72, 78, 84, 142, 146, 164, 187, 196, 229, 284, 294, 306

Serenade 3, 44, **148-52**, *149*, *151*

Seven songs of summer* 27, 235

Shoemaker, The (Lillygay) 193, 194, **196-7**, *196*, **198-200**, *200*, 201, 202, 203, 251

Shrouding of the Duchess of Malfi, The 200, 218, 262, **265-9**, *266*, *267*, *268*, *269*, 272, 339, 341

Sick heart, The 24, **262**, *263*

Sigh no more ladies 225, 226, *291*, **292-4**, *292-3*, 298

Singer, The 118, **178-80**, *179*, *180*, 181, 182

Sleep 168, 170, **184-7**, *185*, *186*, *189*, 280, 282, 289, 298, 322, 339

Sorrow's lullaby **283-9**, *285*, *288*

Spring (Peterisms set II) **171**, 174

Spring of the year, The **269-72**, *270*, *271*, *272*

Suky you shall be my wife (Candlelight) **212**, *213*, 223, 225, 293, 321

Sweet-and-twenty **259-60**, *261*, 342

Sweet content **102-4**, **114-15**, *114*, 159, 229

Sweet o' the year, The **230**, 235

Sycamore tree, The (Three carols) 192, **219-20**, *221*, 221

Take O take those lips away (Saudades) **27-9**, *28*, *30*, 49, 229, 284, 294; (1918) 53, **86-7**, *87*, **108**

There is a lady sweet and kind **93-4**, 97, 98, **111**, 117

There was a man of Thessaly (Candlelight) **212**

There was an old man (Candlelight) **209-10**, *210*

There was an old woman (Candlelight) **212-14**, *213*, *214*

Thou gav'st me leave to kiss (Two short songs) **253-4**, *254*

Three carols* 192

To the memory of a great singer **84-5**, 141; Tom Tyler **228**, 235

Toper's song, The **237-8**

Tordion (Capriol) **330-32**, *332*, *333*, 334, 335

Twelve oxen 220, **236-7**, *237*, 286

Two short songs* **253-4**

Tyrley tyrlow (Three carols) 168, 170, **189-91**, 219, 260

Valses: Rêves d'Isolde 11, 51

Walking the woods **223-4**

Water lily, The 13, 20, **22-4**, *24*, 27, 29, 30, 32, 33, 44, 59, 65, 84, 146, 284

What cheer? Good cheer 249, 252, 303

Whenas the rye reach to the chin 53, **95**, 96, 111, 112, 166, 225

Where riches is everlastingly 252, **303**

Wind from the west, The **18-20**, *19*, *20*, 21, 23, 38

Wine comes in at the mouth 51, 80

Withering of the boughs, The (The curlew) 60, 70, 71, **73-8**, *74*, *75*, *76*, *78*, 104

Yarmouth fair **238**

Youth **230-31**, 235

Warlock Society, The Peter 2, 21;

Newsletter 52, 205
Watkins, Glenn 156
Webern, Anton: *Concerto* 312
Webster, John 255, 262, 339
Whittall, Arnold 252
Wilde, Oscar 53
Williams, Ralph Vaughan 3, 5, 8, 34, 52, 104, 141, 192, 193, 319, 340; *Bright is the ring of words* 107, 107; *Pastoral Symphony* 52; *Roadside fire, The* 145; *Songs of travel* 119, 145
Wolf, Hugo 1, 11
Wood, Sir Henry 7

Yeats, William Butler 54, 55, 56, 67, 77, 80, 118, 177, 193, 338, 341